DETROIT COUNTRY MUSIC

Detroit Country Music

MOUNTAINEERS, COWBOYS, AND ROCKABILLIES

By Craig Maki with Keith Cady

The University of Michigan Press
Ann Arbor

Published in the United States of America by
The University of Michigan Press
Manufactured in the United States of America
⊗ Printed on acid-free paper

2016   2015   2014   2013   4   3   2   1

A CIP catalog record for this book is available from the British Library.

Library of Congress Cataloging-in-Publication Data

Maki, Craig.
Detroit country music : mountaineers, cowboys, and rockabillies / Craig Maki, Keith Cady.
    pages ; cm
Includes index.
ISBN 978-0-472-07201-9 (hardback)—ISBN 978-0-472-05201-1 (paper)—
ISBN 978-0-472-02961-7 (e-book)
    1. Country music—Michigan—Detroit—History and criticism. I. Cady, Keith. II. Title.
ML3524.M335   2013
781.64209774'34—dc23   2013025448

CONTENTS

PREFACE AND ACKNOWLEDGMENTS

In July 1995 I received an unexpected call from Eddie Jackson, a sixty-nine-year-old musician who had entertained in Detroit since the 1940s. Through a Middle Tennessee accent, Jackson invited me to meet him for the very first time at a Detroit bar, at a private party he would play. "You'll be my guest," he said. "Swanee Caldwell will be there, and do you know . . . ?" He bounced several names off my bean.

Jackson got in touch after he heard from a mutual friend that I was spinning his old records on my radio shows at WCBN-FM Ann Arbor and WHND-AM Detroit. While I attended college in 1990, the host of the long-running "Rockabilly Show" at WCBN announced plans to leave town, and I took his seat. As I got comfortable in the studio, local music collectors hipped me to the Fortune Records label of Detroit with some country rockers issued during the 1950s. One of Jackson's records was among them.

A few days after our telephone conversation, I met Jackson at the Golden Greek Lounge, a long brick building on the Detroit side of Eight Mile Road, east of Interstate 75. Without any idea what Jackson looked like, I stepped into a darkened room filled with people of all ages eating, talking, and dancing. Four guitarists wearing cowboy hats stood at the opposite end of the narrow space, playing through old speakers. The bass player and the rhythm guitarist sang. Without drums, the music took me by surprise.

During a visit to Austin, Texas, in 1993, musician friends introduced me to western swing. I fell in love with this music in far-off Texas, and by good fortune I had stumbled upon some of the folks who established western swing in Detroit decades before.

Jackson led the band. Guitarists Marvin Weyer, Cliff Gilbert, and Fran Mitchell (in whose honor the party was held) and bassist and singer Swanee Caldwell joined him. After two more sets of music, Jackson moved the celebration to his cozy home just a few blocks away. Behind the finished basement's bar stood a wall of photographs of Jackson and musicians he knew during the 1940s through the 1970s, when he played Detroit nightclubs. Over drinks, jokes, songs, and games of pool, we discussed the people in the photos, stoking my interest in this particular history of the city's musical past.

As I got to know Jackson and his peers, my concept of Southeast Michigan's country music scene grew from a dozen artists to three or four times as many. I could find no definitive document on country music in Detroit. Most accounts survived as fragments in album liner notes and vintage magazine features. By the 1990s, many country musicians who entertained in Detroit fifty years before were aging fast, had retired to the South, or had passed away. In a region where most residents valued music above other types of entertainment—a community that produced world-class performers in all genres—Detroit's most productive and influential era of country music was unknown to younger generations.

On radio I broadcast local music, information, and interviews with Detroit area musicians. I penned a couple of articles for magazines that specialized in American roots music and continued searching for new leads.

Then I met Keith Cady, who listened to my programs while he earned a degree at broadcasting school. At Swanee Caldwell's funeral in 2000, we discovered we had befriended several of the same musicians, and we joined forces on this project.

Cady worked at classic country station WSDS-AM Ypsilanti, Michigan, from 1998 until its sale in 2005. As "Keith Jason" he broadcast disk jockey programs mixed with live performances by local musicians every day. His managerial position at the station and ready access to recording equipment allowed him to interview Michigan artists and Nashville hall-of-famers. Cady's reputation as a disk jockey, his tireless research, and his skill as an upright bass player let him into social circles that hadn't been accessed by researchers before. Because of his efforts, our perspective expanded, adding several more years to the project as we traveled Southeast Michigan and parts of the South.

Our aim to preserve the early history of country music in Detroit, tracing the activities of local country musicians from the 1930s through the 1960s, is still a work in progress. This volume serves as an introductory account of the impact Detroit country artists had on the greater tradition of country music.

Some artists who made music elsewhere and relocated to Michigan are not included in this work. For instance, the career of the late Wade Mainer, who moved to Flint in 1953 to work at General Motors, didn't meet the parameters of the project. Mainer was most recognized for recordings he made before moving to Michigan, as well as post-1960s efforts that have been well documented elsewhere.

We refrained from presenting full biographies of a few Detroit artists who did fall into the scope of this project, such as Jack Scott, Skeets McDonald, and Johnny Powers, because their stories are easily found online and in print. However, tidbits of interest about them—and many less famous musicians—are scattered throughout the book. We ask fans of Detroit music to forgive our omissions. After twenty years of research, we have a good understanding of how many artists we could not include due to limited space. Hundreds of entertainers dedicated their time and talent for country music fans in Detroit nightclubs, radio, and television during the twentieth century. This book is dedicated to them all.

Please look for more stories, information, and ephemera related to this project online at www.carcitycountry.com. We extend our foremost thanks to our interview subjects, their families, and friends (see Appendix B). We also express our humble gratitude to the following people for their generous help and interest: music historians John Rumble, Charles Wolfe, Paul Kingsbury, Kevin Coffey, Michael Hurtt, and Donald McCatty; record collectors Gerald "Cappy" Wortman, John Morris, Tony Fusco, Sal and Dottie Leczynski, Bob Silverberg, Willie Lewis, Sven Bergmann, J. C. "Dude" Towler, Jeffrey "Loney" Irwin, and Carl Pellegrino; radio broadcasters George Koch, Andy Baron, Jim Petrat, Rob Miller, Dan Moray, and Jim Manheim; musicians Marvin Weyer, Bill Sterling, Bobby Anderson, and Harvey White. And we acknowledge and appreciate the patience of our families, the staff at the Frist Library and Archive at the Country Music Hall of Fame and Museum in Nashville, and the staff at the Detroit Public Library.

Craig Maki
April 2013
Southfield, Michigan

Figure 1. Advertisement from the *East Side Shopper*, December 1944.

Chapter 1

DETROIT'S EVERLASTING
HARMONIZATION

In October 1943 Detroit nightclub owner William Levin realized he had problems, World War II the least of them. After struggling through the Great Depression, earnings from his vaudeville show bar had slipped into the red. From behind picture windows advertising jazz music, theatric entertainers, and comedians, Levin fought pangs of helplessness as he watched hundreds of workers leave shifts at the Chrysler Corporation and Continental Aluminum facilities nearby and head God-knows-where, but not through his doors. Wartime production in Detroit, including the factories surrounding Levin's Jefferson Inn, at 11707 East Jefferson, ran at full capacity, twenty-four hours a day.

Levin's few remaining regulars observed how the neighborhood had changed in the past few years, with newly arrived white workers from the South filling single family homes, rental flats, and apartments. As housing became available, another family from Appalachia materialized, ready to move in. Realizing he couldn't ignore the demographic shift any longer, Levin dialed a telephone.

In the past he had booked entertainers through Detroit offices of national talent agencies, which typically represented few country and folk music artists. Levin phoned the independent Betty Bryden agency in Detroit to hire acts that would appeal to the Southern migrants living and working in the vicinity of his club. Bryden, who led an "all-girl" pop orchestra during the

1930s, landed the York Brothers, two Kentucky transplants, to headline at the Jefferson Inn. Bryden also arranged for Levin to sponsor a radio show for the duo at WJLB Detroit. To his surprise, business improved immediately, and Levin had a happy Thanksgiving.

When he first asked around, Levin discovered the York Brothers, George and Leslie, were famous among the Southern newcomers. He remembered the hoopla their record "Hamtramck Mama" caused in the spring of 1940. Then-mayor of Hamtramck Walter Kanar obtained a court order banning performance of the song within his city's borders.[1] In neighboring Detroit, country music fans wore out that record, and dozens of others the York Brothers made for the Mellow Record Company, based in Edward Kiely's Mellow Music Shops a few blocks away from the Jefferson Inn.

Kiely opened his first Mellow store in 1939, at 13217 East Jefferson, across the street from the former Braun's Music House. In 1927–28 Braun's operated WBMH radio, a one hundred-watt station at 1420 kc. By 1930, WBMH fell silent. WMBC radio Detroit, based in the Hotel LaSalle (later called Hotel Detroiter) at Woodward and Adelaide, claimed the frequency that year.

The Michigan Broadcast Company launched WMBC in 1924, presenting broadcasters and entertainers from a variety of ethnic backgrounds that made up the citizenry of Detroit. The station's most famous incident concerned the shooting of commentator Gerald Buckley in 1930, a murder linked to his support for a successful recall campaign against Detroit Mayor Charles Bowles. Country artists dotted the WMBC schedule during the 1930s, and it may have been the station where the York Brothers first appeared after they moved to Detroit around 1938 from WPAY Portsmouth, Ohio. After purchasing the station in 1939, newspaper executive John L. Booth changed its call letters to WJLB.

The York Brothers' radio work prepared them for making recordings, which wasn't much different from playing music in a broadcast studio. Musicians performed around a few microphones (sometimes just one) in a room lined with sound-dampening material while engineers electrically transferred the sounds into grooves on wax master disks. Metal plates were made from masters, and shellac records pressed from the plates. While the

Depression caused all but the largest record companies to fold, a revival of the jukebox industry in Detroit during the early 1940s led to a new business model in making and selling records, spurred by factory workers with pocketfuls of nickels to spend in jukeboxes.

In 1939 the York Brothers cut "Hamtramck Mama," a musical portrait of a red-hot playgirl, in Universal Recording Studios at 12942 East Jefferson. The sentimental "Going Home" appeared on the flipside of 78-rpm disks sporting blue paper labels and the Universal Recording Studios emblem printed in silver ink.[2] Marquette Music, a forty-year-old Detroit vending company, produced and distributed the records in Michigan and parts of Indiana and Ohio.

"Hamtramck Mama" struck a rich vein of precious metal—coins, that is. Its popularity in barroom and café jukeboxes spread like wildfire. A few months later, Hamtramck Mayor Kanar's court order brought wider attention to it, resulting in sales of 300,000 copies in Detroit alone. With no competition from other independent record companies in Detroit, Marquette Music probably issued the first commercial recordings by country musicians made in the city.[3]

At least three more records by the York Brothers appeared on Universal within a year of "Hamtramck Mama." Marquette Music produced the Yorks' follow-up, "Highland Park Girl." Other Universal records by the York Brothers displayed the street address of Edward Kiely's satellite Mellow Music Shop at 965 Dickerson (around the corner from his first).[4] Besides selling musical instruments, lessons, and records, Kiely serviced a route of jukeboxes on the east side. Perhaps to distance himself from Marquette Music and their use of the Universal imprint, around 1941 Kiely introduced the Hot Wax label, featuring silhouettes of two shapely young ladies. He closed a deal with Buhl Sons Company, another Detroit jukebox supplier, and issued "hillbilly novelty" and "hillbilly blues" records by local country-western groups led by Forest Rye, Billy Casteel, and Eveline Haire. Kiely also produced the Mellow label, resulting in a catalog of thirty-some records dominated by the York Brothers.

The Kentucky voices and guitars blasting "Hamtramck Mama" from area jukeboxes announced to Detroit—and the rest of America—that a substantial number of workers from the South had arrived in Southeast Michigan. William Levin of the Jefferson Inn figured this out relatively late, yet cashed in on the phenomenon. Levin advertised for hillbilly acts in music industry magazine *Billboard*. He hired many groups from Detroit and nearby cities (due to wartime travel restrictions), initiated weekend square dances, and sponsored radio shows by his artists. To improve foot traffic, Levin ended his door charge—an unusual move for show bars, according to *Billboard*. "His idea is a quick turnover," stated an article from December 1943.[5]

Turnovers drove the 300-year history of Detroit. When Antoine Laumet de La Mothe, sieur de Cadillac founded Fort Pontchartrain du Détroit in 1701, he brought French troops and Native American allies to the west bank of an isthmus between lakes Huron and Erie to provide strategic support of the French military and fur trade. By the end of the War of 1812, the region passed from France to England, and then to the United States. Americans completed the Erie Canal in 1825, improving travel between the Atlantic Ocean and the Great Lakes. As gateway to Michigan Territory, the city of Detroit grew dramatically.

After Michigan gained statehood in 1837, Detroit shipbuilding industries expanded to include production of oceangoing vessels. Manufacturers developed internal combustion engines for ships and smaller watercraft. Along with a concentration of carriage makers in Southeast Michigan, engine workshops set the scene for people like Henry Ford to experiment with automobile technology.

Detroit's population ballooned during the early decades of the twentieth century, as manufacturers of stoves, furnaces, automobiles, paints and varnishes, and ships sought employees. Thousands of Europeans, particularly Germans, Italians, Russians, and Poles, settled neighborhoods where their languages and culture served as support systems while managing life in Detroit.

World War I obstructed immigration from abroad. American manufacturers created more than three million jobs, and the industrialized North looked to the South for workers. Congress passed more restrictions on immigration during the early 1920s, swelling numbers of Southern migrants into millions, until the Great Depression.

A second major phase of circulation by Americans from the South be-gan during the mid-1930s as manufacturing in the North revived. Move-ment of Southern migrants peaked during the 1940s and continued through two more decades.⁶

Along with workers from the South came entertainers. During the 1920s and 1930s, musicians often broadcast at radio stations for little or no pay, advertising goods and public appearances. With commercial radio blanket-ing the United States by the start of the 1930s, a generation of performers developed their talents on the road, hopping from station to station, playing local theaters, cafés, and halls.

The first radio stations in Detroit ranked among the broadcasting pio-neers of North America. In August 1920 the *Detroit News* launched station 8MK. The *News* changed its call letters to WWJ two years later. WCX, a *Detroit Free Press* endeavor, began operations in 1922. In 1928, this station moved into the newly completed Fisher Building on West Grand Boulevard to begin a legacy known as WJR "The Goodwill Station." By the close of the 1930s, WJR broadcast at fifty thousand watts with a clear channel sig-nal reaching the eastern half of the continental United States and parts of Canada.

The earliest folk music radio entertainer in Detroit, Tim Doolittle, a.k.a. Bruce Myers, sang with the WCX *Red Apple Club* in 1924. With his six-piece band, the Pine Center Gang, Doolittle entertained on WJR through World War II. After the war, he moved to WKMH Dearborn for a few more years.⁷

Perhaps the first country recording artist based in Detroit was Kentucky-born Joe Steen, who left WHAS Louisville in 1932 for a job with Ford Mo-tor Company. While in Kentucky, Steen sang four songs in mountaineer style for Victor Records' Bluebird label. Because Victor eliminated field re-cordings during the early years of the Great Depression (as did other major labels), Steen visited the company's Chicago studios after he moved to De-troit. The lyrics of Steen's "Kentucky My Home," issued on his final Bluebird record, expressed a traveling man's longing for the land of his youth during a time when record numbers of Kentuckians left the commonwealth (between 1920 and 1930, close to 9 percent of the 1920 population left its borders).⁸

As cowboys on radio and the silver screen grew popular, Steen changed his stage name to Jack West, fronting the Circle Star Cowboys on WJR. Band member "Texas" Jim Lewis departed for New York City with most of Steen's group in 1935.[9] Seven years later, Steen died of a heart ailment.

Detroit musicians often supported themselves and their families with jobs outside of radio and nightclubs. During the late 1930s, when Southeast Michigan transformed into an "arsenal of democracy," folk from across the South arrived with patriotic fever to do their part. Soldiers returning to civilian life followed friends and relatives north. Southern whites lived in sizable sections of the city, including an area surrounding Chrysler facilities, from East Jefferson up to Mack Avenue; near the New Center area, around Woodward and West Grand Boulevard; along West Vernor and Clark Park; and near Cass Avenue and Second and Third streets in Midtown.

The entertainment that William Levin and Edward Kiely presented brought Southern people together and stirred memories of their earlier lives back home. The success of these businessmen publicized the economic power of their customers. Other organizations soon entered the market, making it difficult for both men to stay on top.

Kiely seemed unable to issue new records after the York Brothers joined the Navy in 1944. Universal Recording Studios did not survive the war years. Another recording company in Detroit, United Sound Studios (a.k.a. United Sound Systems, established ca. 1933) on Second Avenue near the New Center area, may have been too inconvenient, or too expensive for Kiely to work with.

In January and August 1946, *Billboard* mentioned Kiely had plans to "have his labels in quantity pressing soon."[10] No reviews of Kiely's records appeared in later editions of the magazine. In March 1947, *Billboard* reported Kiely was "slugged and robbed of $185 by a pair of bandits" as he worked his jukebox route.[11] In June 1950, *Billboard* printed its last direct mention of Kiely under the Coin Machines features page: "Edward Kiely, pioneer music operator who now specializes in the East Side music field, reports business slowly coming out of a three-month standstill caused by the long Chrysler strike."[12]

After the war, new record companies in Detroit (e.g., Fortune, Shelby, Trophy, Citation) and a few labels introduced by jukebox service companies (e.g., Sultan, Alben) took up where Kiely left off by issuing country records by local acts. Kiely probably closed his second shop on Dickerson by the early 1950s.

In May 1954 *Billboard* noted, "Mrs. Lula Kieley [*sic*, Kiely], owner of the Mellow Record Shop, recently sold the fifteen year-old retail outlet."[13] The report made no mention of Edward Kiely, who may have passed away. (Jimmy Work described Kiely as "up in years" when they met during the 1940s.)[14] The Chiodo family, who purchased the Mellow Music Shop, operated it with an emphasis on pop music for the next dozen years or so.

William Levin's Jefferson Inn gave way to scores of bars and nightclubs featuring country-western entertainment across Southeast Michigan. In 1948 the York Brothers, who had moved to Nashville in 1946 and joined the WSM *Grand Ole Opry*, worked Detroit nightclubs for thirty-eight consecutive weeks.[15] Western swing bandleaders such as Chief Redbird, Arlee Barber, Luke Kelly, and Jack Luker kept Detroit bars crowded with dancers.

During the 1950s and 1960s, most Detroit radio stations committed more airtime to country music, and profited by doing so.

With a daily schedule that included live music, WEXL Royal Oak broadcast country music for nearly fifty years. First licensed in 1924 as WAGM, Jacob B. Sparks purchased the station in 1929 and changed its call letters. Sparks oversaw WEXL operations with his two sons. From the 1930s through the 1970s, WEXL broadcast local musicians playing folk and western music live in its studios or via remote broadcasts. Commercial-free religious programs filled the Sunday schedule, including church services performed in the studio and organ music from the chapel of the Sparks Funeral Home.[16] Around 1949 disk jockey "Cousin" George Cross started the *Sagebrush Melodies* program every weekday afternoon, and Jack Ihrie took it to new heights in popularity during the 1950s, before WEXL went country twenty-four hours a day in 1962.

In December 1939, WCAR Pontiac opened studios in the Riker Building downtown. From its beginning through the early 1950s, the station devoted a few hours of its daytime-only broadcasts to local C&W acts.

Cowboy singer Happy Hank (Marc Williams) performed early in the morning over WJR during the 1940s. In 1951 to 1954 Pie Plant Pete (Claude

Moye) and Bashful Harmonica Joe (Joseph Troyan) woke up WJR listeners every weekday with old-time songs and farm animal impressions.

Smilin' Red Maxedon and Dottie Leader sang western songs together at WJBK radio Detroit in 1947–48. Also at WJBK in 1948, disk jockeys Brother Bill (Guy Bowman) and Shorty (Harry Smith) hosted the four-hour *Hillbilly Hit Parade*.

In 1950–51, Bob Newman and the Georgia Crackers performed every Saturday afternoon over CKLW radio's powerful signal from Windsor, Ontario.

Network syndicated shows from Gene Autry, Hopalong Cassidy, *Renfro Valley Sunday Morning Gatherin'* (from Kentucky), Pee Wee King (from Chicago), Judy Canova (from New York City), *National Barn Dance* (from Chicago), *Saturday Night Country Style* (a CBS network production of barn dances from around the United States) and the *Grand Ole Opry* filled out Detroit radio schedules. Possibly the first Detroit-based radio barn dance premiered on WJR as the *Goodwill Frolic* in October 1944, featuring the Goodwill-Billies every Saturday night for two years.

From 1949 to 1952, WKMH Dearborn broadcast *Hayloft Jamboree*, a Saturday night barn dance featuring Charlie Jones and His Kentucky Corn Crackers (who worked at WMBC Detroit during the 1930s and 1940s). In 1951–52, *Hayloft Jamboree* took place at the Hollywood Theater (now demolished) on West Fort Street in Detroit.[17]

In March 1952 WJR began airing a half-hour segment of a Saturday night jamboree called the *Big Barn Frolic*. One of the most popular radio shows in Detroit, the *Frolic* ended in July 1953.

Casey Clark and His Lazy Ranch Boys hosted the *Big Barn Frolic* from the Dairy Workers Hall in Highland Park until his band left the show in late 1952 to start the Lazy Ranch Boys Barn Dance at a United Auto Workers hall at 12101 Mack Avenue (at Conner). WXYZ radio Detroit broadcast thirty minutes of the Saturday night show in spring 1953. A half-hour portion of Clark's barn dance returned to WJR that autumn as the *Goodwill Jamboree*. Clark also served as a country music disk jockey at the station, and the Lazy Ranch Boys played a live set every weekday morning from 1954 to 1956. *Goodwill Jamboree* broadcasts ended in June 1956.

In December 1953 the *Motor City Jamboree* premiered at the Madison Ballroom (at Woodward and Forest, now demolished), hosted by Milton Estes, with Danny Richards and His Gold Star Cowboys, and guest stars from the *Grand Ole Opry* every weekend. WXYZ broadcast part of the Saturday show through March 1954.

Early television often featured programs first heard on radio, including country music variety shows. The *ABC Barn Dance* premiered in summer 1949 on ABC network affiliates. In 1954 ABC syndicated the *Ozark Jubilee* out of Springfield, Missouri, until 1960 when the show was called *Jubilee USA*. A *Grand Ole Opry* show also came through the ABC network in 1955–56. *Ranch Party* from Los Angeles, California, aired coast-to-coast in 1957–58. Detroit stations got in the game as early as 1949, with local stations running music variety shows and cowboy-themed children's programs featuring hosts such as Sagebrush Shorty, Chief Redbird, and Cowboy Colt with Smilin' Red.[18]

In March 1954, WWJ-TV Channel Four introduced the *Michigan Barn Dance* from its downtown studios, featuring Phil Girard and His Jubileers, Chuck Hatfield and Boots Gilbert, and emcee Max Henderson. For nine months, a dozen local musicians and guests performed every Saturday night, from eleven o'clock to midnight.

Casey Clark and his band staged the *Casey Clark Jamboree* every Friday night at CKLW-TV Channel Nine Windsor, Ontario, from 1955 to 1957. In 1957 Clark moved the program to WXYZ-TV Channel Seven every Friday night through August 1958.

WJBK-TV Channel Two also produced a country music show on Saturday nights. *Michigan Jamboree* ran for several weeks during spring 1957.

Weekend barn dances without radio or television affiliation cropped up in Detroit suburbs. These events included live sets of music by host bands, guest entertainers, and round and square dances.

Jimmy Williams of New Baltimore produced Saturday night dances at Bill's Barn in Utica (at Twenty-one Mile and Dequindre Road) and Colonial Hall in Sterling Heights (at Fifteen Mile and Mound Road) from 1955 to 1959. Williams played for as many as five hundred customers on Saturday nights, with twenty-five square dance sets on the floor.[19] After Williams' departure from Bill's Barn in 1956, rockabilly Johnny Powers hosted dances there through 1958.

In 1954–57 Lonnie Barron held Saturday night dances at the White Eagle Hall in Muttonville (on Gratiot Road, between Richmond and Marine City).

Jack Scott of Hazel Park hosted jamborees at Bill's Barn in 1955, then started a weekly dance at May's Barn in Troy (Big Beaver and Rochester Road) for a few more years.

Ralph Davis and the Western Rhythm Boys played weekend dances at Sheldon Hall on Plymouth Road in Livonia from 1957 to 1959.

With a one-two punch from rock 'n' roll and the worst recession since World War II, barn dances in Southeast Michigan died out around 1960. The Packard Motor Car Company, Hudson Motor Car Company, and the last major stove manufacturer (representing the city's largest industry until the automobile boom of the early twentieth century) ended production in Detroit between 1954 and 1958. Chrysler Corporation, the city's top employer, shed eighty thousand jobs. Square dancers moved into smaller venues such as nightclubs and church halls.

In 1958 Casey Clark received an offer he couldn't refuse from WNAX radio Yankton, South Dakota. As it rolled out of Michigan, Clark's flex bus carried away a significant amount of air from beneath the wings of country music in Detroit.

Following completion of Cobo Hall at Detroit's riverfront in 1960, multi-act country music shows with *Grand Ole Opry* stars appeared at the convention center's arena monthly, supplanting the previous decade's barn dance scene.

On television, the NBC network broadcast the full-color *Five Star Jubilee* from Springfield, Missouri, in 1960. The syndicated *Porter Wagoner Show* debuted in 1960 and lasted twenty-one years. Pontiac-based bandleader Billy Martin hosted the *Michigan Jamboree* on WILX-TV Channel Ten Jackson, in 1960. Frankie Meadows, whose band worked steadily at the Wayside Bowling Lounge in Hazel Park, hosted a weekly show on WKBD-TV Channel Fifty Detroit, during the mid-1960s.

In December 1962 WEXL introduced Southeast Michigan's first

twenty-four-hour country music format. They shared syndicated highlights from the *Grand Ole Opry* daily. Remote broadcasts of local bands in Detroit nightclubs such as Caravan Gardens and Tistle's Lounge aired weekday evenings. By 1967 the WEXL Country Club, the station's fan club, boasted more than fifty thousand members. Disk jockeys spun at least one classic record mixed with contemporary hits and Detroit-made music every hour, as well as one religious song during each show. The local flavor of WEXL continued through 1973, when the station celebrated its golden anniversary with an eleven-hour country music fair in Utica. *Opry* member George Morgan performed alongside Michigan-based entertainers.[20]

With a more powerful signal and a top-forty country format, WJBK radio introduced tough competition in 1970. In 1974 the Sparks family introduced an all-Christian format at WEXL.

West of Detroit, near Ypsilanti, WYSI mixed local and major-label country music. In 1964 to 1968 WYSI disk jockeys Farris Wilder, Big Bill Evans, and Col. Jack Wilkerson spun records and engineered live music in the station's studios. They also broadcast remotely from west side venues such as the legendary Club Canton (on Michigan Avenue in Canton).

In 1964 Wilkerson helped establish a Michigan Country Music Association. Its aim was the promotion of country music at radio and television stations, and public venues. Members of the MCMA included local radio hosts, musicians, and fans.

Arizona Weston, a founding member of the MCMA, broadcast an early-morning country music show from 1961 to 1973, at WPON Pontiac. Weston's friend Jimmy Williams hosted a similar program at WSMA Marine City from 1960 to 1988. Both men followed and reported developments in country music through contacts established by frequenting Nashville's annual disk jockey conventions.

In 1966 *Music City News*, a tabloid based in Nashville, granted its name to a Michigan supplement distributed monthly in Southeast Michigan. Paul Wade reigned as editor-in-chief during a handful of years. *Music City News—Michigan Supplement* documented the end of an era when Nashville's stars fraternized with Detroit musicians and fans, on and off the bandstand.

Around the same time Wade's paper spread news and a little history about Detroit country music, Bessemer "Buzz" Rider, raised in Van Lear, Kentucky, organized a jamboree called the *Michigan Hayride* near Saginaw, Michigan. In 1971 Rider created the Michigan Country Music Hall of Fame, to honor Michigan talent at an annual festival. William Aukerman purchased the rights to the Hall of Fame before Rider died in 2001. Aukerman continued adding to the list Rider began thirty years before at events on his property in Prairieville, Michigan.

During the 1970s business competition from around the globe, rising energy costs, and inflation helped slow the growth of Michigan manufacturing, reducing the sixty-year-old river of jobseekers from the South to a trickle.

A strip of country bars grew popular on Eight Mile Road, east of Woodward—an area dominated by jazz and pop music entertainment thirty years before. Sons and daughters of musicians who started careers in Detroit during the 1940s and 1950s joined their parents on stage. Most sang country music learned from radio hit lists, a few wrote their own songs, while others preferred tunes they grew up with, as evidenced by a Michigan bluegrass tradition and large fan base. Some groups of young musicians, such as Commander Cody and the Lost Planet Airmen, followed the example of the 1950s generation and combined country and rock music.

In 1977 musician Dave Atkins quit his day job selling Oldsmobiles to start publishing a magazine called *Country in the City News*. He teamed with Evelyn Harlene (Casey Clark's daughter) and several contributors who updated long lists of nightclubs that continued to book bands for multi-week contracts. Through the 1980s, Atkins' editorials and interviews with disk jockeys, musicians, and club owners provided insightful reports on the changing business of country music in Detroit.

While Atkins promoted country music from a Detroit-centric perspective, most recognized that the music industry of Nashville dominated songwriting, production, distribution, and even radio access. From the late 1970s, a hit record meant that a song had achieved national success, rather than extraordinary regional sales (e.g., "Hamtramck Mama" by the York Brothers). By the mid-1980s, radio stations such as WCXI and WWWW (the first Detroit country station to broadcast FM stereo, in 1981) gave sparse attention to local acts.

Most musicians who began careers in Detroit before and after World War II continued entertaining until the ends of their lives in venues such as older country bars, social halls, picnics, and house parties. Meanwhile, commercial country radio stations spinning contemporary hits for a younger generation earned strong listener ratings. The Detroit Downtown Hoedown, a weekend music festival started in 1982, drew thousands of fans once a year to Hart Plaza (on the riverfront where Woodward and Jefferson avenues meet), to witness the latest stars from Nashville along with Michigan artists.

For most of the twentieth century, talented musicians who lived and worked in Southeast Michigan added fuel to the nation's country music machine. Here we pay tribute to those who took part, reigniting a spotlight on pioneers of country music made in the Motor City.

Figure 2. Chief Redbird and His Western Aces at Scrib's Drive Inn, Pontiac, Michigan, ca. 1948. From left: Skeets McDonald, Chief William Redbird, Walt Lee, and Larry Heath. Used by permission from Della Redbird.

Chapter 2

CHEROKEE BOOGIE
Chief Redbird

> I was playing them old tunes down at a television station, and the announcer said, "Chief, I bet you made a lot of money with that old fiddle." I said, "Well, quite a little bit." He said, "How much did you make on one setting?" So I said, "One setting, you mean? Well, let's see. It was me and my brother Sam, we was a-playin' for a country square dance, and we made nine hundred and five dollars apiece." "Nine hundred and five dollars apiece," he said, "That's a lot of money!" "Well yeah, they paid us five dollars in cash and we had nine hundred dollars worth of fun."
>
> —CHIEF REDBIRD[1]

When the cowboy and the country music singer joined forces during the 1930s boom of western musicals on cinema screens, the two images fused together forever. Before then, most people regarded cowboy songs as a distinct genre from the folk music of the South.

The string band that introduced singing cowboys on radio first broadcast over KFRU in Bristow, Oklahoma, in May 1925. Billy McGinty, a rancher from Ripley who rode with President Theodore Roosevelt's Rough Riders during the Spanish-American War, and a veteran performer with Buffalo Bill's Wild West Show, fronted a group of cowboy musicians who played local dances and social functions. McGinty's Cowboy Band stayed with the radio station through its evolution into KVOO Tulsa in early 1927. By then, the group had performed across the region and witnessed several personnel changes, including the adoption of Stillwater rancher Otto Gray as the organization's manager while McGinty eased into retirement.

Gray took McGinty's Oklahoma Cowboy Band on tours of vaudeville circuits through urban centers of the Midwest and East, bringing a surprisingly successful stage show of cowboys with authentic attire and gear, who sang and performed comedy, rope tricks, and feats of sharpshooting and knife throwing. They introduced western music—a mix of traditional cowboy songs, nineteenth-century pop, and fiddle tunes—to thousands, if not millions of people several years before cowboys began singing on movie screens.

In a photo from about 1927—probably around the time Gray changed the band name to Otto Gray and His Oklahoma Cowboys—Redbird appeared in a group lineup, a grinning, lanky young man holding a cello and bow. Representing American Indian culture of the West onstage, Redbird was known as Chief Sanders then.[2]

INDIAN TERRITORY

The nineteenth-century Indian relocation policies of the United States created a melting pot of Native American culture in Oklahoma before it achieved statehood in 1907. In 1838, a grandmother of Redbird's participated in the Trail of Tears forced emigration of Cherokee from the Southeast United States to an area along the Arkansas-Oklahoma border. Several years later, the federal government merged tribal areas into Indian Territory.

Susan Martin and William D. Sanders, Redbird's parents, married in 1888. In a 1900 interview for the federal Dawes Commission, Sanders testified he was Caucasian, claiming Cherokee citizenship by marriage.[3] The couple had three children at the time. William A. (Redbird) was born April 7, 1899, near Cherokee City, Arkansas. He grew up in Indian Territory, spending his early years in Leach, Oklahoma (Going Snake District), and later in Ponca City.

Although the Dawes Rolls of 1907 listed the blood degrees of the Sanders children as one-quarter Native American, Otto Gray promoted Redbird as a half-blood Cherokee. "He told me that the government designations weren't right," said daughter Della Redbird, "and that someone [possibly his father] decided it would be better for the family to tell the government they had more European blood."[4]

Redbird attended Cherokee Baptist church, where he learned Christian songs in the Cherokee language. He grew up with three sisters and three brothers, and attended school in a one-room log house. He excelled in sports, rode horses, and loved to entertain and sing, learning fiddle, bass, banjo, and guitar. He left behind this tantalizing statement, recorded in 1966 on a reel-to-reel mix tape of records and living-room performances.

> I was the youngest leader of the Cherokee tribe. . . . Old Sam Saia [sp?] and Bird Poorboy, they were the two bigshots in the Cherokee tribe, and they made me a leader when I was about twelve years old.[5]

"He used to say because he was so smart and caught on to everything, some of the elders made him honorary chief," said Della Redbird. Cherokee elders dubbed him "Chief Redbird."[6]

Redbird learned how to make clothing decorated with beadwork, as well as drums, turtle shell rattlers, and headdresses in the style of Plains Indians from a chief named Blue Cloud. President Woodrow Wilson accepted a headdress made by Redbird at some point during his years in office (1913–21). For the rest of his life, Redbird created a traditional headdress to honor every elected president of the United States. "He wished to acknowledge the leader of the country," said Della Redbird, "and remind them that the American Indian played a significant role in defining our nation."

EARLY STATEHOOD

Redbird worked several jobs before joining the Oklahoma Cowboys. He often entered rodeo competitions for calf roping, his favorite event.

He played semi-professional baseball as pitcher for a team based in the oil town of Cleveland, Oklahoma. A 1920s snapshot of Redbird shaking hands with the legendary Ty Cobb showed Redbird dressed in a uniform for a team based in Lamar, Oklahoma.

Redbird and his brother Sam played music for local square dances. Their repertoire included fiddle breakdowns such as "Danced All Night With A Bottle In My Hand" and "Old Judge Parker, Take The Shackles Off Of Me."

A series of snapshots including exotic animals and an impromptu grouping of John R. Van Arnam's Honey Boy Minstrels in a family album suggested Redbird worked with a traveling tent show. In one photo, a grinning Redbird, wearing a stylish white suit and hat, posed with a boa constrictor slinking round his neck and shoulders.

OKLAHOMA COWBOY BAND

No one knows how Redbird met and joined the Oklahoma Cowboys. Redbird's home at the time was probably Ponca City, north of Otto Gray's Stillwater ranch. Gray's practice of booking the band on the road for several months caused a high rate of musician turnover, because most of the band's earliest members preferred living as cowboys in Oklahoma. In a 1929 full-page advertisement in *Billboard*, the band's name appeared surrounded by call letters of thirty-two radio stations they had visited, from Texas to New York, including WJR Detroit.

Otto Gray rarely sang on stage, preferring to serve as emcee and perform with a lasso. His wife Florence, a.k.a. Mommie, also a rope handler, sang parlor songs of the late nineteenth and early twentieth centuries. The Grays' adult son Owen, a.k.a. Zeb, sang novelties, performed comedy (dressed as a rube), and played guitar.

With the Grays at the core of the group, musicians from Oklahoma and nearby states made up a revolving cast of members. Some notable personalities included mandolin and fiddle player Dave "Pistol Pete" Cutrell, who sang the very first recording of "Midnight Special" with McGinty's band (1926); *Grand Ole Opry* member Zeke Clements, a singer who played the dwarf Bashful in Walt Disney's *Snow White* feature; and Benjamin "Whitey" Ford, who performed a comedy act with Zeb Gray around 1932. After leaving the Oklahoma Cowboys, Ford re-invented himself as the Duke of Paducah, and also landed a steady gig at the *Opry*.

Gray's Oklahoma Cowboys did so well during the early years of the Great Depression, they traveled in customized automobiles with steer horns and railroad train cowcatchers mounted to the fascia. Besides touring the RKO Vaudeville circuit, the group worked lengthy contracts at stations WGY Schenectady, New York, and KDKA Pittsburgh, Pennsylvania.

The repertoire of the band, revealed in recordings made between 1926 and 1931, included old-time songs ("Gathering Up The Shells From The Seashore," 1930), fiddle breakdowns ("Cow Boy's Dream," 1926), blues ("Tom Cat Blues," 1928), spoken word ("Coon Hunt," 1928, an audio depiction of an Oklahoma raccoon hunt), pop ("When You Come To The End Of The Day," 1931), minstrel songs ("Plant A Watermelon On My Grave," 1929), and novelty ("It Can't Be Done," 1928). Because of the band's versatility, every performance was ad-libbed.[7]

SANDERS ON RECORDS

Perhaps the first time Redbird recorded was for Gennett Records in May 1930, playing cello while Mommie Gray sang "Down Where The Swanee River Flows" and "Gathering Up The Shells From The Seashore." Other musicians probably included Lee "Zeke" Allen on fiddle and his brother Wade "Hy" Allen with banjo.

In February 1931, while the act broadcast on WGY Schenectady, the Oklahoma Cowboys made their final commercial recording session— arguably their best out of twenty-nine issued performances. Mommie and Zeb took a back seat to vocals by Zeke, Hy, and Redbird.

At the session, Zeb played mandolin and guitar, Zeke played fiddle and guitar, Hy played banjo, and Redbird played cello. Zeke sang the novelty "Suckin' Cider" and a call-and-response blues, "Who Stole The Lock On The Henhouse Door," which offered a foretaste of the western swing that developed a few years later. Hy sang "When You Come To The End Of The Day," a sweet pop performance, and the minstrel tune "Mammy's Little Coal Black Rose," a selection telling of what passed for sentimental songs at the time.

Redbird sang two numbers that hearkened back to his early days in Oklahoma: "The Cat Came Back," popular in vaudeville and traveling tent shows, originally published by Harry S. Miller in 1893; and "Four Thousand Years Ago," an adaptation of the folk song "I Was Born Ten Thousand Years Ago." Redbird's sense of humor and warmth came over the microphone as if he were singing at a campfire gathering.

In 1931 the Oklahoma Cowboys made a film for Veribest Pictures of New York. The fifteen-minute reel documented a high-paced show of comedy, songs, and electrifying scenes of expert musicianship. Among the movie's highlights, Zeke and Redbird performed a fiddle duel on "Pop Goes The Weasel." The fiddlers played each other's instruments and turned their fiddles upside down without missing a lick. At one point, all the musicians gathered into a confusing mass of arms, hands, and strings to perform an old-time breakdown. A newspaper clipping from Schenectady, in Redbird's scrapbook, described a stage show from the same period.

> There's something in those old plaintive tunes like the "Black Sheep," "The Picture From Life's Other Side," and "The Baggage Coach Ahead," that'll set the nerves of the most hardened cynic atingle. And it's these very songs that have made for Otto and his boys a hit that draws them 1,600 letters from fans a day, according to WGY estimates.
>
> Otto's boys sing and play. Their band consists of mandolin, banjo, violin and cello, and they make the old shakedowns sound as they never sounded before. In addition to the six Oklahomans there is a German shepherd dog, "Rex," who has a solo part in the opening and closing numbers with "Pip," a tiny monkey, squealing and screaming an obligato.[8]

The band moved to KDKA in Pittsburgh, where Bennie Ford entered the fold. When Otto Gray signed the Oklahoma Cowboys to NBC Artists Services, Redbird negotiated his own contract with the agency as Chief Redbird. Redbird married a woman who assisted him on stage, holding cigarette targets in her mouth for him to pick off with his rifle.

In 1933 Redbird and two fellow Oklahomans, fiddle player Bob Bellmard and Hy Allen, spent some time in Detroit, performing in local theaters and on WJBK as the Bronc Busters. Felix Holt, the Kentucky-born writer of *Lone Ranger* and *Green Hornet* radio plays at WXYZ during the late 1930s, and author of *The Kentuckian*, worked at WJBK in news and publicity. He was the source for a newspaper clipping from Redbird's scrapbook.

FELIX HOLT of WJBK tells it to me this-a-way:

The Bronc Busters, cowboy musical trio heard each day at 10:30 p.m. over WJBK, are real cowboys from Oklahoma and have been friends since they were children, riding the same horses on the same range and sharing each other's chaps, ropes, guns and grub.

Chief Sanders is a half-blood Cherokee Indian and comes from Ponca City, Bob Bellmard, double-stop fiddle player of the trio, comes from Caw City, and is part Caw Indian. Hy Allen hails from Stillwater, Okla.

Chief Sanders is a trick roper and expert pistol shot. He has been riding at rodeos for years and last year took several prizes at the Madison Square Garden rodeo in New York for riding, roping and shooting.

Only this week Chief Sanders came into the studios of WJBK with a burn scar on his cheek. He got it keeping practise with his rope.[9]

Another clipping, dated "June 29–July 1, 1933" by hand, advertised a show at the Rialto Theater in Lewiston, Pennsylvania, headlined by Otto Gray and His Oklahoma Cowboys. Chief Redbird was named a feature, and his association with Gray ceased about this time. He was the longest-serving musician in the band, besides Gray and his family.

In 1936 Otto Gray officially dissolved the Oklahoma Cowboys and settled at his Stillwater ranch. By then, hundreds of musical cowboy groups had sprung up across North America, due in no small part to the Oklahoma Cowboys' success. In dance halls across the Southwest, string bands experimented with jazz. Gray's act was more about the stage show and telling stories. With Bob Wills and His Texas Playboys going great guns at the same Tulsa station where the Oklahoma Cowboys debuted, Gray felt it was time to retire.

A NEW TRIBE

NBC Artists Services booked Redbird at WTAM Cleveland, Ohio, around 1934. His group, Chief Redbird and His Tribe, included four musicians who dressed as cowboys on stage, while Redbird wore a traditional Sioux bonnet in promotional images.[10] After several months of morning broadcasts, the band moved to WJAY in the same city. By March 1935, Redbird and His Tribe had moved to WMBC Detroit, performing every afternoon.

It's unclear how long they played together, but after the Tribe had run its course, Redbird organized an all-woman band, which included his wife. A handbill from 1940 for the Bliss Theater, a cinema in Blissfield, Michigan, advertised "Chief REDBIRD and the Texas Kids / RADIO STARS / Sharp Shooting, Roping, Acrobatic Dancing / SEE THE UPSIDE DOWN GIRL!" Apparently, Redbird still led a vaudeville-styled show.

During World War II, Redbird joined the defense industry in Detroit, working as a tool and die maker. He continued making music at night, and performed as an occasional guest with Charlie Jones and His Kentucky Corn Crackers at WMBC (late 1930s) and WKMH (1946–49). On New Year's Eve 1944, Chief Redbird and His Famous Cowboys began an extended booking at the Jefferson Inn on Detroit's east side.

WESTERN ACES

After the war ended, Redbird organized bands to play dance music, with three to six pieces, working clubs from Detroit to Pontiac. Redbird's showmanship, combined with some of the best country swing musicians in the region, made for a popular act booked for weeks at a time.

Around 1949 Chief Redbird and the Western Aces performed six nights a week at Scrib's Drive Inn, on Telegraph Road (near Elizabeth Lake Road) in Pontiac. Redbird used different themes for nightly floor shows between dance music. Tuesdays featured "guest artist nite—everybody sings." Wednesdays included "sharp shooting, trick roping." On Thursday nights, the band followed Redbird across the dance floor as he led a Cherokee stomp dance.

Singer Danny Richards described Redbird's trick shooting act: "He used a pellet gun, actually. People thought it was a .22. He would put a blackboard up and stick little things on it, shoot. If he hit close to 'em, it would bust them.

"He went to the West Fort Tavern and was doin' it one night, when the police come in. They put a stop to it right there," said Richards.[11]

REDBIRD ON RECORDS

Veteran song publisher Joe Guinan opened an office in the Dime Building downtown in 1948.[12] Guinan contracted the WXYZ orchestra to record pop music productions, which he manufactured on his Shelby Records label. Redbird participated in four songs for Guinan around 1949–50. The arrangements featured western swing with trio vocals. Redbird played fiddle with Norman "Blackie" Blackburn on accordion, and Paul Perry on bass. Members of the Bobby Stevenson Trio, including jazz pianist Stevenson and guitarist Bob Mitchell, probably made the rest of the music.

Redbird sang "They're Gonna Hang Old Pappy Tomorrow," a cowboy satire, and led a vocal trio on "When We Said Goodby In Algiers." The other two songs featured vocals by Blackburn and a female pop singer. These were probably commissioned performances, as Redbird didn't write the material.[13]

In 1950 Texas pianist Aubrey "Moon" Mullican played some dates in Detroit with Redbird (probably at the Roosevelt Lounge, which opened that year). Mullican left town with Redbird's composition "Cherokee Boogie," in which Redbird honored his early mentor, Chief Blue Cloud. Mullican recorded the song October 8 for King Records. Four days later, the two friends signed a song-publishing agreement, and Mullican placed his name next to Redbird's as co-writer. "He didn't write that a bit more'n I did," said singer Arizona Weston. "Chief Redbird was singing that for four or five years before Moon Mullican got ahold of it. But he made a good hit out of it."[14]

"I worked with [Chief Redbird] a lot of times," said Danny Richards. "Him and Moon Mullican were big buddies. Moon recorded that 'Cherokee Boogie' for him." King released Mullican's single around May 1951.

The triumph of Mullican recording his song was tempered by the loss of Redbird's wife, who died of cancer in October 1950. Perhaps Richards' statement about Mullican recording Redbird's song "for him" implied a friendly gesture by Mullican, to generate some income for Redbird during trying times.

Mullican paid his dues working in several Texas bands during the 1930s and 1940s, and rode the gravy train in 1950–51 with two smash hits. "I'll Sail My Ship Alone" (1950) reached number one in *Billboard* magazine's country charts, while "Cherokee Boogie" proved popular not only in autumn 1951, when it reached number seven, but through the following decades. After several C&W and R&B remakes during the 1950s, a 1996 version by BR5-49 rose to number forty-four on *Billboard* country singles charts.[15]

Redbird remarried in February 1952. The couple's daughter, named for Redbird's oldest sister Della, was born later that year. "For the first couple of years after I arrived, we lived in an apartment above a drug store on Joseph Campau [Street], in Hamtramck. Then we moved to Hazel Park," said Della Redbird.

Through the 1950s, Ed "Red" Reeves (piano), Tom Peterson (guitar), Bernie Watts (bass), and Tony Bigda (accordion) worked steadily with Redbird, entertaining at nightclubs, movie openings, fairs, and theaters. Redbird also participated in cultural activities of the North American Indian Association (NAIA) of Detroit. He often invited NAIA dancers, musicians, and singers to participate in his nightclub engagements.

REDBIRD ON TV

In 1949 *National Hillbilly News* columnist Gene Roe, of Melvindale, Michigan, reported Redbird and bandleader Paul Perry were on Detroit television.[16] Roe didn't identify the station, but Redbird returned to the medium in 1952 through 1954. Redbird starred in the *Tom Tom Matinee*, a thirty-minute program for children broadcast on WWJ-TV Channel Four, Detroit. Sponsored by Farm Crest Bakery and airing Sunday afternoons, the show featured Redbird, guitar and banjo player Phil "Smokey" Girard, accordionist Tony "Cook" Dannon, a bass player ("Clem"), and Betty and Bobby Payne (child dancers).[17] "I grew up thinking I was famous [*laughs*]," said Della Redbird, "because I thought my dad was famous. He was a star. He was on TV and he was a cowboy."

In June 1955 Chief Redbird and His Cherokee Braves cut Redbird's "Big Chief Yodel" and "No Need To Cry" at United Sound Systems in Detroit. Fortune Records issued the songs in 45- and 78-rpm formats. "Yodel," which began with Redbird pounding his tom-tom, told a humorous story about a yodeling Indian chief who became a star on television.

While Redbird included more percussion in his music than most country artists, he was not immune to the public's changing tastes during the rock 'n' roll years of the late 1950s. Redbird began devoting more time to NAIA cultural events, especially entertaining children.

In July 1958, he opened a store attached to Guffin's Frontier Town restaurant on Grand River in Farmington. Chief Redbird's Post Exchange sold traditional Indian clothing, art, crafts, and children's toys. Pony rides were also an option. "We used to take Nine Mile right off Grand River and go [east] about a couple of blocks," said Della Redbird, "and there was a little barn that these people owned, and that is where we kept the ponies. We would sometimes just ride them over to the store."

FINAL TRIBUTES

In 1969 Della Redbird and her father met Johnny Cash and June Carter on a day they headlined at the Michigan State Fair in Detroit. Cash's 1964 album "Bitter Tears: Ballads Of The American Indian" and his well-publicized concern for Native Americans touched Redbird. Seated in Cash's trailer with Della at his side, Redbird presented Cash with a headdress of the same style he sent to U.S. presidents. When she vacationed in Nashville, Tennessee, a decade later, Della Redbird saw the bonnet on display at the House of Cash museum.

"He wasn't rich in money," said Della Redbird. "He was rich in friends. Everyone—adults, children, family, and strangers—gravitated to him. He knew how to bring out the best in people."

In 1975 Redbird presented programs about his heritage to grade schools throughout Metro Detroit. A *Detroit Free Press* article noted his Sioux headdress and clothing, and the luck inherent in eagle feathers. After closing his program by singing "What A Friend We Have In Jesus" in Cherokee, Redbird told his audience if they believed in "Almighty God, everything else will take care of itself. Of course, an eagle feather helps a lot, too."[18]

In 1977 Redbird sent President Jimmy Carter a headdress. To his surprise, Carter's team returned it with a note explaining the administration's policy against accepting gifts from the public. "He didn't complain about the incident to anyone," said Della Redbird. "He just said, 'Well, he sent it back. He sent it back.'"[19]

Following a cancer diagnosis, in February 1978 doctors removed Redbird's larynx. He regained the ability to speak with an artificial larynx several weeks later. Meanwhile, the Associated Press got wind of the Carter administration's rejection of the headdress. Redbird's family and friends, including leaders of the NAIA, posited it as a "symbolic tribute," not a "gift."

After weeks of mounting publicity, Carter's office relented. "Channel Four [television] got involved," said Della Redbird. "When the president's wife said she would accept the bonnet, my dad said, 'Okay, let's go!' Channel Four was going to pay for the trip."

While the media presented meeting the president as Redbird's last wish, his daughter said he expressed more concern for watching his infant grandson grow up. "He would say things like, 'I'd just like to see him hit a baseball some day.' And I knew that he knew he wouldn't be around much longer," said Della Redbird. "He died June fifteenth, before he could take the trip to Washington."

Redbird's family kept the headdress he made for President Carter. "We buried him in his Indian suit. It seemed the right thing to do, because that was how we knew him," said Della Redbird. "Even when he wasn't wearing his Indian clothing, he always wore cowboy boots or his hat, because that was part of who he was."

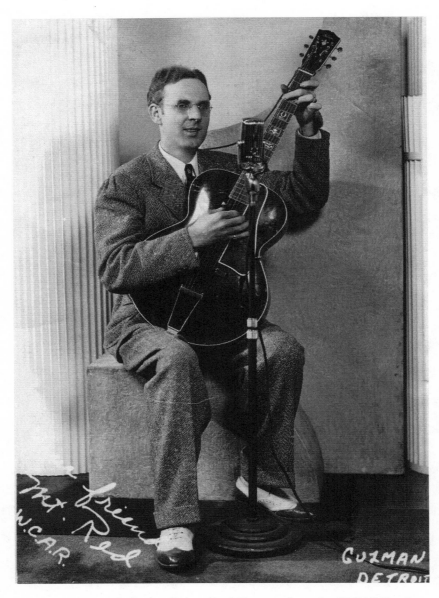

Figure 3. Mountain Red, a.k.a. Robert Ford Hogg, performed at WCAR Pontiac through the 1940s. Used by permission from Robert James Hogg.

Chapter 3

THE KENTUCKY TROUBADOUR
Mountain Red

> To sing successfully on these [Kentucky radio] stations as Mt. Red did, he
> had to know his backwoods strains and deliver them as they should be, for
> Kentuckians know their "Coming around the Mountain" as citizens of Naples
> know their "O Sole Mio."
>
> —PAUL WADE, MICHIGAN-BASED COUNTRY MUSIC PROMOTER[1]

> What you don't see anymore are the real hillbillies, who used to just get out
> there and have fun.
>
> —BOBBY HOGG, MOUNTAIN RED'S SON[2]

Dressed in his suit of navy blue jacket and cream-colored slacks, the
eighteen-year-old man with slicked red hair sat stiffly in the waiting room of
WMBC radio, his guitar case at his side and harmonica in his coat pocket.
Operating from the mezzanine level of the 700-room Hotel Detroiter on
Woodward Avenue, a few blocks north of Detroit's main entertainment district, WMBC featured a daily variety of commentary and music programming. The July heat caused the man to mop his brow with a handkerchief.
He was thinking on his one-way bus ride from Kentucky and the relief he
felt when he found his brother in Detroit, just two days before. A click from
a door disrupted hopeful thoughts as a well-dressed man entered. Following introductions, Hy Steed, the station's music director, ushered the young

man into an empty room with a baby grand piano. "And what is your radio act called?" asked Steed.

"I've gone by Mountain Red since my first job at thirteen," said Red with a smile, and rattled off the call letters of several stations in Kentucky and Ohio. He pulled on his resonator guitar and assembled a wire rack around his neck, placing a silver harmonica within reach of his mouth. Red picked his guitar as he alternately sang and blew his harmonica to a song he'd lived within for so many years, the vocal nuances he added to its ancient lyric enkindled the verses with a fresh blaze of meaning.

> I'd rather be in some dark holler where the sun don't ever shine
> Than to hear you call another darling, when you promised to be mine
> I don't want your greenback dollar . . .

Toward the end of the song, Red shifted his performance into high gear by thumping a foot on the polished wood floor of the studio. Steed noted the locks of hair that fell out of place during the man's presentation. "That's fine, fine," he said. "Do you know any cowboy numbers?"

"Yes, sir. As I like to say, this one's for the children to ride home on," and Red slid into a song about an old pony. "Is music your sole livelihood?" asked Steed as he considered the salability of the young man's act. When Red confirmed the question, Steed hired him on the spot.

On May 17, 1914, Mountain Red, a.k.a. Robert Ford Hogg, was born in a three-room house near the Kentucky River in Letcher County, Kentucky, near Blackey, in the Eastern Coal Fields. His father George Matt operated a store of general merchandise and groceries in the remote village, and the family got by with few hardships to endure.[3]

His mother Polly Ann purchased a $12.95 guitar and a harmonica, from a Sears-Roebuck mail order catalog. Red took to playing music and singing like a fly on molasses. In 1927 Red left home for Berea, Kentucky, where he enrolled in secondary school, and washed dishes afternoons and evenings to pay for his room and board.

He made a wire shoulder rack to hold the harmonica as he strummed guitar, and performed at churches and talent shows. Clyde Foley, a popular student a few grades ahead, admired Red's Eastern Kentucky "high and lonesome" vocals. He suggested Red audition at a nearby radio station. (Foley later entered a career in radio, calling himself "Red," too.)

At age thirteen, Red adopted a character type popular among folk music singers at the time, the mountaineer, as "Mountain Red" at WFBE Cincinnati, Ohio. Within a few years, he dropped out of school to pursue a career in entertainment. From the late 1920s until 1932, Red worked programs on WLM and WKRC Cincinnati, Ohio; WHAS Louisville, Kentucky; WLAP Lexington, Kentucky; and WCKY Covington, Kentucky.[4]

MOUNTAINEER MIGRATES

His repertoire expanded from the ballads he learned in Letcher County to popular songs on records by the likes of Jimmie Rodgers and Bradley Kincaid. He purchased a resonator guitar (or dobro) from Grinnell's in Cincinnati and added kazoo, knee cymbals, and jaw harp to his act. The instrumental combination changed Red from a singer with guitar to a one-man band, capable of playing almost any song with unique rhythmic effects.

After learning one of his brothers had moved to Detroit, Red took a bus to the Motor City in July 1932. Just two days after arriving in Michigan, he joined artists Gernert Case (another solo mountaineer) and Uncle Henry and His Harvesters at WMBC radio. A program called *The Happy Hour Club* gathered WMBC performers for a daily jamboree, which included comedian Danny Thomas performing as Amos Jacobs.

Mountain Red, "The Kentucky Troubadour," played coffee shops, bars, and cafés throughout the city. General Motors, Ford Motor Company, and C. F. Smith Company hired him to entertain at western-themed corporate events. He serenaded crowds on the Bob-Lo boats as they cruised the Detroit River from downtown to the Bob-Lo Island amusement park. Red also performed for the benefit of churches and charities.

WCAR CITY

The *Mountain Broadcast and Prairie Recorder*, a magazine that documented folk music entertainers on radio across North America, published a photo and letter from Mountain Red in November 1939. He was broadcasting on WMBC and had also appeared on WXYZ radio.[5]

Following the sale of WMBC in 1939, Red moved over to WEXL Royal Oak, where he crossed paths with Dixie Lee Walker, Sliver's Oregon Buckaroos, and the Lonesome Cowboys, a western-styled group led by the Buffington brothers, Tex, Clayton, and Ive. Vocalist and bass player with the Lonesome Cowboys, Enos "Skeets" McDonald, became a fast friend to Red.

In December 1939, WCAR signed on the air from studios located on the sixth floor of the Riker Building on West Huron Street, in downtown Pontiac. The growing city lay at the northernmost end of Woodward Avenue, connected to Detroit by the wide road and its electric streetcars. Pontiac featured a regional hospital and auto-related manufacturing within its borders. In 1940, Mountain Red was among the first country acts at the station (musicians from WMBC and WEXL soon followed).

With "I Hear Kentucky Calling Me" as his theme, Red performed twice a day at WCAR. The *Sears-Roebuck Farm Hour* featured most of the staff musicians from eleven o'clock to noon, and Red's show aired at a quarter past two, Monday through Friday, and at a quarter past ten Sunday mornings. During the rest of the day, he worked in sales at the nearby headquarters of his radio sponsor, the People's Credit Clothing Store, on North Saginaw. Red made the slogan of People's Clothing, "Where you get that e-e-e-easy credit," a familiar saying across Southeast Michigan. Often performing on the front sidewalk, he passed out coupons that bore his image and the text "My personal discount of $1.50 on any purchase of $15 or more."

Red met and courted Virginia Ferree, a young nurse. In 1940 Red and Virginia married at a double wedding in Toledo, Ohio. Skeets McDonald and Peggy Powell of Flint were the other couple in the ceremony. McDonald and his bride separated a few years later. "I know they weren't married as long as we were," said Virginia Hollar.[6]

In 1943, the army took McDonald overseas. Red did his part by promoting war bond rallies and other charities. He performed with Sgt. Gene Autry during Autry's personal appearance at the WCAR *Michigan Roundup* program in 1944.

Red stayed with WCAR for nearly fifteen years, performing every day. Red's first child, Shirley Grace, often joined him during broadcasts. Red's bookings took him around Michigan and Ohio, and into Ontario. For many years, he hired a driver to deliver him to personal appearances. He sold hundreds of songbooks with his name and picture on the cover. Pontiac songwriter and publisher Earl Boyt wrote folios of songs for Red to sing. In the 1947 *Mountain Red Special Song Folio Vol. 2*, printed by the M. M. Cole Publishing Company, Boyt's fare included western, sacred, war, love, and mountain songs.

During the late 1940s Red worked Pontiac nightclubs with fiddler Forest Rye and His Sagebrush Ranch Boys. Originally from Erin, Tennessee, Rye had lived in Detroit since 1924, working as a welder by day and entertaining at night. During the 1930s Rye and his band worked at WXYZ radio, where Red may have become acquainted with the bandleader.

Red also performed at showcases with the likes of Ernest Tubb, Minnie Pearl, and Hank Williams. He remained a favorite of local country fans from his time at WCAR through his return to WEXL in 1952. Sponsored by Sam Benson Men's Clothing Store on South Perry Street in Pontiac, Red's show followed Jack Ihrie's popular disk jockey program, *Sagebrush Melodies*, every weekday afternoon.

CATCHING CURVEBALLS

In 1955 Red moved to WPON radio, which had opened its Pontiac studios the year before. In 1956 he suffered a heart attack, which forced him to give up his radio show for six months of rest. After the minimum number of weeks passed, Red returned to the nightclub scene. A few months later he suffered a stroke that paralyzed part of his mouth and right hand. "He was doing good until he had that stroke," said Bobby Hogg. "I watched him have the stroke right up on the house. He was up there fixing some shingles, and he had a sunstroke. From there, he had all kinds of stuff happen to him."

Changing times presented fewer options for Red to make a living. In previous decades Red was a star on radio. After World War II, most country musicians played dance music and made records for jukeboxes and disk jockeys to spin. Red cut homemade disks for friends and fans, but never made a commercial record. He opened a store on South Paddock in Pontiac, where he sold and repaired household appliances. The family moved to an apartment across the street. Red continued performing at night, while his wife worked at the state hospital. Then his marriage hit the rocks. In 1963 a judge granted a divorce.

RESURGENT RED

Red opened a new repair shop on North Perry Street. With Dixie Lee Walker and her husband's convenience store up the street, the back of Red's shop was the scene of many jam sessions. In September 1966, promoter Paul Wade tracked down Red living at a friend's house. Wade's feature on Red's life story in the very first *Music City News—Michigan Supplement* gave him a boost.

Wade booked Red for a variety of public showcases, such as a January 1967 in-store performance at Recordland in Wayne.[7] In September, at Wade's first annual Michigan Country Music Convention in Frontier City, an Old West theme park in Michigan's Irish Hills, Red accepted an award acknowledging his contributions to country music in Michigan.[8]

Red spent his last years in Pontiac, never hesitating to strum his dobro for an audience when the opportunity arose. On June 26, 1976, another heart attack silenced the Kentucky Troubadour. His ex-wife and children buried him at the top of the Drayton Plains Cemetery, north of Pontiac. In 2007, years after the disappearance of the original marker, Mountain Red's children placed a heart-shaped stone at his grave.

Figure 4. George (left) and Leslie York teamed up as the York Brothers at WPAY Portsmouth, Ohio, in 1936, just a couple of years before they moved to Detroit and began making records. Used by permission from John Morris.

Chapter 4

THE YORK BROTHERS,
GEORGE AND LESLIE

Someone in Hamtramck tried to sue George and Les about that song....
Said, "You're putting our city down." We got a lot of requests for it.

—TOMMY VENABLE, BASS PLAYER FOR THE YORK BROTHERS,
REGARDING THE SONG "HAMTRAMCK MAMA"[1]

Leslie York's brother George knocked at the apartment door. "Les, you in there?" he called. Leslie set down his glass, and swung himself up from his chair. "Yeah, it's open," he said. George entered with the half-smile he wore when something bothered him. "Have a chair," said Leslie.

A few drinks and cigarettes later, George had shared his news: Nearly four years on WSM radio and the *Grand Ole Opry* couldn't save Leslie's job after his blunder on the Ryman Auditorium stage.

George looked up and said, "Eddie can get us back on the *Louisiana Hayride*."

"You don't have to leave," chuckled Leslie. "They didn't fire you."

"If you're going, I'm going. What am I gonna do? I can't just sit and stare at the walls."

"Well, I'm not crazy about Shreveport. But I guess it's better than nothing."

George stared at his brother. "We can always go back to Detroit," he said.

In the Cumberland Mountains, Louisa, Kentucky, sits on the border of West Virginia. U.S. Route 23, the "hillbilly highway," runs through the town, and the region has long been regarded as an excellent place to fish for bass and hunt deer and wild turkey. Growing up in Louisa, George and Leslie York learned hunting and fishing, as well as music. Both played guitar and developed decent singing voices.[2] Born February 17, 1910, George York won his first talent show at age eleven. After completing the eighth grade, he frequented theater stages at night, while working days in coal mines at Wheelright, Burdine, and Jenkins.[3] During the late 1920s, George moved to Denver, Colorado, and caught the ear of a local bandleader who hired him to work in nightclubs and on radio.

Leslie York, born August 23, 1917, left school after completing the ninth grade. He earned a few dollars by catching and selling wild game and fish, and working at neighboring farms. At a talent show in Lexington's Kentucky Theater, he won a four-week spot on a local radio station. In 1936 Leslie joined George in Portsmouth, Ohio, where his older brother sang at WPAY radio.

The York Brothers' voices sounded with similar timbre and blended well as George sang most of the lead vocals, and Leslie sang harmony. A master of old-time guitar picking, George combined single-note runs with chords with a style traditionally played behind fiddles. Leslie played melody and improvisations that echoed the music of Southern speech. Although he avoided the "virtuoso" tag, Leslie got the job done in his own way.

Born on the banks of the Ohio River in Portsmouth, the York Brothers act matured along the Detroit River in Detroit, where George and Leslie settled by 1939. Perhaps Portsmouth's annual floods—particularly the devastation of 1937—convinced the Yorks to head north.

UNIVERSAL APPEAL

Hamtramck, a city within Detroit's borders, began as a township in 1827, named after Jean François Hamtramck of Quebec, who fought for the American cause during the Revolutionary War. In 1796 Commander Hamtramck took charge of Fort Shelby in Detroit for the United States. One hundred years later, several hundred German families farmed Hamtramck Township. After John and Horace Dodge constructed the Dodge Brothers Auto Car Company facilities on the township's south end in 1910, Polish immigrants moved in by the thousands. In 1922 citizens incorporated Hamtramck to prevent Detroit annexation. Despite the Poles' efforts to spread Catholicism, Prohibition-era mobsters brought booze, drugs, and prostitution to Hamtramck, giving the young city a wide-open reputation.

At the start of the 1930s, state authorities directed a clampdown on the most obvious illegal activities, resulting in the arrest of several politicians, including the city's first elected mayor.[4] Perhaps the Yorks were inspired by stories they heard, or scenes they witnessed firsthand, to write their most famous song. In the spring of 1940, months after "Hamtramck Mama" first appeared in jukeboxes throughout Detroit, Hamtramck Mayor Walter Kanar sought a court order to stop play of the song within his city. The publicity led to more record sales. (Two years later Kanar was indicted on vice and corruption charges, and resigned his position.)[5]

The York Brothers cut "Hamtramck Mama" backed with "Going Home" at the Universal Recording Studios on East Jefferson for the Marquette Music Company, which serviced jukeboxes across Michigan's Lower Peninsula, northern Indiana, and Ohio. Marquette Music had existed since 1900, when founder John Marquette supplied rolls for coin-operated pianos in Detroit beer joints.[6]

She's a Hamtramck mama, and she sure does know her stuff
She's the hottest thing in town, Lordy how she can love[7]

"Hamtramck Mama" was comparable to the popular "Deep Elm Blues" in melody and lyrics about visits to good-time women, lawless law enforcers, and corruptible preachers. Les York played a signature guitar lick that established a style the Yorks milked for several more years.[8] The B-side, "Going Home," an adaptation of Bradley Kincaid's "Little Whitewashed Chimney," appealed to the York Brothers' audience of Southern transplants by expressing regret for leaving the South to find work in Detroit.

Marquette Music followed up the York Brothers' first record with a double-sided scorcher. In "Highland Park Girl" (1939), George related a lusty encounter with a married woman in Highland Park, a bustling city of middle-class residents employed in its local factories. Blistering steel guitar (probably played by Art Brooke or Taft "Rosebud" Blevins)[9] opened "Detroit Hulu Girl" on the flipside.

The Yorks made at least one more record issued with the Universal label, produced by Edward Kiely, owner of the Mellow Music Shops located around the corner from Universal Recording Studios. The York Brothers' last Universal singles featured another steel guitarist on "Gamblers Blues" (1940) and "It Taint No Good" (1940). The latter, with verses about the spoiled charms of a love-crazy woman, was backed with "Sweetheart Darling." "Gamblers Blues" was coupled with "Conscription Blues," a reference to the draft instituted that year.

BLOWIN' TO THE WINDY CITY

In February 1941 the York Brothers traveled to Decca's Chicago studio where they delivered subdued, yet sparkling vocals in the style of the Delmore Brothers (who also recorded for Decca at the time). The session resulted in three records. Highlights included Leslie York's "Speak To Me Little Darling," with a traditional "dead lover" theme, along with the tongue-in-cheek original "Naggin' Young Woman," sung by George York. For Decca the York Brothers picked acoustic guitars and presented well-rehearsed music without the ad-libs or hollers heard on their next Detroit recordings.

While the York Brothers promoted their Decca records, Edward Kiely issued a clutch of C&W novelties on his Hot Wax and Mellow labels. Vocalist Billy Casteel with WEXL radio artists the Silver Sage Buckaroos cut "Hollywood Mama" (1941), a rewrite of "Hamtramck Mama." Forest Rye's Red River Blue Yodelers recorded "On Down The Line" (1942). Eveline Haire and Her Swingtime Cowgirls cut "Triflin' Woman" (1942). When their Decca contract lapsed in 1942, the York Brothers cut dozens more for Kiely.

DETROIT'S CALLING ME

Leslie York acquired an electric guitar and amplifier in 1942. Compared to the Delmore Brothers' records of the 1930s and 1940s, the Yorks' Detroit recordings came across with more volume and spontaneity, no doubt inspired by their noisy, urban surroundings.

More than ten years before Elvis Presley and Johnny Cash cooked up a similar formula at Sun Records in Memphis, Tennessee, the York Brothers formed a rockabilly trio by adding Jonnie Lavender on upright bass. Lavender slapped the strings, whooped and laughed maniacally on "Going To The Shindig" (1942) and "I've Got My Eyes On You" (1942).

Around 1941 Kiely got his hands on the original stamping plates and reissued the 1939 version of "Hamtramck Mama" backed with "It Taint No Good." He also paired "No Good" on Mellow with a 1942 version of "Hamtramck Mama," cut with an upright bass (probably Lavender). Kiely arranged a deal with Buhl Sons Company, a record distributor with offices in Detroit, Toledo, and Grand Rapids, while he maintained a jukebox route in the neighborhood surrounding his shops. In September 1942, *Billboard* reported, "Edward Kiely, operator, has formally registered as sole owner of the Mellow Record Company."[10]

The York Brothers made more than thirty recordings in Detroit. Leslie York wrote most of the songs, covering a broad range of subjects and styles, for example, blues ("York Brothers Blues" and "Got To Get Rid Of My Worried Mind"), patriotism ("Hail, Hail Ol' Glory"), cowboys ("Riding And Singing My Song"), and heart songs ("If I Would Never Lose You"). In close harmony they yodeled on one record ("Conscription Blues") and whistled on another ("Kentucky's Calling Me"). Locomotive sound effects introduced "We're Gonna Catch That Train."

In December 1942 *Billboard* noted, "The Detroit area is paying plenty of nickels to hear the York Brothers' *Not Over 35*."[11] Beginning with the wail of a police car siren, a talking blues made light of the thirty-five-miles-per-hour wartime limit on vehicle speeds to conserve gas and tires, while celebrating that the new law treated "big shots" in limousines the same as more humble folk.

From 1939 to 1943, the York Brothers were the most prolific of any hillbilly songsters based in Michigan. Wartime shortage of shellac likely caused Kiely to stop manufacturing in 1943. The American Federation of Musicians recording ban from August 1942 until October 1943 may have also played a role in the confused, yet preeminent legacy of the Mellow Records Company.

FROM UNCLE SAM TO UNCLE SYD

In April 1944, *Billboard* reported, "The two York Brothers, who until recently were playing at the Jefferson Inn, Detroit, have joined the navy."[12] Leslie York served with amphibious forces in Europe, while George York joined a unit that entertained soldiers in the Pacific theater.

Upon receiving discharges in 1946, they headed for WSM radio Nashville, Tennessee. The York Brothers debuted on the *Grand Ole Opry* in January. They worked an early morning program on WSM and broadcast Saturday afternoons coast-to-coast over the Mutual Network's *Checkerboard Show*, sponsored by Purina. The Yorks hired Henry "Swanee" Swan as bass player. During the week, they often worked bookings in Detroit, where they maintained ties to friends and extended family.

In 1946 the York Brothers recorded for Bullet Records, one of the first independent labels in Nashville. Besides pop, gospel, and blues artists, Bullet signed *Opry* stars such as Pee Wee King and Minnie Pearl. Although cut with better technology than their pre-war sides, the Yorks' songs came from the salty vein they mined in Detroit. Their first single, "I'm Not Foolin'," sounded like the country blues Detroit jukeboxes played before the war. And they reprised "Hamtramck Mama." Four more recordings in 1947 included fiddle by Curley King and accordion (possibly John "Rocky" Norocki, who worked with C&W groups at Ted's 10-Hi in Detroit).

In January 1947 *National Hillbilly News* published a photograph of Charles H. Muggleduck, comedian of the York Brothers act, sneaking up behind an unsuspecting George York with a cream pie raised high, ready to press into his scalp. Leslie York played Muggleduck dressed in the colorful rags of a backwoods clown.[13] The York Brothers participated in Bill Monroe's traveling tent show that year and worked beside Monroe and His Bluegrass Boys on the WSM *Carter's Champion Chicks* program at seven o'clock Saturday evenings.

As the York Brothers established themselves in Nashville, Detroit musicians Eddie Jackson and Hugh Friar both remembered the Yorks performing at Ted's 10-Hi on East Jefferson at Fairview, a few blocks up from the Mellow Music shops. Friar first met them in 1946. "If George was gonna take a night off or . . . gonna be out of town, I would go and set in with Leslie. We got to where we could do pretty good duets together. 'Swanee' was with 'em at that time," said Friar. "'Chubby' Wise, . . . he played quite a while with the York Brothers. He played fiddle for them at Ted's 10-Hi. This was years before [Wise] went with Hank Snow."[14] In 1947 Jackson's band alternated sets with the Yorks at Ted's.[15]

In mid-1947 the York Brothers inked a contract with King Records of Cincinnati, Ohio. During the next nine years, the Yorks cut eighteen sessions for King, owned by Sydney Nathan. His operations, housed in a former ice warehouse on Brewster Avenue, included recording and mastering studios, record manufacturing, and a distribution hub. Nathan retained a top-notch C&W band for studio work, including guitarists Zeke and Red Turner and steel guitarist Jerry Byrd.

The first couple of King sessions occurred near the end of 1947. James C. Petrillo, president of the American Federation of Musicians, called for a ban on recording by members of the American Federation of Musicians, starting January 1, 1948. Petrillo wished to pressure record companies into making larger royalty payments to musicians. The York Brothers recorded some tunes they had made in Detroit for Mellow, including "It Tain't No Good," "Riding And Singing My Song," and "Long Gone." With accordion, steel, guitars (two electric), and fiddle, the music during the first King sessions sounded close to western swing.

Although working with King Records improved the overall quality of York Brothers recordings, Nathan refused to allow Leslie York to play guitar on sessions. His love for gin and Squirt soda was "the reason they didn't use him on the records. [They] used Zeke Turner," said bassist Tommy Venable, who worked with the Yorks in 1953 and 1954. "George, he played open chords all the time, and they got Red Turner to smack rhythm [guitar]." However, the cutting tone and punchy style of the guitar on most 1947 numbers made it clear Leslie York played lead guitar at the sessions, while Zeke Turner picked some harmony. Aside from George York and Swanee Swan, other musicians included Jerry Byrd, Curley King, Rocky Norocki, and Drury Russell "Dink" Embry.[16]

In March 1948 the King Records promotional tabloid, *Record Roundup*, reported, "York Brothers, King recording stars, back on the Grand Ole Opry after several months of successful personal appearances in Michigan plan to return to that state in March at which time their agent, Eddie Johnson, has them booked for 38 weeks."[17]

In late 1948, the York Brothers left the *Grand Ole Opry*, moving to the KWKH *Louisiana Hayride* in Shreveport, Louisiana, for six weeks. *Opry* managers allowed the York Brothers to come back, but after a while, they again wound up on the *Hayride*, never to return to the *Opry*. "They wouldn't let 'em play the *Opry* anymore 'cause [Leslie] went on the stage loaded," said Venable. "He came out on stage, they mentioned one song and he kicked another one off." Joining the *Hayride* was a move not uncommon for WSM artists who broke rules barring alcoholic drinks from performances. Hank Williams moved from the *Opry* to the *Hayride* in 1952 for the same reason.

In July 1949 *Billboard* reported the York Brothers had left KWKH to "work permanently on a Michigan outlet."[18]

MOTOR CITY BOOGIE

After moving into an apartment building on Parkview, north of East Jefferson, the Yorks were welcomed back to Detroit with the reissue of their 1939 Universal recordings "Hamtramck Mama" and "Highland Park Girl" by Fortune Records. Owners Jack and Dorothy Brown started Fortune in 1946 with their hopes set on the pop market, but some of their earliest successes were in the country music field, including Roy Hall's jukebox hit "Dirty Boogie" (1949) and "Skeets" McDonald's "The Tattooed Lady" (1950). To the chagrin of proud Hamtramck folk, Fortune kept "Hamtramck Mama" in print through the 1970s.[19]

The York Brothers booked into the Caravan Gardens, a new country music nightclub at Woodrow Wilson and Davison. During the day they wrote songs and gambled. "They were both horse racin' fans," said guitarist Chuck Oakes. "They'd play on weekends, or three or four nights a week, and then you'd see 'em out at the race track every day to go play the horses."[20]

At King studios in January 1950, the York Brothers cut an ode to Detroit called "Motor City Boogie," as well as "Gravy Train," originally recorded by King R&B artist Tiny Bradshaw. Sometimes, as on "Motor City Boogie," the brothers rushed the meter, or held back for an extra beat, but they always came in singing together.

"They'd look at each other, and they could read each other's mind, I believe," said Venable. "If I missed timing, George would turn around and say, 'Hey, next time we do this, I'm gonna look at this and get this straight.' I tried to tell 'em [what they were doing wrong], and George knew. He said, 'Yeah, we know that, Tom.' When I mentioned it to Les, . . . I swear, he got mad, boy! He said, 'Hey, you can be replaced!' Their timing was real funny."

During the early 1950s musical crossovers—where C&W, pop, and R&B artists recorded each other's songs—sold well. King producer Henry Glover, who worked with both black and white artists, may have assisted the York Brothers during 1951, when they recorded tunes originally cut by Wynonie Harris ("Tremblin'") and the Dominoes ("Sixty Minute Man" and "Chicken Blues"). The York Brothers did not sing like Harris, or Bill Brown of the Dominoes, expressing the drama of the moment. Rather, their interpretations typified a traditional country approach with mellow, tongue-in-cheek delivery.

TRIUMPH OF THE TANGO

Johnnie and Jack's "Poison Love" was the first country hit with a Latin-American beat, and the York Brothers tried similar rhythms, beginning with "That's Why I'm Crying All The Time" in 1952. Redd Stewart's "Tennessee Tango," cut by the Yorks that year, proved to be the big hit they were searching for. The flipside, "River Of Tears," also attracted jukebox spins and sales.[21]

In 1952–53 the York Brothers appeared regularly on the WJR *Big Barn Frolic* Saturday night jamboree. During a special June 24, 1953, broadcast for tornado disaster relief in Flint, Michigan, a WJR announcer referred to the York Brothers as "stars of the *Big Barn Frolic*."[22] With Chuck Hatfield on steel guitar and Horace "Horsefly" Wilson on bass, the group began with "Raise A Ruckus Tonight," the *Frolic* theme song. The York Brothers sang "River Of Tears" and "Tennessee Tango," sounding as good as—if not better than—their recordings. During "Tango," after the verse "I know that she'll always love me," they carried an extra beat to accommodate Wilson yelling,

"I hope! I hope! I hope!" With a nationwide hit under their belts, the York Brothers had reached a plateau of their career.

Tommy Venable, born in Tazewell, Tennessee, joined the act in 1953.

> Me and Carson Wagner was playing [music together], but one night we didn't have to work. He called me and said, "Do you wanna ride up with me to see the York Brothers?" I said, "Yeah, let's go." We went to the 3-J's bar [on West Vernor in Detroit] and they didn't have a bass player. They had a bass—they just didn't have a bass player. . . . I got on that upright bass and got to work on it. Les looked at me and said, "Hey, you're doing a good job with that." I said, "Well, thank you." He said, "You wanna work tomorrow night?" I said, "Yeah!"

Venable participated in recording sessions at King. They traveled to New York City once, to perform on a television program. They played few shows outside Detroit, such as the jamborees held at the Circle Theater in Cleveland, Ohio. They also appeared a few times on the WSM *Ernest Tubb Midnight Jamboree*, broadcast from the Ernest Tubb Record Shop in Nashville.

"We were kinda under contract there at Ted's [10-Hi]," said Venable. "We'd go to work on Tuesday, Wednesday, Thursday, Friday and Saturday. Or sometimes we'd let someone take the Friday and Saturday, and we'd go to Nashville. We'd leave on a Friday evening and make it down there for Saturday. When we worked the 3-J's bar, I think that was a contract. I'll put it this way: Them two guys were business, and the only two who knew their business was them. George and Les didn't tell me nothing 'til about a day or so before it's time to go. And Les would never tell me. It was always George. George would stand between me and Les, playing his rhythm. George would look around on a Wednesday or Thursday and say, 'We gotta be at so-and-so place at a certain time. Do you wanna drive or do you wanna go with me?' I'd say, 'Hey, somebody pick me up.'"

In 1953–54 the York Brothers performed on Casey Clark's Lazy Ranch Boys Barn Dance, broadcast on WJR radio. Clark's wife Mary recalled, "They were so good with their ears that they could come from opposite sides of the stage and take off singing, immediately. They didn't have to strike a note, hum or nothing. They just hit it."[23] Clark reproduced a photo of the York Brothers on its own page in his 1953 Lazy Ranch Boys souvenir book.

FROM ONE BIG D TO ANOTHER

The *Big Barn Frolic* ended in July 1953. Later that year, the York Brothers and their families moved to Texas. George established a restaurant in Dallas. The brothers appeared as guests at the WFAA *Saturday Night Shindig* in Dallas, as well as the KRLD *Big 'D' Jamboree* in Dallas. However, during 1954–55 the York Brothers returned to Detroit for several months at a time to work in theaters and nightclubs.

KING CUTS

Syd Nathan probably planned a York Brothers country-to-pop crossover hit, but it never happened. Several of the York Brothers' King sides featured piano accompaniment played in a pop style, a few years ahead of its time. And instead of cutting songs about contemporary events or issues, the majority of the Yorks' King records concerned affairs of the heart.

Rock 'n' roll jumped into the mainstream in 1956, more than ten years after the Yorks cut their most rocking music in Detroit. Still, their influence on contemporary musicians appeared in remakes of their songs by artists such as Carl Butler, who cut "River Of Tears" in 1957. Slim Whitman remade the song in 1958. Although the liner notes to the Everly Brothers' album "Songs Our Fathers Taught Us" stated that "Long Time Gone" was an Appalachian folk song, the Everlys sang a version that resembled the Yorks' 1950 recording for King. In 1960 Reno and Smiley changed the York Brothers' "Mountain Rosa Lee" (1947) into a bluegrass classic.

LES IS MORE

In 1955 Ted's 10-Hi changed its house entertainment from country to Latin music. In summer 1956, Leslie York returned to Michigan without George, and continued to do so for several years, playing with Danny Richards' Gold Star Cowboys. Besides sharing vocals with Richards, Leslie did most of the announcing for the band. He recorded solo for King in 1956, during the York Brothers' final two sessions. On sides attributed to "York Brothers," Leslie sang his and George's parts, using overdubbing technology. Danny Richards attended these sessions, singing on "Lightning Struck My Heart" and "Blue River."

In 1957, the Gold Star Cowboys opened radio station WBRB Mount Clemens and performed in the studio every morning for nearly two years. At night, the band played the Dixie Belle on West Vernor and other venues. "[Leslie would] go down there [to Texas] for seven or eight months, then come back up here [Detroit] for three or four—'til about '63," said Richards.[24]

In July 1957 Leslie met George in Nashville to cut a session for Decca. They made four recordings at Owen Bradley's Quonset hut studio, and Decca issued one single, the bopping "Everybody's Tryin' To Be My Baby," based on a 1930s Texas swing number, coupled with "I Want My Baby Back." The record went nowhere. With their 1957 hit "Bye Bye Love," the Everly Brothers had redirected the industry's focus to younger harmony acts. Besides that, George had all but quit the music business.

One night at the Dixie Belle in Detroit, Leslie York and Danny Richards ran into Sage and Sand Records producer Pat Nelson, who offered them a record deal. Quick-like, the Gold Star Cowboys went to a building on Woodward Avenue and Selden in Detroit, where Nelson's engineers set up a temporary studio. Richards recorded "Better To Be Safe" and "The Last Curtain" on which Leslie sang harmony. Leslie remade the 1954 pop hit "River Of No Return" and delivered a smooth vocal for his own "I'll Cry Again Tomorrow," on which Richards sang harmony. Issued on the Sage label, "I'll Cry Again Tomorrow" was the company's bestseller of 1957. Four years later, Bob Wills and Tommy Duncan revived it for Liberty Records as "Tomorrow I'll Cry."

YORK BROTHERS RECORDS

In Dallas and Fort Worth, the York Brothers performed as occasional guests on local television and radio shows. Radio emcee Lawton Williams hired them as regulars for a strictly country revival of the *Big 'D' Jamboree* during the mid-1960s, and the Yorks appeared on Lloyd "Cowboy" Weaver's Saturday night country music program on KTVT-TV Fort Worth Channel Eleven.

Around 1960, the York Brothers started making records again. They pressed their own singles on custom labels called York, York Brothers Records, and York Records Inc., issuing eighteen sides by the end of the decade. Their Texas recordings featured a mix of musical styles such as country and pop in Marvin Rainwater's "Gonna Find Me A Bluebird" and Earl Carson's "Big Blue Diamonds,"; and traditional numbers such as Cliff Carlisle's "The Girl In The Blue Velvet Band," along with blues—as only the Yorks could deliver—with "Monday Morning Blues," an ode to a working man's post-weekend hangover.

Of more than a hundred recordings, the York Brothers' most enduring title remained "Hamtramck Mama." During the late 1960s, Detroit disk jockey Dick Purtan used it with an on-air game during his popular show at WKNR radio Dearborn.[25] Through the years, Detroit-area country and rock bands revived the song.[26]

George York died in July 1974. Leslie, playing music to the end, passed in February 1984. "The last time I seen him, we was over at Hatfield's Old Town Tavern [near Cadieux Road and Harper Avenue]," said Danny Richards. "He come into the club and I didn't feel good. . . . So I said, 'Hey Les, you wanna take over for me tonight?' He said, 'Yeah!' He grabbed his big ol' guitar and I went home to bed.

"I went down there and visited. The last year [1983] I didn't get to see him. I wrote him but I didn't get no answer. He must have been a little sicker than I thought he was," said Richards.

Guitarist Paul Williams, who played music in Detroit with the Lonesome Pine Fiddlers, and Jimmy Martin, said, "I really liked those guys. . . . They had been on top of the heap, you know. And we kind of looked up to those people because they had been on top for a long time. They were good people."[27]

Figure 5. The Prairie Pioneers performed at WCAR Pontiac when the station opened in 1939. Clockwise, from lower left: William Harvey "Arizona" Breeding, Bernard "Sleepy" Heldt, and Grover "Smokey" Breeding. Used by permission from Margueritte Breeding.

Chapter 5

TENACIOUS TRAILBLAZER
Arizona Weston

> I've done everything a guy can do in this business.
>
> —ARIZONA WESTON[1]

During the first half of the twentieth century, country and western singers often invented alter egos. As cowboys and mountaineers grew popular
through radio, stage, and motion pictures, musicians found it necessary to
invent new names and appearances. Arizona Weston, a.k.a. William Harvey
Breeding, began his career as a country and western singer, with an emphasis
on the "western," and never veered from the course he set early on: to participate in and promote country music. Weston followed the chivalric ideals
presented in the books of Zane Grey and movies of Gene Autry through
eight decades as a musician, singer, emcee, square dance caller, songwriter,
recording artist, storyteller, radio disk jockey, television host, booking agent,
friend, husband, father, and grandfather.

He was born April 15, 1921, to Frank and Alma Breeding in the small community of Washburn, Tennessee, east of Knoxville. Months after his arrival,
Weston's parents moved to Middlesboro, Kentucky, northwest of the Tennessee and Virginia state lines, between Pine Mountain and the Cumberland Mountains.

> We lived there five years. . . . Then we moved back to Tennessee. . . . Then we
> moved to Detroit, Michigan, in 1928. Then we moved to Pontiac on New Year's

Day 1929. The Depression hit us in '31, and we went back to Tennessee. It was worse down there than it was up here, so we came back [to Pontiac] in '34.

Eventually, Weston found himself the big brother to six boys, but he played music with just one. Seventeen months younger, Grover "Smokey" Breeding was as large as Weston by the time he was five years old. "The two of us grew up together, and everybody thought we was twins," said Weston. "When we started playing music, we were called . . . the Arizona Twins. I went by the name of Arizona, no last name or anything. . . . Zane Grey's books, . . . I read all them books and I liked the name Arizona."

Weston's dad played music, providing entertainment for house parties, churches, and other community functions.

Before we came up here, we went to a singing school in Tennessee. . . . I'd have been about eleven, twelve years old. We went to a singing school at the church, and they taught us how to read shape notes. . . . We wound up [with] my dad singing bass, my mother singing alto, and I was singing tenor, and my brother was singing the lead. We had a quartet in our family. When we came up here, my dad always had a guitar—I can't remember when there wasn't a guitar at the house—and he played banjo and the fiddle.

In 1929 and '30, everybody [made their own] homebrew. The house that we lived in, in Detroit, was a two-story family flat. The house next door was raided one time. Police brought out big jugs and dumped it right in the backyard. Broke it all to hell.

So everybody had their own homebrew and stuff, and they'd have house parties on weekends, Friday night or Saturday night. [The parties went] on 'til three or four o'clock in the morning. The band would get tired, and that's how me and my brother Smokey, we got to play in the band. We'd get up there and play the guitar because we was sober, and [the band wasn't]. That's how we learned to play the guitar. . . . My dad could play fiddle for old-time breakdowns and stuff like that, square dances and stuff. . . . Before I was seventeen, I was calling square dances.

After the family's move to Pontiac in 1934, Weston's father befriended

Steve "Mack" McDonald, who operated an auto service station. Mack McDonald was an older brother of musician Enos "Skeets" McDonald, and the first of his family to move to Michigan from Arkansas. "The first day Skeets arrived in town, my dad was introduced over at Mack's garage. My dad invited Skeets to a house party he was playing that night. Skeets showed up, and my dad and him were good friends after that."

Skeets McDonald grew up in rural Arkansas (born in 1915 near Greenway) and moved to Pontiac around 1935 (his mom, dad, and another brother followed). He found work in a factory and fell in with Tex, Clayton, and Ive Buffington's band the Lonesome Cowboys, playing bass and singing. The group performed cowboy songs and western swing in cafés and bars around Pontiac. "When we were about fifteen, sixteen years old, my dad used to take us over to the club where Skeets was playing with the Buffington boys," said Weston, placing the years around 1936–37. "They were playing in . . . Bob and Myrtle's, a little bar over on East Boulevard, in Pontiac." Because the boys were underage, their father took them to see Sunday matinee performances of the Lonesome Cowboys. "We'd go over and drink a Coke and listen to 'em play music," he said.

The Arizona Twins also knew songs by Wade Mainer, whose popular radio broadcasts they listened to back in Kentucky. In 1938 the Twins accepted an invitation from the Lonesome Cowboys to be their guests at WEXL radio Royal Oak. "That's the first time we was on the air," said Weston. "Me and my brother Smokey went down and sang [Carson Robison's] 'Carry Me Back To The Mountains.'" They made their first public appearance at the Oasis, on Hatchery Road and Dixie Highway in Waterford.

ROAD BUSTERS

Soon after appearing at the Oasis, a man called Doc Johnson invited the Arizona Twins to join his group, the Arizona Bronc-Busters. Johnson led the band, played banjo, and performed comedy and tricks with a sixteen-foot-long bullwhip. Bernard "Slim the Fiddlin' Fool" Heldt played fiddle, Lamar "Curly" LaFave (son of a Rochester Hills dentist) played accordion, and Jeff "the Wrangler" Stover played bass. Arizona and Smokey both played guitars and formed the Black Canyon Trio, a singing group within the band, with Heldt.

"We used to stand [Heldt] on his head. We'd hold him by his feet, . . . and he'd stand right on the top of his head and play the fiddle. Then he'd play it behind his back, and on top of his head, and under his arm, and every other place. . . . He could play anything, from Stokowski to 'Comin' Around The Mountain,'" said Weston.

> Ted's Trailer [had] the original foot-long hot dog, [and was located] on Square Lake and Woodward. It was there for years, and they had swinging doors. . . . They stayed open twenty-four hours of the day. We had come back from playing down in Detroit some place, and we walked in the swinging doors. Just as the fiddle player, Sleepy, went through, somebody grabbed his cowboy hat and slung it back through the building. We had a gang fight! There was six of us, and that's when we was playing with Doc Johnson, and we was all going in there— and boy, you talk about fights! Everybody was into it in a few minutes [laughs].

On January 2, 1939, the six men set out for New York City to audition for the *Major Bowes Original Amateur Hour*, a famous talent show broadcast on the CBS radio network. Weston drove them in his 1936 Ford. "Couldn't keep oil in it," he said. "We even got down to a point where we carried a five-gallon can and at every gas station we'd get used oil, if we could." They stopped at clubs and cafés to earn traveling money. "[We] asked them if we could play some music and pass the hat," said Weston. "That's the way we earned our way down through there."

Stover's parents lived in Charleston, West Virginia, and they stopped to visit. "They had a telephone system where you rang a firebell and you got everybody on the line. That's what they done, and we sang over the telephone," said Weston. The telephone audience included a representative from WCHS Charleston, and the Arizona Bronc-Busters received an offer to perform on radio every day. "We was there three months, doing two [shows] in the morning. And every Friday night they had a *Farm and Home Hour* that everybody was on."

A mail-order chicken hatchery sponsored the Arizona Bronc-Busters. Other entertainers with the *Farm and Home Hour* included the Bailes Brothers, Budge and Fudge Mayse, the Holden Brothers (Milton Jackson and Fairley Holden), Clarence C. "Nimrod" Clere (fiddle and comedy), Lloyd "Cowboy" Copas, and Natchee the Indian (a.k.a. Lester Storer, a trick fiddler). "Cowboy Copas, he played with Natchee," said Weston. "We used to go up to their hotel room and watch them practice."[2]

> Just at the last week of March, . . . we played a dance hall and got twenty bucks for the whole band. And when we come back, [Doc Johnson] went out for a coffee, and that's the last we seen of him—twenty bucks and all! [*laughs*]
>
> Anyway, he run off and left us, so we was there to shift for ourselves. We checked with the boss at the front end, and they gave us some money because of the chicks that we were selling on the Friday night *Farm and Home Hour*. We had about twenty, twenty-five dollars to get outta town. We didn't have sense enough to come home—we went to Knoxville, Tennessee. . . . My uncles and aunts lived there. . . . We went to the *Midday Merry-Go-Round* [at radio station WNOX].

Their audition for producer Lowell Blanchard, who created the *Midday Merry-Go-Round* at WNOX after leaving WJR radio Detroit in 1936, was a success. But because the station didn't pay musicians, the penniless men decided to return to Michigan. "The first day of April, we got back here about four o'clock in the morning. And my license plates run out at midnight," said Weston.

PONTIAC PIONEERS

Weston re-organized the Black Canyon Trio, with Smokey and Sleepy (formerly Slim), as the Prairie Pioneers for bookings in Flint at Jessie's bar and Frances' Tavern. Frances' Tavern, on Industrial Avenue just south of East Stewart Avenue, kept the Prairie Pioneers busy through February 1940. Across the road from the bar sat Buick City, General Motors' sprawling complex on the Flint River. "We used to get a lot of people from the plants come out. After they'd get out of work they'd come over and listen to us sing," said Weston. "We was up there . . . five nights a week. . . . They promoted us in the daily paper" and a local entertainment magazine.

On December 17, 1939, WCAR radio began broadcasting at 1300 kc from the sixth floor of the Riker Building on West Huron Street in downtown Pontiac. Aside from a few syndicated shows, the station's daily programming was live, six a.m. to quarter past six p.m. every day. From news broadcasts to religious hours to musical entertainment, every voice participated in person. The Prairie Pioneers was one of the first musical acts on the air, and the first country-western group. "We went on between the holidays [Christmas and New Year's Day]," said Weston. "And we was there until '43, almost four years."

In February 1940 they began working with Prairie Maid Norma. "She was from South Lyon [Michigan]. . . . She used to get shows booked, and we'd go out and play music for her. She could yodel up a storm. She done more yodeling than any girl yodeler I ever heard," said Weston. "She did a fifteen-minute show every day, just like we did. She stayed here [in Pontiac] with her aunt, and she'd go home on weekends. She couldn't have been older than eighteen or nineteen years old at the time.

"When WCAR went on the air, it was just wide open for anyone that wanted to come. . . . Nobody got paid," said Weston. During the station's first decade of business, musicians included solo acts Gernert Case, Mountain Red, and Fred Nelson, as well as members from groups that first broadcast at WEXL, such as the Rambling Cowboys and Sliver's Oregon Buckaroos. "Tommy and Ruth . . . had a show," recalled Weston. "Tennessee Gal and Tiny Chuck, and Ozarkie, . . . these people traveled all over the country, playing at different radio stations. . . . Blackie and the Roving Cowboys was on WEXL [Royal Oak] before they came up to WCAR. And Dixie and Her Ranch Boys. Skeets played bass for her for a long time."

Dixie Lee Walker, from Missouri, led western swing bands in the Pontiac area. Walker entertained at the Old Dutch Mill in Auburn Heights through the 1940s. With McDonald and his mellow vocal delivery, steel guitarist Taft "Rosebud" Blevins, a vocalist called the "Singing Kid," and Dixie herself,

Dixie and the Ranch Boys proved one of the most versatile and popular bands in Pontiac. "Me and Dixie did a show on WCAR. . . . Just called it *A Boy And A Girl*. . . . I'd play guitar and she and I'd sing, and we'd do duets," said Weston.

THE MICHIGAN JAMBOREE (1)

"We were all on in the afternoon [at WCAR], from 3:05 until four," said Weston. "We had a jamboree—*Michigan Jamboree*—and we had Dixie and Her Ranch Boys, Prairie Pioneers, Blackie and the Roving Cowboys; we had Prairie Maid Norma, Mountain Red, Gernert Case.

"We had an hour from eleven to twelve every day, for *Sears-Roebuck Farm Hour*," he said. "We used to play at eleven o'clock, and we'd come back at three o'clock. . . . [The studio] had big windows, and the schoolkids in the afternoons would come watch us. That place would be packed with seventy-five, eighty, a hundred people in that hallway, watching us broadcast. . . . Gene Autry stopped in there, one time. . . . [He] was . . . recruiting for the air force."

In 1943, Skeets McDonald joined the army and served in North Africa, India, and Japan. "He was a friend of my dad's and the family," said Weston. "When Skeets went in the Army, he got rid of his instruments and everything. When he came out, he didn't have a bass fiddle. So he used my bass fiddle out to the Old Dutch Mill, where he was playing with Dixie."[3]

THERE WAS ALWAYS A CROWD

In January 1941 Weston married his sweetheart, whom he started dating before the Arizona Bronc-Busters left town. "On the night I got married, a Saturday night, we played at the Jockey Club, on Southfield and Twelve Mile," he said. "That was our first night to play [there]. . . . We played Friday and Saturday night. The next week, we wound up going to Sunset Inn over on John R. and Seven Mile Road. Got a job playing there on Sunday afternoon. After a couple, three weeks, we talked him into Thursday night, so we played two nights there. And then we went down to the ... St. Jean Bar [in Detroit]. Played the St. Jean Bar Sunday night and Wednesday night. So we played Wednesday, Thursday, Friday, Saturday, Sunday [afternoon], and Sunday night. Six times a week. Five bucks a piece [*laughs*]. Thirty bucks a week.

"We was [at the Sunset Inn] on a Sunday, the day [the Japanese attack on] Pearl Harbor happened," said Weston. "I remember we was going down Woodward Avenue, right at the cemetery at Twelve Mile Road, when it come over the radio that Pearl Harbor had been bombed. That was about twelve, 12:30 in the afternoon. We was on our way down to play music. Was supposed to play at two o'clock, and we listened to the radio all afternoon. We didn't play very much music."

Through the war years, Weston often performed at the Wayside Bowling Lounge (John R. and Ten Mile Road). "We all used to play down at the Wayside bowling bar. The Wayside bowling bar was a country joint from the word 'go.' Fight after fight after fight! ... There was always a crowd, and they played music down there five, six nights a week," he said.

Weston also performed western-themed events at the Saddleridge Club in Salem (Curtis and Joy Road, west of Detroit), where an association of Ford dealerships sponsored parties, picnics, rodeos, and barbecues for its members.

> We'd stand up on the platform where the announcer was and sing cowboy songs. A guy named Harry Mack, ... he give us a fifty-dollar bill one night to sing "Cool Water" and "Tumbling Tumbleweeds." This was for a New Year's Eve party they had down there.[4]

During the war Weston drove a cab for a couple of years, then worked the midnight shift at a factory. "I got laid off V-J Day," he said.

HILL-BILLY OPRA

In May 1947 Weston organized a Friday night barn dance at the Pontiac Armory on Water Street. It featured the Prairie Pioneers, Tommy and Ruth,

Mountain Red, and others. He called it the Hill-Billy Opra. The house band included Paul Lane (fiddle), Jimmie Lott (bass), Howard Auger (accordion), and Sleepy Heldt (fiddle). Weston played guitar through the first part of the show, which included comedy, and called square dances after guest appearances by stars such as Patsy Montana (best remembered for her 1935 hit "I Want To Be A Cowboy's Sweetheart").

After several weeks, Weston closed the Opra. In May 1948, Weston reorganized the Prairie Pioneers to play at WCAR. The new Prairie Pioneers were Arizona (vocal, guitar), Smokey (guitar, vocal), Jimmy Lott (bass, vocal), and Curly (steel guitar). Star Cleaners, for which Weston drove a truck, sponsored a fifteen-minute spot. A transcription disk of the first program featured Smokey singing the 1946 Bob Wills hit "The Kind Of Love I Can't Forget"; the trio sang "What A Friend We Have In Jesus" and the Sons of the Pioneers 1935 favorite "Echoes From The Hills," and Weston sang Eddy Arnold's then-current hit "What A Fool I Was (To Ever Let You Go)."

Weston joined Oklahoma and the Westerners at Scrib's Drive Inn and at WCAR in 1948. "Oklahoma was the gal singer. She played bass," said Weston. "She was married to Tony Gray. . . . Tony Gray played accordion. He had an accent. I can't place what it was . . . Italian? Tony Gray wasn't his real name." Along with take-off guitarist Rosebud Gailey and rhythm guitarist Larry Heath, the band cut a single for the Vargo label of Owosso, Michigan, in 1948.[5] I was playing with 'em, in the band at the time," said Weston, "but for some reason I didn't go over with them to make [the record]."

From there, Weston played with a variety of musicians across Southeast Michigan, including Bob Norton and Phil Girard at Ted's 10-Hi in Detroit. Weston described Ted's 10-Hi as "one of the roughest damn bars in history. . . . Everybody played there. Bob Norton was our leader, more or less. He was the one that got the job. And Howard Auger was the accordion player. Me and him were buddies for years. Wherever he'd go, I'd go."

Weston started another barn dance at a venue on Dixie Highway, called the Dixie Barn Dance. "That was me and my brother," said Weston. "We played maybe two months, about seven or eight Saturday nights." The band included Primo Manni, an Italian who sang country; Jack Stockwell (fiddle); and George Sloan (steel). Weston got acquainted with Sloan, a tool and die maker, after he married Weston's wife's sister. A letter printed in the March 1945 *Mountain Broadcast and Prairie Recorder* noted Sloan was from St. Louis, Missouri.[6] Before settling in Detroit, Sloan played steel with Doc Williams in Wheeling, West Virginia. Sloan also worked with Bill Turner and His Ozark Valley Boys, and Bobby Sykes at the Wayside Bowling Lounge.

SO LONG, SKEETS

In 1948, Skeets McDonald joined Chief Redbird and His Western Aces at Scrib's Drive Inn, before playing with steel guitarist Johnnie White and guitarist Benny Walker. White specialized in telling humorous stories and jokes. White's Rhythm Riders broadcast from WKMH radio Dearborn and worked Detroit nightclubs. In 1950 they recorded a jukebox hit for Fortune Records, "The Tattooed Lady" backed with "Mean And Evil Blues," both sung by McDonald. After the group cut five sides for the Citation label, McDonald re-joined Chief Redbird at the Roosevelt Lounge. In early 1951, Capitol Records musician Merle Travis appeared at the Roosevelt. Impressed by McDonald's style, Travis invited him to move to California. "[Skeets] was with Chief [Redbird] when he left here and went to California, and got on Capitol Records," said Weston.

In April, McDonald began recording for Capitol. He scored his biggest hit in December 1952 with a cover of Slim Willet's "Don't Let The Stars Get In Your Eyes," which reached number one for three weeks. McDonald stayed with Capitol through 1959. Then he signed with Columbia Records, scoring a hit with "Call Me Mr. Brown" in 1963–64.[7] Columbia issued McDonald's last charted single, "Mabel," in 1966.

"We went out to their house, when we was visiting out there [in California].... Skeets was on a trip overseas at the time, so we missed him," said Weston. "That was probably about 1967." McDonald was likely touring U.S. military facilities in Asia. In March 1968, McDonald suffered a fatal heart attack after performing in a San Diego nightclub.

THROUGH THE WILDERNESS

During the 1950s, Weston came to terms with supporting a family and supporting country music. "He was a kind father," said daughter Karen Cusumano. "We never heard him raise his voice or swear. He took us on trips across the country, often squeezing my sister and I into the back of the car with his big old bass."[8]

In spring 1955 Weston's band opened Spattafiore's, located on North Cass Avenue, near downtown Pontiac. "They enlarged it—two buildings into one—and when they did that, they started having music," he said. "Me and Walt Lee on the accordion, and Larry Heath on the guitar, just a trio.

"That's where I wrote my song, 'If I Can't Live It Down, I'll Live It Up.'... A friend of mine came in to see us. He'd just got out of jail for not paying his back alimony. I told him, 'Jimmy, you come in here to the bar, and they'll slap you right back in the cooler.' He said, 'Well, if you can't live it down, go out and live it up' [laughs]." Weston cut the song for Howard Walker's label Walker around 1967. "When we left [Spattafiore's], they brought Jimmy Martin in, with his Sunny Mountain Boys," he said.

During the late 1950s, Weston began servicing vending machines. While working his route, he got to know Brace Beemer, the voice of WXYZ Detroit radio's *Lone Ranger* program of the 1930s and 1940s. "He lived out there at Oxford," said Weston. "I used to run into him all the time when I was doing my cigarette route.... He'd be in one of them bars out there, and he could really get loud. Had a boisterous voice. When he was in there, you knew it." Weston wrote a cowboy song called "So Long, Partner" and changed its title to "So Long, Lone Ranger" after Beemer's death in 1965.

THE MICHIGAN JAMBOREE (II)

In 1957 Missouri-born bandleader Billy Martin made records in Detroit for the Fortune and Bart labels. Martin and his family lived in Pontiac, where he worked in a factory and performed early in the morning at WPON radio. By 1959 Martin worked as a disk jockey at the station, spinning country records Monday through Saturday. He called his show *RFD 1460*. Martin served in the U.S. Army in Italy during World War II, and RFD meant Ready For Deployment, while 1460 was the station's dial frequency. "He would go on from five until six, and he had to go to work at [General Motors] Truck and Coach," said Weston. In 1959, Martin signed with the "D" label based in Dallas, Texas, which issued two singles.

In 1960 Martin launched a weekly country music show called *Michigan Jamboree* at WILX-TV Channel Ten in Jackson, and Weston joined Martin's band. "We did a television show . . . every Saturday afternoon for twenty-six weeks," said Weston. "We also did a lot of the *Grand Ole Opry* shows throughout Michigan, Ohio, Indiana, and Illinois." Musicians with single names were out of style by then, and Weston tagged a surname onto Arizona.

With banjo picker and comedian Ford Nix added to the mix, Martin and Weston made a go of it, booking talent such as Flint's Dottie Moore,[9] Charlotte Harden,[10] and Patti Lynn. "We done a show down in Lima, Ohio, with the Glaser Brothers and Billy Grammer," said Weston. "We was just traveling on the weekends, running here and there, . . . doing shows and then driving all night to get home."

THE ARIZONA WESTON SHOW

In summer 1961 Martin left his radio gig. After listening to two months of filler programming, Weston approached the station about continuing country music in the mornings. "They wanted to know if I'd had any experience, and I said, 'Not playing records. Hell, I know everything there is to know about country music.' And he said, 'Well, we'll give you a try.' This was Bill Morgan, . . . who was on WCAR with us in 1939," he said.

Weston started at WPON on October 16. "I was just doing an hour show when I first went on WPON, five until six," he said. "Then they give me 4:30 until six. Don McLeod came to be our program director, and he said, 'How would you like to do another hour in the morning?' I said, 'That's fine with me.' He said, 'I'll sleep in and you can go on until seven.' [*laughs*]"

PLATTER PARTY

Former WJBK Detroit disk jockey Don McLeod, a reluctant participant in the Detroit radio payola scandal of 1959, helped Weston cut his first commercial recordings in 1962. "I'd talked to him about making a record," said Weston, "and he said, 'I'll go up with you, and maybe I can help you out a little.' So he was kind of the [producer] on that record." Archie Grammer, a brother of Billy "Gotta Travel On" Grammer, split the session with Weston. Pontiac singer Bobby Brandon launched the Emcee label to issue Weston's and Grammer's recordings.[11]

They took a band to Flint radio broadcaster Bill Lamb's studio in Grand Blanc, and Weston recorded "Don't Walk Away." For the flipside, Weston sang the up-tempo "My Baby Just Walked In" and played upright bass. "I wrote that while playing in a bar in Detroit," said Weston. "The bandleader was named Tommy [Whisman], and every time a pretty girl would come in, Tommy would say, 'My baby just walked in.'" Weston overdubbed a second vocal on "My Baby Just Walked In" at United Sound Systems in Detroit.

Weston visited annual disk jockey conventions in Nashville from 1962 to 1967. "The first time I went down, in '62, . . . they'd give [Patsy Cline] an award of some sort or another, and while they were doing it, somebody stole her fur coat! So she was without a coat, and I was just standing around, seeing what was going on at the Andrew Jackson hotel," he said. "She came into the lobby and I recognized her. I just walked right up and introduced myself, and she gave me a big ol' bear hug. She said, 'If it wasn't for you disk jockeys, I wouldn't be nobody.'"

Weston wrote more songs, such as "Beautiful Waltz Of Michigan," and in 1964 he made two records for the Glenn label based in Hammond, Indiana.[12] The connection to Glenn was Kit Wright, who lived in Detroit. "We just met him at a country music show somewhere," said Weston. "Said he was a promoter. We went to his house two or three times. Had a real nice wife. He went to the disk jockey conventions all the time, and she went with him one time, and we was all down there—my wife, my daughters. . . . We had a ball."

Weston cut two dance numbers, his "Two Of A Kind" and "Don't Keep Stepping On My Heart" with members of Frankie Meadows' band, at Sound Incorporated in New Haven. They also remade "My Baby Just Walked In" backed with "Mabeline," a pop number with rockabilly guitar.

About a year later, a surprise regarding "My Baby Just Walked In" arrived in the mail. "That record was playing on the radio down in Arkansas, and I got a royalty check for thirteen dollars and thirty-three cents from plays that they done on the radio," he said. "I'd only [earn] something like two cents a play, when they was playing it. So they played the hell outta that for a while."

MICHIGAN COUNTRY MUSIC ASSOCIATION

Around 1964 Weston joined Gladys McKeon, WYSI Ypsilanti disk jockey Col. Jack Wilkerson, WEXL radio disk jockey Jim Mitchell, and singer Buddy Sanders in forming the Michigan Country Music Association. "I was a vice president, along with two other guys," he said. "I think we had three vice presidents. . . . [McKeon would] send out write-ups to let us know what was going on. We had meetings once a month, . . . mostly at the Wayside bowling bar." At the time, country shows at Cobo Hall in Detroit occurred monthly. "They told us that if we helped to promote it, we could come and go as we pleased, free of charge," said Weston. "So we got to just run around. . . . Went into the back room, where everyone was drinking [laughs]."

OXBOW LAKE DANCE RANCH

In autumn 1966, Weston organized the Oxbow Lake Dance Ranch, a monthly show headlined by Nashville stars. Weston hosted entertainers for matinee and evening programs every fourth Sunday with his band the Westerners, at the Oxbow Lake Pavilion (on Elizabeth Lake Road). The

Westerners included Lindy Larson (lead guitar), Chet Cutshall (steel guitar), Gene Farris (bass), and Bob Warman (drums), along with local guests such as Frankie Meadows, Patti Lynn, and the Gibson Sisters. "We got Nudie suits," said Weston. "We sent away and got them suits for a hundred dollars apiece. . . . Mine's purple, and the rest [were] chartreuse."

"The Oxbow Lake Dance Ranch was a family affair," said Karen Cusumano. "My mom would handle the tickets and my sister and I ran concessions." Over fourteen months, Weston booked stars such as Red Sovine, Bill Anderson, Tompall and the Glaser Brothers, George Morgan, Lefty Frizzell, Jim Ed Brown, Billy Grammer, Charlie Walker, and the Stanley Brothers. One of Carter Stanley's last shows took place at the Oxbow in 1966.[13]

Weston had hit his stride, until he and Cutshall went with other musicians to back Ferlin Husky at the Pontiac Armory in 1967. It caused a misunderstanding with the owner of the Oxbow Pavilion, who ended Weston's dance ranch. "The boss got mad at us and fired us, after we'd brought in all them shows for a whole damn year," he said.

He left the vending business and opened the Lakeland Record Shop. From his store, Weston chartered and hosted bus tours to Nashville.[14]

In 1972 Weston landed on *Country Corral* at WXON-TV Walled Lake, Channel Sixty-two. "We had Malcolm Paul and the Country Images, and Ronnie Wolf and the Runaways on that," he said. Weston produced a record of Wolf singing "Beautiful Waltz Of Michigan" and sent the proceeds to the March of Dimes. "I worked thirteen years for the March of Dimes," he said. "We used to do wild game dinners, and I was the chairman one year. We took in forty-three thousand dollars for just dinners from different bars. That was the record at the time. . . . I got to go to San Diego and meet Doctor [Jonas] Salk." *Country Corral* ran through November, when station owners shook up the schedule and moved down the dial to Channel Twenty.

Weston's WPON program ran for some months from midnight until six a.m. In June 1973, it ended abruptly. The man supposed to read the six o'clock news got into a habit of showing up late, so Weston continued playing his music. When manager Bill Morgan heard about it from a sponsor, he exploded at both disk jockeys. The six o'clock host quit, and when Weston couldn't persuade Morgan to let him go until nine o'clock, he quit too. "It wasn't a year after I left WPON that they sold the station and it went all country," he said. "Ain't that ironic."

CHASING RAINBOWS

In late 1976 Weston traveled to Nashville and recorded another single, this time for his Lakeland Records label. "Johnny Gimble, who played fiddle with Bob Wills' Texas Playboys, was our bandleader," he said. "We cut four songs in that three-hour session, at the Glaser Brothers studio." Weston pressed the record in February 1977. He paired "I'm Through Chasin' Rainbows," a song he wrote in 1956, with "Beautiful Waltz Of Michigan," which Weston always hoped could be adopted as Michigan's state song.[15] Weston closed the Lakeland Record Shop later that year.

From 1978 to 1982, Weston and his wife lived in Arizona, where he frequented the Reata Pass Steakhouse in Scottsdale. "Bud Isaacs was playing up there, . . . [with] his wife [Jeri Mapes], just the two of 'em. She handled the . . . drums and bass, and he played steel guitar. I used to go up there and sit in with 'em," said Weston.

"[Isaacs] worked with the Sons of the Pioneers at one time. . . . They was in town one day, and . . . we're up there singing, and here comes [guitarist] Roy Lanham and [singer] Rome Johnson. Both of 'em played for the Sons of the Pioneers. They walked in as we're singing their songs. That's a thrill, boy, I'm telling you."

In 1991 Weston underwent triple-bypass surgery on his heart. During his recovery at a Clarkston seniors center, he created a local access cable television show called *The Arizona Weston Show—Portrait of a Country and Western Superstar.* "I [profiled] the Sons of the Pioneers first. Then I did Gene Autry. Then I did Red Foley, Jim Reeves, and Eddy Arnold," said Weston. "I did eight different shows. . . . After I got it done, my grandson . . . was going to college up in Marquette, and we went to see him. Just for the hell of it, we took it over to the TV station, and they took it. . . . They played it three years in a row." The program aired over the Waterford cable station as well.

Booking agents sent him into assisted living facilities across Southeast

Michigan during the 1990s. "I must have done two hundred, two hundred fifty shows all over: Ypsilanti, Detroit, Pontiac, Flint, clean over to Lake St. Clair," said Weston.

He also returned to WPON radio. "I got some sponsors [for] twenty-five dollars a spot, and I went down there every Thursday night, from five 'til six, . . . playing nothing but country music," he said. By 2000 Weston's deteriorating eyesight caused him to leave the radio show. In summer 2006, he picked guitar and sang his songs at his induction into the Michigan Country Music Hall of Fame. Arizona Weston passed away April 22, 2007.

Figure 6. During the late 1940s, the Chuck Oakes band included, from left, Emerson Lee "Happy" Moore, Chuck Oakes, Jimmy Franklin, and Marvin "Whitey" Franklin. Used by permission from Keith Cady.

Chapter 6

HEY! IT'S CHUCK OAKES

When I was a young man, I didn't make much money. Back then, if I made fifteen or twenty dollars a night, plus tips, I was doin' great. . . . When I ran out of money, I'd take my guitar down and hock it at the [pawn] shop. Sometimes I'd hock my guitar and by Thursday or Friday, I'd have to figure out a way to go and get it back out. I told a guy one time, "My guitar's been in Lou's Loan shop so much that Lou can play it better than I can."

—CHUCK OAKES[1]

Guitarist Chuck Oakes set himself apart from most players by never using flat picks, but instead employed finger-style techniques that he learned from his father, who was taught in the army by an African American soldier during World War I. "Chuck had a following," said bandleader Bill Hayes, who worked on stage, radio, and television with Oakes. "He could play boogie woogie—he'd turn the volume up [on his guitar] and not use his right hand [to pick the strings], just note it [on the guitar neck with his left hand's fingertips]. . . . People go for that. I mean, he'd play with one hand! We bought thirty-dollar boots, and he'd order his out of Arizona. Snake skin boots and western clothes. He was sharp."[2]

Charles Oakes Jr., born September 5, 1922, in Knoxville, Tennessee, and raised in Cookeville, learned guitar from his father. Oakes referred to his dad's picking as "the old blues style guitar, with your fingers and your thumb." By age thirteen, Oakes and his brother Leroy were playing guitars they ordered from a Sears-Roebuck catalog at school functions and parties.

In July 1940 WHUB Cookeville opened. "I think it was probably two hundred fifty or five hundred watts," said Oakes. "It covered a couple of counties." He assembled a band with some friends, and they performed on WHUB weekday mornings. "On Saturday night, they'd have a remote broadcast of a jamboree in the courthouse. Local musicians from surrounding counties would come play on the show. You didn't get any compensation for it, just a little publicity. One of the guys was from Sparta, eighteen miles from my home. You probably heard of Lester Flatt. He played with Earl Scruggs for years. He was right in on that whole deal."

ON THE ROAD

Around 1941 Oakes went to Dayton, Ohio, to find work. Relatives employed by General Electric invited him to move. "It wasn't long 'til I was playing clubs in Dayton," he said. "I got married and had a couple of kids. I had two kids and was married when I was drafted into the army."

He served in the Eighty-second Airborne Division in the European theater, and participated in the Battle of the Bulge during the winter of 1944–45. After the European armistice, Oakes entered the honor guard in Berlin, where British, Russian, French, and American armies occupied the city. "There was one [band] down there, they were [military police]. They had a group in the [non-commissioned officers] club, and I got a job with them," said Oakes. "Downtown, American Forces Network broadcast in the thirty-meter shortwave band, and you could get it around the world. We had a radio program, and I found me a bass violin in an old German building. It was a beautiful German bass. I played that some, and I played guitar some. . . . I used an old earphone from a German glider and one of those two hundred forty-volt German radios to make me an amplifier."

Oakes returned to Dayton toward the end of 1945 and resumed entertaining in nightclubs. Smilin' Ernie's Radio Jamboree, an act from Downeast, Maine, came through town and left with Oakes and his family in tow. "They had a big bus and everything, and they needed a guitar player, so they hired me," he said. "We played all over Maine and New Hampshire. Used to broadcast on WABI of Bangor. We even went into Canada and broadcast on CFOS [Owen Sound, Ontario] and CFNB [Fredericton, New Brunswick]."[3]

Ernie's troupe ordered suits from Ben the Rodeo Tailor in Philadelphia, Pennsylvania. "We had ultraviolet [black] lights and we had these suits that was treated," said Oakes. "We'd turn off the lights and turn on the ultraviolet lights, and our uniforms would glow."

They toured the region while Oakes' family lived with Ernie's mother-in-law in Avesta, Maine. "We'd go visit towns ahead of time and put up our advertising, posters and things. We just made a living," said Oakes. "I never did get used to touring, . . . because you couldn't stay in one place long enough to get your clothes cleaned. You had to drive a town or two ahead and drop 'em off. . . . At most of these places where the farmers lived, we put on a show for about an hour and-a-half. [Then] we'd fold up the chairs and line 'em up around the walls. Everybody would do a square dance and the two step and waltzes. It was a lot of fun."

Oakes kept a metal plate of his image, dressed in a western suit and hat, holding a blond Gibson archtop guitar. "I'd take it to a printing shop and get the pictures run off," he said. "They'd run off three or four hundred of 'em. Then we'd sell 'em at the shows for a quarter apiece. Most people'd buy 'em just 'cause they liked to have your autograph. They were just a cardboard picture. We never had the money to do any glossy prints."

In 1946 Oakes and his wife had another child, born in Maine. "I sold my blond guitar to Ernie's mother-in-law for enough money to pay the hospital bill. [Then] I said, 'It's time for me to get out of here and go back to Ohio.' So we went back to Dayton."

Oakes worked with rhythm guitarist Emerson Lee "Happy" Moore in Dayton. "I used to like to hear syncopation on a guitar," said Oakes. "[Hap] could make it sound like a set of snare drums when he played it." Guitarist, bass player, and singer Jimmy Franklin joined the band, along with his brother Marvin "Whitey" Franklin, who played steel guitar. "Jimmy and Whitey Franklin came up from West Liberty, Kentucky," said Oakes. "Jimmy had a real nice voice. He could sing pop music as well as country and western. . . . Jimmy's wife played the upright bass a lot, Dimples. . . . They were a pretty good team, kinda like Chuck Hatfield and his wife Boots Gilbert."[4] The group worked an early morning broadcast at WSAZ Huntington, West Virginia, for several weeks, before Oakes left Ohio.

CHUCK WAGON BOYS

"I had a friend who told me about numerous jobs they were playin' and the opportunities in Detroit," said Oakes. In 1947 he moved to Michigan. Oakes worked with singers Lawton "Slim" Williams and his cousin Jack Luker. "At the time they [Luker and Williams] were playing at a little bar out there at the Oak Gardens on John R," he said.

Eventually Moore and the Franklin brothers followed Oakes north. The quartet found a steady gig at Vandewall's downtown (on Woodbridge, a block below Jefferson). "I used to like to sing a lot of trios—Jimmy Franklin, Hap [Moore] and I. When we first came to Detroit, we used to do [songs by] Sons of the Pioneers, Foy Willing, . . . artists like that. I'd do novelty stuff like 'Smoke That Cigarette,' 'John Henry,' and 'Nine Pound Hammer.' It went over big."

Oakes first appeared on record in 1949 with Bob Durham's band doing "Down Indiana Way" backed with "Rainbow In The Rain" on Fortune Records.

At some point between 1947 and 1950, Jack Luker and Lawton Williams took Oakes to WSM radio Nashville. "We went down there and they had an audition set up for us," said Oakes. "They said, 'Don't call us, we'll call you!' You know how that story goes."

> I worked a lot with Jack at the West Fort Tavern; also over to the Dixie Belle on West Vernor. Over to the Dixie Belle, we had two bands. It was Jack Luker, me, and an upright bass player, . . . Otis Morrell. He had a brother named Royce Morrell who was a staff musician at WJR. The Dixie Belle didn't have intermissions. We played a set and Eddie Jackson and his band would play a set. We had continuous entertainment going all the time at the Dixie Belle.

The first commercial record with Oakes' name on it was "Hey! It's Chuck's Boogie" by Chuck Oakes and His Chuck Wagon Boys around 1950. Oakes' guitar and Don "Lucky Lee" Larsh's accordion traded fiery riffs that pushed the performance beyond the limits of respectable hillbilly boogies.

The band worked at Vandewall's when Jack and Dorothy Brown of Fortune invited Oakes to cut the record.

> Mrs. Brown of Fortune Records wrote songs, and she wanted to use "Waltz of Virginia" on the reverse side of the record. . . . So Danny [Richards] sang the song. But the lady that sings harmony with Danny. . . . Her name was Sylvia, and she was in town working in a club. . . . We went to United Sound Studios, over on Second Avenue. There used to be a guy named Jimmy Siracuse, who owned United Sound. He dubbed her voice right in, singing with Danny.

BETTER TO BE SAFE

"One night Danny's girlfriend got mad at him 'cause she thought he was flirtin' with some girl. So she threw an ashtray through the front of his bass. Some of those bars we played back then—they would fight for a while, . . . then we'd play for a while. When they'd get too violent, I'd unplug my guitar and I'd run and hide in the kitchen 'til it was all over," said Oakes.

Oakes said he wrote a notebook full of songs. Danny Richards cut two: "One Way Ticket" (Fortune, 1963) and "Better To Be Safe" (Sage Records, 1957—Oakes' name didn't appear on the label).

In 1956, Oakes teamed up with Bill Hayes and John Fraley, and cut a record at Fortune. "Everyone in town knew about Fortune Records and we decided we'd like to go over and see if we could get on recordings," said Oakes. "It wasn't real hard to do. We'd pay them a bunch of money and they'd make a master, press some records and give us two or three hundred of 'em. We'd have to peddle 'em where we played." By 1956 most country artists who wanted to make records with Fortune had to buy a package deal such as Oakes described.

"Bill Hayes played upright bass, and John Fraley played rhythm guitar and we sang a lot of harmony together," said Oakes. The trio, Will Hayes and His Ozark Valley Boys, recorded Hayes' "Honeymoon In The Mountains" and "I Could Never Walk Alone." With Glen Ball on fiddle, the band played a show sponsored by Miller Beer at WJR Detroit for several weeks.

Around 1957 Hayes found a job playing music for television in Florence, Alabama. Fraley and Oakes moved to Alabama and performed with Hayes every weekday, along with a Saturday night jamboree. A booking agent sent them on the road, playing within the station's broadcast reach for several months before Oakes and Fraley returned to Detroit.

Fraley worked in machine shops and factories in Detroit and played music at night before retiring to Virginia, where he built mandolins and guitars by hand.

Originally from Arkansas, Hayes moved to Nashville by 1960. While operating carpet shops, he wrote songs such as "I'll Pour The Wine," recorded by Moon Mullican.

From the time Oakes arrived in Detroit until about 1962, he played music full-time. He also worked in Lansing with Bill Sova's Ranch Boys; with Don "Sonny" Sexton in Flint; and with Primo Manni in Pontiac. "We didn't make a lot of money, but we made enough to get by. 'Course back then, you didn't have to have a lot of money. You could rent a furnace room for eight or ten dollars a week," he said.

END OF THE WILD GOOSE CHASE

Oakes remembered gigging with vocalist Jess Childers in Detroit. "We used to work a lot on the east side, at a place called the O'Mack Bar. That was a bar down below with a hotel above. When you got ready to go to sleep, you'd just go upstairs and get yourself a room. If you were lucky, you didn't have to go by yourself [*laughs*]."

Through the GI Bill, Oakes attended electrical engineering courses. "I took calculus, physics, . . . everything they taught," said Oakes. "I got my first class broadcast engineer's license, first class radio and telephone. I could have operated as a chief engineer in any radio or TV station in the United States. I had that back in the 1950s. I never did use it for broadcasting."

In 1962 Oakes hired into a communications shop where he tuned transmitters on freighters, yachts, and ships that sailed the Great Lakes. He later opened his own television and radio repair shop and played music on weekends. "Eddie [Jackson] and I, and [guitarist] Johnny Clem, we worked quite a bit, at Eagles and Moose lodges, and things like that, around Mount Clemens, and Roseville," he said.

Oakes maintained a membership with the Detroit Federation of Musicians for forty-two years. "I imagine I know just about any musician that you've ever run into or heard of in Detroit," said Oakes. "I never did try to go anywhere with music much, because back then, when you had a family and a job makin' a few dollars, you'd hate to just pull off and leave, and go some place on a wild goose chase. Nine times out of ten you're gonna be on the wrong side lookin' in, like most of 'em were. Down in Nashville, it wasn't what you knew a lot of times—it was who you knew." He retired to Gladwin, Michigan, in 1992, and passed away on May 23, 2001.

Figure 7. Casey Clark and the Lazy Ranch Boys on the stage of the 12101 Mack Avenue U.A.W. hall in Detroit, 1955. Top row, from left: Buddy Emmons, Smitty Smith, and Chuck Carroll. Middle row, from left: Casey Clark, Fairley Holden, Charlie Miller, Honey Miller, Evelyn Harlene, Bronson "Barefoot Brownie" Reynolds, Herb Williams, and Dick McCobb. Kneeling, from left: Sonny Osborne, Bobby Osborne, and Jimmy Martin. Used by permission from Evelyn H. Atkins.

Chapter 7

HERE THEY ALL COME
Casey Clark and the Lazy Ranch Boys

> Everybody said, "Well, you can't get by with country here [in Detroit]." And I
> guess if they hadn't of told me that, I would have left. But when they told me
> I couldn't, why, I decided I would.
>
> —CASEY CLARK[1]

From 1952 to 1958 Casey Clark and the Lazy Ranch Boys, a nine-piece western swing unit, dominated country music in Michigan. Every week, Clark
hosted *Grand Ole Opry* stars at the Lazy Ranch Boys Barn Dance in a United Auto Workers hall at 12101 Mack Avenue, broadcast over clear channel
WJR radio Detroit, and performed at CKLW-TV Windsor, Ontario. Like
a magnet, amplified by Detroit's Southern-born population and the wealth
generated by the region's manufacturing industry, Clark attracted up-and-
coming artists such as the Davis Sisters (Skeeter and Betty Jack), Jimmy
Martin, the Osborne Brothers, and Buddy Emmons. He gave countless
young musicians their first glimpses of careers playing music, securing his
reputation in Michigan, Tennessee, and points in-between, for generations
to come.

Weighing close to three hundred pounds in his prime, Casey Clark, "Your
Big Fat Buddy," forged a public persona of modesty and self-deprecating humor, masking an unstoppable drive to excel as musician, bandleader, broadcaster, promoter, and mentor. When comparing other bands in Detroit to
the Lazy Ranch Boys, musician Cranford "Ford" Nix said, "They all had a

shot at it, but they didn't have the talent to pull it all through. [Casey's] was the biggest band of any of these bands up here."[2]

Born in Soldier, Kentucky, July 24, 1918, to John and Sarah Clarke, Harlen Nathaniel "Casey" Clark (he dropped the "e" in Clarke during the 1940s) grew up in Carter County surrounded by three brothers, seven sisters, and a large extended family. His Irish grandfather played fiddle and proved to be no small influence. The oldster fashioned a fiddle out of a cigar box for the youngster, who began learning how to play from watching his grandfather and an older brother who took violin lessons.

At age twelve, he fiddled old-time melodies as Kid Casey, on his first radio show at WCMI Ashland. In 1932, the award-winning young fiddler and his brother joined three cousins at WSAZ Huntington, West Virginia, performing for the Sandy Valley Grocery Company.

WPAY Portsmouth, Ohio, opened in 1935, and Clark worked a jamboree program that included singers Lee Moore (who later worked with his wife Juanita in West Virginia radio), "Indian" Bill Stallard (a.k.a. Billy Starr, who later managed Lloyd "Cowboy" Copas), and, in 1936, the York Brothers.

Inspired by groups such as Clayton McMichen's Georgia Wildcats, and Bob Wills and His Texas Playboys, Clark moved to Fort Worth, Texas, around 1937–38 and played for Bill Boyd and His Cowboy Ramblers. "I remember going out to play a dance with Bob Wills' band at a great big hall that looked like a barn, out in the middle of nowhere," said Clark. "By the time the sun went down, hundreds of cars were parked around the building, as far as the eye could see."[3] Decades later, Clark summed up his impression of Wills: "He wasn't a great fiddle player, but he was a great man. If it hadn't been for him, I probably wouldn't have stayed in the business."[4]

KENTUCKY SWING

Upon his return to Kentucky in 1938, Clark couldn't help but notice the ruckus Eldon Baker and His Brown County Revelers made over WLW

Cincinnati, Ohio. The group performed a style reminiscent of the Texas bands Clark had witnessed, with swing fiddle by Charlie Linville and jazz-styled vocals by Wade "Pee Wee" Baker. Guitarist Harry C. Adams delivered unusually fast and fiery picking with his acoustic instrument. The group featured comedian Bronson Lee "Barefoot Brownie" Reynolds, who played harmonica and bass. In June 1938 the band made recordings for Columbia Records' Vocalion label, including "Lost John" with vocal by Reynolds. The sessions went against a WLW policy forbidding contracted performers from making records while in their employ. Resulting tensions at the radio station caused the Revelers lineup to shatter, with Adams leaving, and Linville and Reynolds joining the station's *Top O' The Morning Show* with Pa and Ma McCormick.

It's a good bet Clark found himself a job with a similar act in Mel Steele and His Oklahoma Ramblers that year. West Virginia guitarist Bob Pauley imitated Adams' punchy style. Steele, a guitarist and comedian who also played bass and old-time fiddle, took the band from WCHS Charleston, West Virginia, to WJLS Beckley, West Virginia, WING Dayton, Ohio, WMMN Fairmont, West Virginia, WWVA Wheeling, West Virginia, and down to WOPI Bristol, Tennessee. Steele's wife Patsy Jean, a.k.a. Blue Eyed Jean, also sang with the group.

While working in Beckley, Clark met and befriended a teen-aged Jimmy Dickens who longed for a career entertaining. "I met Casey in 1939," said Dickens (born in 1920 at Bolt, West Virginia). "Casey was working with ... Mel Steele and his group. Casey was playing fiddle with them, and they took me in, ... as their child, or something [*laughs*]. ... Bob Pauley was the guitar player, a big old husky guy, and Casey was a big guy, and I slept between 'em! [*laughs*]"[5]

"Casey was working in West Virginia, and Jim ... wanted a job for the summer," said Clark's wife, Mary. "Casey and the guitar player, Bob, they told the boss, 'If you'll just let him sing and play with us, we'll feed him.'"[6]

Dickens sang one song per radio show and performed at the band's personal appearances. He left high school to continue with Steele's band at WING Dayton for a few months. After taking a break, Dickens joined them at WMMN Fairmont. By 1940 the Oklahoma Ramblers split up.[7]

BIRTH OF THE LAZY RANCH BOYS

While visiting family in Soldier in 1939, Clark met Mary Evelyn Smith, a college student from the nearby village of Haldeman. Although she didn't play music, Smith could carry a tune, knew good music when she heard it, wrote poetry, and conspired to further Clark's ambitions. On June 21, 1940, Clark and Smith married during a country music festival in Ironton, Ohio, broadcast live on WCMI.

In September 1940, *Mountain Broadcast and Prairie Recorder* printed a letter from Clark in which he reported working with his brother Bruce.

> The other members of our band are Howard Atkins, guitar; "Frosty" Allen, so-loist; and "Red," the bass man. Also vocal trio. We are now located with Asa Martin's famous Morning Roundup Gang, WCMI, and doing fine. I would like to know the whereabouts of Riley Puckett, Bert Layne and Harry C. Adams....
> We are on the air from 6 to 7 o'clock each morning.... So long, Casey Clarke [sic], Soldier, Ky.[8]

When his first child, Evelyn Harlene, arrived the following year, Clark left his musical pursuits for work that offered more security. "He was in West Virginia and I was in Kentucky," said Mary Clark. "He quit out there and came home, and got a job in a brickyard, wheeling brick.... There would be times when he'd be listening to a [radio] barn dance out of Cincinnati.... He would get such a faraway look in his eyes. And I knew, 'He's not here right now. He's in that studio.' I understood that, and I understood his desire to play like that."

In 1943, Clark took a job at WIBC Indianapolis, Indiana, where Jimmy Dickens had teamed with T. Texas Tyler. O. J. Kelchner, manager of WMMN when Clark and Dickens played in Mel Steele's band, worked at WIBC.[9] The Saturday night *Hoosier Barn Dance* featured Dickens, Judy Perkins, Emma Lou and Her Saddle Pals, Bill Stallard, the Blue Mountain Girls, comedian Raymond "Quarantine" Brown, guitarist Verne Morgan, bassist Chick Holstein, and Clark. Hugh Cross, former member of Gid Tanner's Skillet Lickers, served as emcee.[10]

In January 1944 Clark formed the first incarnation of the Lazy Ranch Boys, as a trio.[11] Original members included guitarist Verne Morgan, Clark, and Bill Stallard. Bassist and lead singer Chick Holstein replaced Stallard in July. Clark and Morgan alternated with tenor and baritone, performing Western and spiritual songs during the barn dance. "They asked their audience to send in ideas for names, and the Lazy Ranch Boys came in through the mail," said Mary Clark. During August 1944, the Lazy Ranch Boys toured the Midwest with Gene Autry sidekick Lester "Smiley" Burnette.[12]

GOODWILL-BILLIES

In October, WJR Detroit, the Goodwill Station, introduced a country music program Monday through Saturday from five to six a.m., hosted by the Goodwill-Billies. Singer John "Smilin' Red" Maxedon, who had worked with Mountain Pete at WXYZ and WJBK, as well as with Tim Doolittle's Pine Center Gang, and solo at WJR, joined three entertainers who moved from John Lair's Renfro Valley in Kentucky: singer Ernie Lee, steel guitarist Jerry Byrd, and "Barefoot Brownie" Reynolds.[13] Clark, accordionist "Pee Wee" Linden, and a vocal duo called the Milk Maids (Helen and Mary) also joined the show. The band performed old-time and western music in a modern, swinging style. After several weeks, WJR initiated a Saturday night show called the *Goodwill Frolic Barn Dance*, which may have been the first barn dance program produced by a Detroit station.

Ernie Lee, born Ernest Eli Cornelison in Berea, Kentucky, in 1916, started in radio at John Lair's Renfro Valley jamboree in 1940, broadcasting over WHAS Louisville. Lee's upbeat, easygoing baritone made him a popular emcee and singer.

Jerry Byrd, born in 1920 in Lima, Ohio, purchased his first steel guitar at age fourteen. Four years later, John Lair hired him at Renfro Valley. Byrd introduced a type of C6 tuning for the steel guitar at Renfro Valley that established his reputation as an innovative musician.

"Barefoot Brownie" Reynolds joined Renfro Valley during the early 1940s. Born in 1912 in Spring Station, Kentucky, Eldon Baker's Brown County Revelers provided Reynolds with his breakout radio gig at WLW during the late 1930s.

The Goodwill-Billies played bookings across Michigan, avoiding bars and nightclubs for family-friendly fairs and events such as the State Sheep Shearing Contest in Manchester, Michigan.[14]

WJR allowed fans to view live performances from their broadcast studios. Singer Arizona Weston recalled, "We used to play in Detroit 'til two o'clock in the morning, then go to a restaurant and hang out until [five], and stay and watch them," said Weston. "We lived up here in Pontiac, and we'd drive back and forth. Three or four different times, . . . we would eat breakfast and just hang around. . . . Then go up [in the Fisher Building] and watch. . . . Smilin' Red Maxedon, Ernie Lee, . . . he could sing. Man, he had a voice."[15]

Ernie Lee established Smiley Burnette's "Hominy Grits" (1946) as his theme song and cut a version of it for the Victor label in 1947. The lyrics described lip-smacking Southern food, including black-eyed peas, biscuits, and sorghum molasses.

The group attracted mentions in the October 1946 *Mountain Broadcast and Prairie Recorder,* including a list of comedy acts within the ranks: "Nat and Les, the Kentucky Boys, and Melba, the Sweetheart of the Goodwill Frolic Gang—and especially the sweetheart of Barefoot Bonnie."[16] Melba and Barefoot Bonnie were female alter egos of Maxedon and Reynolds, respectively. Nat and Les were Clark and Byrd, who played rhythm guitar as Les.

Billboard reported that the band began a tour October 5, 1946, in Richmond, Michigan, with plans to continue through the winter. "Advance sales and bookings point to what looks like a record tour," it read.[17] However, the November edition of *Mountain Broadcast* declared the end of the WJR program, which may have lost sponsors. Lee moved to Chicago, Illinois, for a few weeks, then to the WLW *Midwestern Hayride* in Cincinnati, Ohio.

Reynolds and Byrd moved to Nashville, Tennessee. Reynolds joined Red

Foley's Cumberland Valley Boys, and Byrd went with Ernest Tubb's Texas Troubadours for about four months before settling with Foley's band, too.

Maxedon remained in Detroit, broadcasting at WJBK radio and recording more than a dozen western sides for the local Arcadia label. Clark and his family went home to Kentucky where, during the long winter nights, Clark decided he should organize and lead his own bands from then on.

SPRINGTIME IN SAGINAW

At the start of 1947, WIBC manager O. J. Kelchner and announcers Howard "Foxy" Wolfe and Bill Edwards, who helped run the *Hoosier Barn Dance*, prepared to launch a new station in Saginaw, Michigan. "They knew Casey, and knew what he could do, and they got in touch with him. They wanted him to get a band together and start," said Mary Clark. "He went before they'd even finished soundproofing the studios, and he helped them do that."

During April 1947 WKNX began broadcasting a thousand watts, daytime only. Jimmy Dickens also received an offer before the station opened, and he moved from a radio job in Kansas. He and Clark hosted disk jockey programs, read news reports, and tackled other types of announcing duties while assembling bands.

Dickens called his group the Down Home Boys. "I had a half-Polish and half-country act," he said. "I had a country fiddle player [Don Boots], a country guitar player [Morrie Jones], another guy that doubled on clarinet and guitar [Bernie Kimes]. Romie Nentwig played accordion and sang like [pop singer] Vaughn Monroe. Coy Crank played steel, [he came] from Indianapolis. So, we had it pretty well covered in the [Saginaw] Valley, because we could play polka rooms or we could play the country rooms.

"I worked a lot, when I first went up there, with Casey Clark," said Dickens. "When I wasn't making any money, I'd stay with him and his wife until I'd get straightened out. You don't forget folks like that."[18]

Clark re-organized the Lazy Ranch Boys with guitarists Bob Pauley (who had been working at WIBC) and Curly Cagle (formerly with the Radio Rangers at KFAB radio Lincoln, Nebraska), vocalist and fiddler Billy

(Bob) Williams, and bassist Gene Starr from Moscow, Michigan. Cagle left after a short while. Clark continued the Nat and Les comedy duo with Pauley (as Les), who also sang solos. All musicians at WKNX worked interchangeably with the Clark or Dickens bands as needed.

BOY WITH THE GOLDEN VOICE

Gene Starr, a.k.a. Eugene "Smoky" Sauber, was born in 1927 on a farm between Hillsdale and Jackson, Michigan. The first of eighteen children, Starr began singing on WIBM Jackson with Tex Powell and the Rhythm Rangers in 1946. Starr also performed a fifteen-minute show, *Smoky and His Guitar*. Powell, who presided over the *Cheshire Op'ry* at WKNE Keene, New Hampshire, before moving to Michigan, had a Saturday night gig at the Villabee restaurant in Jackson.[19] Along with Powell's wife Jenny on accordion, Charlie Flannery played fiddle, and Luke "Buddy" Ratcliff played bass. Ratcliff, who also played fiddle, grew up with Flannery in Floyd County, Kentucky. "When Tex needed a bass player, Chuck called me and I came up from Kentucky," said Ratcliff. "Chuck and me worked in a furniture shop in Jackson, when we played for Tex."[20]

Ratcliff married Starr's sister Mona. When Powell disbanded his group at the end of 1946, the couple moved to Kentucky. Clark hired Starr to play bass at WKNX.

"One day, Casey and I were in the studio and we heard him sitting in there with a guitar, just playing and singing," said Mary Clark. "I said, 'Casey, listen to him!' Casey was really impressed, . . . and he said, 'Well, Eugene, what would you say if I told you I would like for you to be a vocalist, and we'll get somebody else to play bass?' . . . So Casey hired Gene and then he hired his brother-in-law [Buddy Ratcliff]." Mary Clark suggested Starr's new radio name and title—Gene Starr, the boy with the golden voice. With a smooth vocal style, Starr grew popular at WKNX, hosting his own program, writing songs, and sitting in with Dickens and Clark.

Starr also assisted Mary Clark with promotions. "He would drive her. She did not drive," said Clark's daughter Evelyn Harlene.[21]

The Lazy Ranch Boys played at the station every day, picking through the WKNX record library for material. The station didn't pay musicians, but they could come and go as they pleased, and promote their personal appearances on the air.

A daily program from a quarter past noon to a quarter to one o'clock, called the *Dinner Bell Roundup*, featured all WKNX musicians in freestyle collaborations. The Clark and Dickens bands also performed fifteen-minute shows for sponsors at other times of the day. Tex Ferguson and His Drifting Pioneers arrived during the second half of 1947, and all three acts played together every Friday night at a skating rink in Bad Axe, Michigan.

Ferguson, from Grassy Creek, Kentucky, rode boxcars around North America during the Great Depression. He led bands at WLOK Lima, Ohio, in 1941, and in Findlay in 1944. Ferguson's band at WKNX included Chuck Flannery, Don Boots (guitar, fiddle, and comedy as Denny BoomFoozle), and Dick Weston (bass).[22]

Besides playing halls and schools, the WKNX bands opened for traveling artists, such as Roy Acuff in Flint and Saginaw in October 1947. WKNX disk jockeys "Uncle Don" Andrews and Bob Maxwell (who hosted an afternoon disk jockey show called *Luke the Spook*) helped book local events.

In summer of 1947, Clark and Dickens discovered singer May Hawks at the Bad Axe roller rink, when she approached the bandleaders to sit in. "They said, 'Well, come on and sing us a song.' And I did," said Hawks. "The crowd seemed to like it. The next week, WKNX radio station sent me a letter and asked me if I'd like to have my own program." Hawks sang and accompanied herself with guitar, with Andrews as her producer. Although she lived with her husband in Troy, Michigan, Hawks rented a room in Saginaw during the week, and worked with the WKNX bands on radio and personal appearances.[23]

DEPARTURES AND A RELEASE

In February 1948 Roy Acuff invited Dickens to appear on the WSM *Grand Ole Opry* in Nashville, Tennessee. Acuff was so impressed that he asked

Dickens to move to Nashville. Dickens accepted, and invited his band at WKNX to make the move with him. Coy Crank followed Dickens south, but not before he made a record with the Lazy Ranch Boys.

"They cut it at the radio station," said Starr's brother, Jim Sauber. "One side was Casey Clark and the other was Gene singing 'Prisoner's Plea.' That was written by a guy in Jackson prison."[24] Personnel included Ratcliff, Crank, Pauley, Clark, and Starr. The performances sounded similar to contemporary records by Roy Acuff and Eddy Arnold. Clark and Pauley sang the Sons of the Pioneers' "Cigareets, Whusky And Wild, Wild Wimmen" as Nat and Les, the Kentucky Boys, on the flipside of the 78-rpm disk. The label was PhonoCraft and included the note "Mfg for Casey Clark," confirming Clark paid for the records. "We sold pictures and copies of the record at our shows," said Ratcliff.

Clark established a Saturday night barn dance after Dickens left in June. Dickens' first regular appearance on the *Opry* occurred in August, and he performed in Saginaw with Clark the following month.

A couple of new voices arrived in 1948: "Blind" Bob Hall and Herb Williams. Mary Clark discovered Hall during a visit to her mother in Kentucky. "I was listening to WSAZ in Huntington, West Virginia, and I heard this beautiful tenor voice," she said. "I went back to Saginaw and I told Casey, 'There's a guy on WSAZ who is fantastic! He's got the clearest tenor voice that I ever heard in my life.' Bob always said that was from growing up in the mountains. He was from Martin, Kentucky, and he was born blind." Hall learned piano and guitar while attending a school for the blind in Louisville. Herbert Williams (Eyler), a tall, dark-haired baritone singer born 1927 in Maryland, was performing with Hall when Casey Clark called him. After Williams auditioned over the telephone, he moved with Hall to Saginaw.

In September, Ferguson moved his group to KFEQ radio St. Joseph, Missouri. Clark's family moved back to Kentucky around January 1949, and Clark took a job at a radio station in Fort Madison, Iowa. "The Lazy Ranch Boys just fizzled out," said Ratcliff, who spent a few months at WKNX playing bass with Andy Kletzgavitz and His Polka Boys. Guitarist Morrie Jones also played in the band. When that group folded, Ratcliff moved his family to Kentucky. Jones took a radio job in Arkansas, eventually settling in Des Moines, Iowa, where he worked as a musician and cabinetmaker.

May Hawks left WKNX too, after a call from Dickens. He heard Royal Flour Mills was looking for a young woman to represent Martha White Flour on WSM radio. Hawks moved to Tennessee and sang commercials and songs during early morning shows, as well as *Opry* broadcasts.

The owners of WKNX carried on with country music before adopting a top-forty pop format during the 1960s. In the immediate wake of Dickens', Clark's, and Ferguson's departures, *Country Song Roundup* magazine ran a profile of disk jockey "Uncle Don" Andrews and a new musical act, Bob Shaffer and His Saddle Pals.[25]

A STARR IN HEAVEN

Starr spent October 1948 in Arizona, before returning home. Around 1945 Starr had been diagnosed with Bright's disease, a problem of the kidneys. He kept his condition a secret from most of his friends. One day in early 1949 Starr showed up unexpectedly in Soldier, Kentucky. "He'd come to visit Casey and me, and I said, 'Casey's not here,'" said Mary Clark. Her husband had just told her over the phone he wanted to come home from Iowa. Starr offered to drive her out to pick him up. "On the way out there, [Starr] got such a nosebleed, oh I thought he was going to bleed to death," she said. "We got Casey, and on the way back, we stopped in a little town in Illinois [Centralia], and Casey got him a job at the radio station." He hired Starr and Bob Pauley. After two weeks, Clark moved his family from Kentucky to Illinois. "When we got back [to Centralia], . . . Gene was gone, and he had left us a note. It said that he had gotten really ill and he felt like he needed to go home," said Mary Clark.[26]

A musician in Little Rock, Arkansas, where Starr worked his last radio job in May 1949, called Starr's parents to fetch him. They brought him home, and Starr's condition quickly worsened. "Finally he had to go to bed. The doctor came out and gave him a shot of morphine every once in a while," said Jim Sauber.

I remember he got out of bed one afternoon, brought his guitar into the dining room and played "Beyond the Sunset." That was when that [song] was first popular. (I think Red Foley had it.) My mother got all excited. We didn't have a telephone here at the time, so she went down the road and phoned the doctor and said, "He's getting a lot better!" And he said, "No, he's not getting better. It's just [that] his insides are getting all numb. He will pass away probably tonight." And he did. About ten o'clock that night. . . . It was too bad, because he had so much going for him.

Starr died May 26. Fans and radio station representatives gathered at the Sauber farmhouse for the funeral. "Driving ahead of the Hearse, I looked back from that curve [in the road] and you couldn't see the end [of the procession]," said Sauber. "Cars were parked on both sides of the road as far as you could see, and all the people shuffled through the house." Starr was buried in a family plot at St. Anthony Cemetery in Hillsdale.

BAREFOOTIN'

After a month in Illinois, Clark moved to WKLX Lexington, Kentucky, joining the Hershel "Cowboy" Smithers band. Then he hopped over to WVLK Lexington, where Clark hosted a disk jockey show overnight, and began using the tagline "Ma Clark's Little Fat Boy." He led a new version of the Lazy Ranch Boys during the midday *Burley Jamboree,* including Bob Hall, Buddy Ratcliff, Bob Pauley, and Don Boots. "Barefoot Brownie" Reynolds joined the band and entered into a business partnership with Clark.

In 1947 Reynolds left Red Foley's band. He had been active not only in radio but in recording studios as well. Reynolds played harmonica on Lonzo and Oscar's "Cornbread, 'Lasses And Sassafras Tea" (1947), and he cut a handful of numbers—including "Hoe Down Hattie" and "How Corny Can You Get?"—for Radio Artist Records in Cincinnati, Ohio. In 1948 he played rockabilly bass on Hank Williams' first session for M-G-M Records, including classics such as "Move It On Over" and "I Saw The Light." Reynolds brought his network to the table, and Clark was happy to share management of the business with a seasoned and well-tempered musician.

Clark's wife Mary worked as talent agent and handled publicity for WVLK. "The station started a barn dance at Clay Gentry Arena," said Mary Clark. "Lester Flatt and Earl Scruggs and their group were on the station at the same time, . . . Molly O'Day and her husband Len."

"I used to go home at lunchtime from school, go to the radio station and do the fifteen-minute broadcast, and go back to school," said Clark's daughter Evelyn Harlene. "I was nine. . . . It was all children's [songs] that were popular at the time. I think at that time, there were a lot of kids that worked with their parents [in music]."

BUCKEYE FROLIC

When Clark and Reynolds moved to WRFD radio in Delaware County, Ohio (north of Columbus), in June 1950, Pauley, Ratcliff, and Boots moved on.

Ratcliff settled in eastern Kentucky where he played music and operated a luthier workshop. In 2006 Morehead State University honored Ratcliff with their Appalachian Treasure award.

Don Boots eventually entered the field of law enforcement, working as a police officer in northeast Ohio, where Tex Ferguson also settled with his second wife and family during the 1970s. Ferguson, who spent a few years during the 1950s broadcasting on television and radio in Bay City, Michigan, spent his final years working as a security guard in Attica, Ohio. He died in 1991.

Bob Pauley joined the Dixie Playboys at WDBJ Roanoke, Virginia, until 1951, when he briefly rejoined Clark and Reynolds at WIMA Lima, Ohio. By 1958, Pauley had settled in Indiana. Bob Pauley and the Plantation Playboys backed singer Tommy Lam on his rockabilly "Speed Limit" for the Nabor label that year. Two more Nabor singles by Earl Brooks also featured Pauley's band.

Inside a Lazy Ranch Boys book of sacred songs, a photograph of the

WRFD band revealed Herb Williams had returned. From Saginaw, Williams moved to KXXX Colby, Kansas. He married a Nebraskan woman, and they had a son in 1949. Williams moved to WGAY Silver Spring, Maryland, before returning to WKNX in September. Then he moved to the *Old Kentucky Barn Dance* on WHAS Louisville, Kentucky. From there, Williams met up with Clark and Reynolds in Ohio. Guitarist Joe Tanner and steel guitarist Floyd Starr also appeared in the photo, standing next to a 1948 Chrysler limousine with "WRFD / 880 on your dial" and "CASEY CLARK / Lazy Ranch Boys / Barefoot Brownie" painted on the side.

Clark worked as a disk jockey and led the band on the WRFD *Buckeye Frolic*. Clark and Williams reprised the Nat and Les duo as Nat and Bill, and when they required other voices for trios and quartets, Reynolds and Tanner probably stepped up.

Tanner was at the dawn of a long career in music. During the mid-1950s, he joined the Bluetones in North Carolina. He played guitar on sessions for Colonial Records in Chapel Hill, including George Hamilton IV's "A Rose And A Baby Ruth" (a pop hit in 1956 after ABC-Paramount reissued it). Tanner moved to Nashville during the 1960s and played the famous twelve-string guitar lick on Roy Orbison's "Pretty Woman."[27]

By 1951, the Clarks had four children: Evelyn, Carol, Billy, and Mike (born 1950). They moved to Lima, Ohio, where Bob Pauley briefly replaced Tanner, and the band teamed up with Red Kirk at WIMA.[28]

Late that year, Clark traveled to Detroit and met with David Abadaher and Norman J. O'Neill (O'Neill was in the construction business, a booming sector in and around Detroit). The two men planned to stage Saturday night barn dances at the Dairy Workers Hall in Highland Park. Clark agreed to provide the house band. During the chilly weeks of January 1952, Clark, Reynolds, and Williams moved their families to Detroit.

BIG BARN FROLIC

Clark and Reynolds accepted Williams as a third partner in the Lazy Ranch Boys. Their first Detroit hire was guitarist Chuck Carroll. Born in Richard

City, Tennessee, Carroll was thirteen when his family moved to Michigan in 1940. In 1947, after service in the army, "I started listening to Chuck Oakes," said Carroll. "He played in a bar . . . I wasn't old enough to get in. I used to stand outside the door and watch him, . . . and go home and hunt for it!"[29] Guitarist Chuck Oakes schooled Carroll on his technique. "He'd sit there on a Saturday night and watch me," said Oakes. "Then we'd get over in the corner and he'd say, 'How'd you do this? How'd you do that?' And he finally started taking up something on the same style I played. Sometimes he plays with a straight pick and his fingers both, . . . sometimes he plays with a thumb pick, too."[30]

Dwight Harris, who played steel guitar in the style of Jerry Byrd, also joined the band. Harris, like Byrd, had a strong interest in Hawaiian music and had been gigging around Detroit with Chief Redbird, Eddie Jackson, Skeet Ring, Hal Clark (no relation), and Bob Norton.

An advertisement for the new barn dance, the *Big Barn Frolic*, ran in the March 1, 1952, *Detroit Free Press*. The *Frolic*, of which WJR broadcast thirty minutes live, included a stage show and round and square dances. Clark also booked the band for family-friendly dances during the week in Michigan, northern Ohio, and southwestern Ontario.

On the show, Bob Quinn from Bay City sang western-styled songs. Banjo picker Ford Nix performed comedy and mountain music. After performing on WSM and the *Grand Ole Opry*, May Hawks returned to Michigan, where she was given a warm welcome by the cast.

In spring or summer 1952, Clark hired Myrl "Rusty" McDonald, a native Oklahoman who had worked with Tex Ritter and briefly with Bob Wills' Texas Playboys. (McDonald sang the vocal for Wills' 1950 hit "Faded Love.") McDonald played fiddle with Clark and occasionally sang a solo. He may have been touring through the region with Ritter and decided to stay for a few months before moving to Southern California.[31]

Lonnie Barron, the "Mississippi Farm Boy," made guest appearances on the show. "Casey tried his best to put Lonnie on every promoted show he could," said Mary Clark. "We just thought the world of that boy." In 1953 through 1956 Clark and Barron sometimes traveled to perform together at the WWVA *World's Original Jamboree* in Wheeling, West Virginia.

Clark also invited Mary Ann Johnson, a singer from the Detroit sub-urb of Redford, to appear as a guest. Johnson had recently begun singing in west side cafés. She wrote "Honey Baby Blues," which singer Neal Burris cut for Columbia Records in late 1952. Johnson and Burris also collaborated on "You're Stepping Out" in 1953.[32]

The most talked-about act Clark brought to Detroit was the Davis Sisters. In reality just close friends, Betty Jack Davis and Mary Frances "Skeeter" Penick came from Covington, Kentucky. During 1951 they performed on the WLEX *Kentucky Mountain Barn Dance* in Lexington with Flatt and Scruggs. Their television broadcasts caught the attention of Reynolds, who often made trips down to his old stomping grounds at John Lair's Renfro Valley.

Clark convinced the Davis Sisters to move to Detroit in mid-summer 1952, setting them up in a flat around the corner from the Clark household. While Betty Jack sang a bold, spirited lead, Skeeter harmonized with an in-tuitive, emotional style that didn't fit traditional harmony rules. They wrote their own songs ("Sorrow And Pain" and "You're Gone"), adapted others (Hank Williams' "Kaw-Liga" and "Jambalaya"), and brought a gigawatt of energy to the show.[33]

In August, poll results in *Billboard* magazine revealed the *Frolic* as the only non-network Saturday night radio show among the top five most popular in Detroit (ranked number three).[34] Despite this, Clark, Reynolds, and Williams quit the show, after a disagreement with the producers. "In November, Casey left, . . . and started his own barn dance," said Mary Clark.

Clark retained Chuck Carroll and hired Mary Ann Johnson. The Lazy Ranch Boys quickly found and negotiated the use of a U.A.W. hall at 12101 Mack Avenue (near Conner Street). The long building featured a wide stage at one end. Its open floor plan allowed hundreds of spectators to move chairs to the sides of the hall and participate in round and square dances.

In November the Lazy Ranch Boys distributed a handbill for a prom-ising premier on Saturday, December 6, starting at eight o'clock. The "Big Barn-Dance Jamboree" featured "WJR favorites," although Clark hadn't found sponsors to broadcast a segment of the show. Evelyn Harlene joined the cast as a named feature. Hugh Cross appeared as a guest, and Clark booked his old friend Ernie Lee, then working the WLW *Midwestern Hayride*, as star of the evening.

DAVIS SISTERS

Clark's only regret about leaving the *Frolic* concerned the Davis Sisters. "[After] we started our own barn dance, . . . the Davis Sisters only worked our barn dance as guests," said Mary Clark.

Norm O'Neill managed the duo and arranged recording sessions for them during late 1952 and early 1953. Most sessions were cut with musicians who played on the *Frolic* after the Lazy Ranch Boys' departure, including Roy Hall, the Lonesome Pine Fiddlers, and steel guitarist Chuck Hatfield. Jack and Dorothy Brown of Fortune Records issued a few singles, beginning December 1952 with "Jealous Love."

"Curly" Ray Cline, a member of RCA-Victor recording artists the Lonesome Pine Fiddlers, suggested the Davis Sisters travel to RCA offices in New York City to meet with artists and repertoire agent Steve Sholes. A brief meeting with Sholes resulted in the Davis Sisters going to Nashville in May 1953, where they signed a contract and cut their first session. The Davis Sisters moved home to Kentucky in June and began performing with entertainers associated with the *Grand Ole Opry*.

RCA-Victor issued the Davis Sisters' first single, Cecil Null's "I Forgot More Than You'll Ever Know" backed with "Rock-A-Bye Boogie," around July. "I Forgot More" steadily gained sales and radio spins through the summer.

After a performance at the WWVA *World's Original Jamboree* on August 2, they drove home to Covington that night. A young man on leave from the army fell asleep while driving the same road outside of Cincinnati, and he struck the girls' car in a head-on collision that killed Betty Jack. Skeeter Davis survived with injuries. While she recovered in the hospital, "I Forgot More" reached number one in *Billboard* C&W charts.

"Skeeter didn't go back to singing for quite a while," said Mary Clark.

Skeeter teamed with Betty Jack's older sister Georgie until 1956. She soon found her way as a solo artist, achieving some success with country singles before her biggest hit, "The End Of The World," climbed to the top of pop charts in 1963.

FLINT STEEL

With a banner that read "The Lazy Ranch Boys Barn Dance" stretched across the back wall of the stage, Clark and his group entertained at 12101 Mack every weekend. For just a dollar, one could spend a few hours watching and listening to country music and comedy, and participate in round and square dances at the end of the show. Active servicemen received free admission. Clark and his partners engaged major talent from the start, including the York Brothers, Hawkshaw Hawkins, Lew Childre, Lulu Belle and Scotty, Ernest Tubb, and Skeets McDonald.

Singer Don Rader remembered Reynolds wearing an alarm clock at the end of a chain for comic effect. "Old Brownie, he was a character," said Rader. "Sears used to have a coat called 'seersucker.' Old Brownie, he asked Herb, 'Where'd you get that jacket?' And he'd say, 'It's a seersucker!' 'Well, whattaya mean a seersucker?' He said, 'Well, Sears sold it and I'm the sucker who bought it!'"[35]

Clark hired Bishop "Bobby" Sykes, a Tennessee-born Detroit singer who dabbled in steel guitar. Sykes soon departed, and Clark called the Honolulu Conservatory of Music and Dance in Flint, where teacher Russell B. Waters had mentored a talented pool of steel guitarists for years.

In 1926, during a rise in popularity of Hawaiian music in the United States, Harry G. Stanley and his half brother George Bronson established the Oahu Publishing Company in Flint. Stanley also opened the Honolulu Conservatory of Music, where music teachers used Oahu materials with lessons. In 1930 Stanley moved to Cleveland, Ohio. Through the next decade, Honolulu Conservatories opened across the United States, supplied by Oahu lesson books. Instructors gave Oahu brand instruments to students upon completion of fifty-two weeks of lessons. Annual music conventions sponsored by Oahu Publishing assembled students from around the country. Some instructors, such as Flint's Russ Waters, directed students in musical programs for local radio stations.[36]

Born in 1911 in Terre Haute, Indiana, Waters moved to Flint in 1927. He began teaching at the Honolulu Conservatory in 1935. Proficient in steel guitar and other string instruments, Waters played Hawaiian music in nightclubs with the Honolulu Ambassadors. He also moonlighted with Flint bandleader Max Henderson during the 1940s and 1950s.[37]

By the time Clark contacted the Honolulu Conservatory of Flint, a few graduates had already pursued careers playing steel guitar, including Chuck Hatfield, Jim Baker, and Chuck Adams. Baker, born in 1933 in Eldridge, Alabama, grew up in Flint. While a student at the Honolulu Conservatory, he worked Saturdays with Tommy Vaughn's Wonder Valley Boys in Saginaw (at WKNX). "I was probably about twelve or thirteen, fourteen maybe, when I started taking lessons," said Baker. "Russ Waters was my teacher. . . . You couldn't speak much higher of a man."[38]

Baker played nightclubs in the Flint area, picking a double-neck steel with bandleaders such as guitarist Cliff Gilbert, Max Henderson, Sonny Sexton, Jimmy Tate, George Pearson, and Lucky Sikes. Then Casey Clark telephoned.

"Evidently someone quit [the Lazy Ranch Boys], 'cause he called me a couple, three times," said Baker. "I guess he was getting desperate! [*laughs*]"

Clark hired Art Dakes, a.k.a. Art Dakasian, to play drums, making the Lazy Ranch Boys one of the first country acts in Detroit to use them. Charlie and Honey Miller, the "West Virginia Sweethearts," joined the cast as well. They had worked radio shows and jamborees at WCHS Charleston and WHTN Huntington, as well as Renfro Valley. Charlie played standard guitar, Hawaiian steel, mandolin, five-string banjo, and piano.[39] Mary Clark likened them to Lulu Belle and Scotty, the popular duo of the WLS *National Barn Dance* in Chicago. "[Casey] knew of them before, but they came out to the barn dance to see him," she said. "They were with the show for about four years."

RADIO ROUNDUP

Steady weekend crowds allowed Clark to maintain a large band and book guest stars. Clark printed souvenir books of photos and biographies of himself, Reynolds, and Williams to sell at personal appearances. In February 1953, WXYZ radio Detroit began broadcasting a thirty-minute segment of the Saturday night barn dance at nine o'clock. The broadcasts ended in May, but the shows continued at the hall. During the summer, Clark produced daily programs for WEXL Royal Oak. These were scripted and performed either at WEXL or in the Clarks' family room. Clark often recorded fifteen- and thirty-minute shows in a home studio for a WEXL salesman to pick up and deliver to the station.

During the last week of June 1953, *Billboard* ran results from another poll that showed the WJR *Big Barn Frolic* rated second most popular Saturday night radio show in Detroit.[40] The final listing for the *Frolic* appeared the same week in the *Detroit Free Press.*

With Clark's barn dance the only production of its size in Detroit, business improved. By the end of August, Clark negotiated with WJR to broadcast part of the Lazy Ranch Boys Barn Dance as the *Goodwill Jamboree* in the same slot the *Frolic* once held. On September 5, Herb Williams opened the show with his standard line, "Here they all come!" (Williams ended each show with "There they all go!") In the weeks leading up to the show's radio debut, Clark began spinning country records daily at WJR from 5:05 to 6:00 in the morning. "That [program] was *Your Big Fat Buddy*," said Mary Clark.

HARLAN HARMONY

During a trip south in spring 1953 Reynolds discovered the Callaway Sisters singing sweet harmony, dressed in old-fashioned gingham gowns and high-button shoes at Renfro Valley. He bent Clark's ear about the group. Knowing they could stay with an aunt in Detroit, Sudie Mae, Coleida, and Clara Callaway joined Clark's barn dance.

Originally from Harlan County, Kentucky, the Callaway Sisters grew up surrounded by music. "We pretty much had relatives on every side playing music at our house on the weekends," said Sudie Mae.[41] "We started singing harmony. . . . We thought we invented it ourselves! [*laughs*] . . . Then we started singing in church. . . . Then we went on up to Renfro [Valley], . . . went into Mr. Lair's office and we did a few songs. . . . We worked there about three years, off and on, because we were still in school."

Sudie Mae had finished school when they moved to Detroit. "We sang things like 'The Old Lamplighter,' some hymns, gospel, old fashioned songs, . . . 'Red River Valley' and some of those. We learned the new ones and sang them as they came out, too," she said.

"We were very professional, because we were used to John Lair at Renfro Valley, and everything [at the Lazy Ranch Boys Barn Dance] was done with the clock. . . . It was all mapped out, what was gonna happen next. . . . First part of it was a live show, broadcast on [the radio]. And then they would move all the chairs off part of the floor and have a big dance. And I'll tell you: It was packed, every Saturday!" she said.

BARN DANCE SHUFFLE

The Lazy Ranch Boys played tunes from the country music hit parade and pop standards, with the sophisticated sound of top western swing acts such as the Hank Thompson, Pee Wee King, and Tex Williams bands. To avoid getting pigeonholed in one particular style, as well as to attract a broad audience, Clark sought variety for his show. Besides booking guest stars, Clark scheduled vocal trios and solos by every member of the band.

In November 1953, Mary Ann Johnson left to join the cast of the *Motor City Jamboree*, a new barn dance in Detroit. Clara Callaway returned to Kentucky in late summer 1953, to prepare for school. Mary Clark sang with the remaining two Callaway Sisters. Sudie Mae Callaway and Jim Baker dated, and after Baker received his draft notice from the army, they married. The couple left the Lazy Ranch Boys in October and Coleida went home. Baker and his bride set up house in Flint, but not before helping Clark find steel guitarist Buddy Gene Emmons.

"I got him to call Buddy," said Baker. "We went down there and seen him at Buck Lake Ranch [in Angola, Indiana]. . . . I said, 'Hey man, that guy plays good.'" A private campground with its own lake, Buck Lake Ranch presented country music shows on weekends, with the biggest names in the business, along with acts such as the Lazy Ranch Boys. Joe Taylor and the Indiana Redbirds of Fort Wayne held sway at Buck Lake during the 1950s. When Baker and Clark first met Emmons, he played steel for Taylor's Redbirds.

"[The Redbirds] were the opening act for all of the *Opry* acts the owner booked in, each Sunday," said Emmons. "I worked with them for a couple of years."[42]

Born in 1937 at Mishawaka, Indiana, Emmons grew up in South Bend, where local radio played big band music during the day. "My dad would come home at night and he would turn a country station on. It was WJJD in Chicago, and WCKY in Cincinnati, and, of course, the *Opry*," said Emmons.

At age eleven, Emmons began learning steel guitar at the Honolulu Conservatory in South Bend. "Most of the time it was pop and Hawaiian tunes," he said. Emmons taught himself to reproduce the steel guitar he heard on records by country artists such as Hank Williams (with Don Helms), George Morgan (with Donald Davis), and Red Foley (with Billy Robinson).

After leaving home in 1953, Emmons worked full-time for Joe Taylor. One night at Buck Lake, *Opry* star Carl Smith asked for his phone number, but Smith's manager thought Emmons was too young. Emmons moved to Calumet City, Illinois, before joining a group in Kennett, Missouri, in spring 1954.

Carl Smith had given Webb Pierce my number, and they called my home. . . . So I quit the job in Kennett, came right straight home and called Webb. By that time, he had hired somebody else. So I hung around my mother and father's house until we got a call from Casey. And he just wanted to know if I'd be interested in coming up to Detroit. He talked about a few local dates and then the Sunday thing, and some WJR stuff.

That Joe Taylor's band, it was fabulous. And Casey's band, it was about the same. He had good caliber musicianship, as far as I remember. . . . It was a fine band. They covered a lot of ground.

Just after Emmons' move to Detroit, bluegrass trio Jimmy Martin and the Osborne Brothers (Bobby and Sonny) made a guest appearance at Clark's barn dance. "We were playing a little ol' nightclub in Dayton, Ohio," said Bobby Osborne. "Sonny and me worked in Wheeling, West Virginia, with Charlie Bailey in late 1953 or early '54. We kind of got halfway acquainted with Casey back in them days. . . . We went up there for . . . an audition, first. . . . We moved up there when we knew we had something definite."[43]

Osborne recalled living in southwest Detroit, working the Saturday night barn dance with the Lazy Ranch Boys and taping daily programs for WEXL. "We did one song on every one of 'em, each day," he said. During the week, Jimmy Martin and the Osborne Brothers played nightclubs throughout the city, including Ted's 10-Hi, Jefferson Beach, Rose's Bar, Dixie Belle, and West Fort Tavern.

"Just about every Sunday, Casey would have *Grand Ole Opry* shows up there," said Osborne. "Sometimes he'd run a tour all the way up into Michigan—about a week's tour. . . . We'd travel right along with Jimmy Dickens, Ernest Tubb, Carl Smith. . . . He had a lot of the *Grand Ole Opry* people, and we got acquainted with a lot of them through that there."

Entertainer Fairley Holden came aboard at the end of summer 1954. Holden, with his humorous songs for King Records, particularly "Keep Them Cold Icy Fingers Off Of Me" (1947), had been a favorite at Renfro Valley. "Carl Smith had a hit song, 'Hey Joe!' [in late 1953]," said Mary Clark. "We had Carl up here for a Sunday show, and everybody told him Fairley did that, so Carl insisted that Fairley do it before he did it. I thought Carl was going to die. He just laughed his head off.

"Casey would hire somebody if he thought they were real good, and [if] he thought they would draw and people here would like them," said

Mary Clark. "If they needed a place to live until they got their paycheck, they lived at our house. I bet you I have made more sandwiches and more orange juice . . . I don't think the Detroit River would hold the orange juice that I have squeezed [laughs]. Buddy Emmons, I used to just feed him orange juice all the time."

"I was at a point in my life when I would play at any time, night or day," said Emmons.

"Me and Emmons used to go down to the Roosevelt Lounge [on Mack near Montcalm] after we'd get off playing. Go down there and sit in," said Chuck Carroll. "Casey blowed his stack and said, 'Next time you go down there, you're fired.' I'd say, 'Well, I guess you'd better fire me now. We're going down there tonight [laughs].' He said, 'No, no.' He'd just rant and rave, but he didn't fire us. . . . We'd just go down there and sit in 'cause there was bunches of musicians always in the Roosevelt. . . . I just didn't like drinking, so I didn't go into a bar except to see a musician or to play a job."

COUNTRY TUNE TIMES

From the start of 1954 through the summer, Clark moved from his early morning radio gig to spin country records at a quarter past four in the afternoon, on a show called *Country Tune Time*. "I made out the program at home, according to the mail," said Mary Clark. "If we had twenty-six requests for Hank Williams, . . . that would be number one, but that would also be the last. Then I'd go to the station, pull the records and put them in order for him. . . . Because immediately after he got off the air, he'd go on a personal appearance, and I'd already be there selling tickets."

Just before WJR began broadcasting the *Goodwill Jamboree* in 1953, singer-songwriter Jimmy Work visited Clark at his early morning disk jockey program.

"I went up to [WJR]," said Work. "He had a little program up there, and . . . I took him one of [my] records. . . . I also told him that if I was makin' records, . . . I asked him if he would be interested in playing the music for me. 'Oh yeah,' he said, just let him know."[44]

In 1948, a Detroit jukebox company issued Work's first hit song, "Tennessee Border." Before meeting Clark, Work cut records for Decca, Bullet, London, and Capitol labels. Work hired the Lazy Ranch Boys to cut his first recordings for Dot Records of Nashville in mid-1954. Clark, Carroll, Reynolds (on bass), and Emmons accompanied Work at United Sound Systems in Detroit. "Chuck Carroll, he was a good guitar player," said Work. "He played that smooth, two-string stuff . . . on that record, 'Don't Give Me A Reason To Wonder Why.'"

The teen-aged Emmons came across remarkably sure of his licks and up-to-date despite playing a steel guitar without pedals. Webb Pierce's record "Slowly," a hit earlier that year, featured the new sound of Bud Isaacs' pedal steel. "We (I mean the whole band, and all the musicians I knew) were just dumbfounded by the sound," said Emmons. "We hadn't heard pedals any other way than Alvino Rey—you know, the chord raking style—up to that point. But I could tell what it was! I knew it was pedals. . . . All the pedal work that I'd heard was with the C6 neck before that. Just hearing those simple triads moving within the chord was quite a different experience, and it got my attention."

With a stripped-down style similar to Webb Pierce or Faron Young, the session yielded two hits, one of which was a monster. Work's original "Making Believe" darted up the C&W charts, but Kitty Wells' Decca cover hit number one in 1955. "That's What Makes The Jukebox Play" also topped the charts. Work recorded several more sessions in Detroit with Clark.

20/20 VISION

As Martin and the Osborne Brothers perfected three-part harmony vocals (Martin sang lead, Bobby sang tenor, and Sonny sang baritone), they cut demonstration records at the home studio of Detroit musician Bill Callihan. A disabled man, Callihan played Hawaiian steel guitar and made recordings of local musicians on acetate-coated disks. "We made them there and sent them to RCA-Victor for an audition, to get that contract with RCA," said Bobby Osborne.

In November, Martin and the Osbornes recorded for RCA-Victor in Nashville. Although Martin had recorded for King Records in 1951 (with Charlie and "Curly" Ray Cline of the Lonesome Pine Fiddlers), his first RCA-Victor single, "20/20 Vision" and "Save It! Save It!" brought more attention to the bluegrass style in Southeast Michigan.

Gene Autry cut "20/20 Vision (And Walking Around Blind)" earlier that year. "Save It! Save It!" was written by Charles "Rufus" Shoffner. In 1950, Shoffner moved from Tazewell, Tennessee, to Monroe, Michigan. Shoffner cut "Save It! Save It!" as "Got Anything Good" for the Country Side label in Lexington, Kentucky, in 1954. "We played down in Monroe, and we met Rufus," said Osborne. "Rufus had a little group of his own, and he played around there a little bit. He'd written a couple of songs. That one, 'Save It, Save It,' . . . we liked it, so we got acquainted with him like that."

NEW RIGS, NEW RULES

Don Rader's parents sometimes invited the Lazy Ranch Boys over to their Hazel Park home for backyard barbecues and suppers. Rader recalled when Emmons started in the band, "he didn't have the pedals, and he used to take that bar, and he'd almost turn it sideways to get that pedal style. You couldn't even get that type of steel."

Playing a four-neck Fender steel guitar, Emmons often led the band through instrumentals introduced by steel guitar pacesetters such as Leon McAuliffe and Joaquin Murphey. "[I did] some Speedy West things. I was pretty heavy into him at the time," he said. "We would do 'Remington Ride' and I would sit on the front neck of the guitar and play behind me while I was facing the crowd."

In early 1955 he took delivery of a Standel amplifier, custom made by Bob Crooks in California. Crooks' "Butcher Paper List" noted the completion of Emmons' amplifier in January.[45] Standel amps included fifteen-inch premium JBL (Lansing) speakers—unheard of in those days. Emmons' Standel was probably the first of its kind in Detroit. Crooks got into the business two years before, when he was asked to create a concept for Paul

Bigsby, a manufacturer of solid body guitars and steel guitars. Bigsby lost interest in the amplifier, but Crooks persevered. He created a cutting-edge legacy of high-quality amplifiers used by musicians such as Merle Travis, Speedy West, Joe Maphis, and Hank Thompson.

Around the same time, Emmons purchased a three-neck Bigsby steel guitar. "I had it set up exactly like Speedy West's—that's the way I ordered it. And when 'Slowly' came out, I called Paul Bigsby and told him to put the Bud Isaacs tuning on the outside neck. . . . That was about two months before I was supposed to have it shipped to me. So he changed it at the last moment, and when I got it, it was all set up with the Isaacs setup, and the other two necks were [set up like] Speedy West's. . . . I'd been so used to standing up, moving around, dancing, or doing whatever I wanted to do. All of a sudden I found myself in a chair, hobbled, couldn't move around. That was uncomfortable for a long time," he said.

CASEY CLARK JAMBOREE

In spring 1955, the P. L. Grissom and Son car dealership on West Fort Street in southwest Detroit began sponsoring a weekly television broadcast of the Lazy Ranch Boys on CKLW-TV Channel Nine Windsor. The *Casey Clark Jamboree* broadcast for an hour every Friday night, from a quarter past eleven. Dewey "Smitty" Smith replaced Art Dakes before the television shows got under way.

Mary Clark typed and mimeographed program scripts listing songs and names of musicians expected to perform them. Many titles included a roster of soloists below them. Boxes decorated with the Grissom dealership name and "Casey Clark" painted in a fanciful script hid music stands. The set was made up with bales of straw, country cabin walls, and a rock fireplace for a homey atmosphere.

After the first several episodes of the TV show, drummer Ted Bay replaced Smith. Despite a hearing problem, Bay's sense of timing added a driving beat to the proceedings. "He had a heightened sense of touch," said Mary Clark.

Just a few weeks into the television shows, guitarist Chuck Carroll left the band. Clark paid the Lazy Ranch Boys a weekly salary to be on call for any work he lined up, such as public appearances and recording sessions. "We was on call twenty-four hours a day," said Carroll. "I mean, ten o'clock at night he'd say, 'We got a recording over here. Come over here. Blah, blah, blah.' That'd get kind of old. Then he started traveling, and man, I can't take that. I told him I was gonna miss two weekends. I was gettin' married and I was gonna go away on a honeymoon. He said, 'You can't. You gotta stay here. We got jobs lined up.' I said, 'Well, we'll get somebody to take my place.' He said, 'No. You go, and you're fired.' I said, 'Well, I guess I'm fired.' So he fired me [laughs]. We remained on good terms. . . . I just didn't work with him."

Carroll played with a variety of local entertainers, including Danny Richards, Lonnie Barron, and Frankie Meadows. He found a day job and picked guitar on weekends. In September 1966, his doctor diagnosed multiple sclerosis and Carroll put away his guitar. Almost a decade later, he picked up his guitar and regained most of the skill he thought he'd lost, playing it until he died in 2004.

OUT OF THE DARKNESS

Clark hired twenty-year-old guitarist Donnel Hemminger of Toledo, Ohio. Born in Millersville, a wide place in the road southeast of Toledo, Hemminger was a little rough around the edges when he arrived. "I think that Chuck [Carroll] was a little 'deeper,' theory-wise at the time," said Emmons. "Don got into that pretty quick, but he was more in the 'speed' end of it. He enjoyed playing a lot of notes. . . . But he progressed really fast. The last time I was in contact with him, he was real deep in jazz, which he was partially, at the time."

Shortly before Hemminger joined the band, pianist Dick McCobb, a neighbor of the Clark family, began to sit in. "He just wanted me to play the piano with him, and he didn't really consider me full-time," said McCobb.[46]

"Casey Clark's wife would give me a ten and a five [dollar bill] every Saturday evening. I was just a kid [from] across the street. . . . They did that as a neighborly thing. But it started to get me some experience."

A 1952 graduate of St. Gregory High School in Detroit, McCobb played organ part-time at a local church and jammed with the Lazy Ranch Boys during morning broadcasts at WJR, besides weekend and evening bookings. "They traveled quite a bit," said McCobb. "And they'd also gone to Toledo Beach [amusement park] every Sunday [in summer 1955], . . . and other places that we traveled to, in and around the Detroit area."

"I remember doing the 'Bumble Boogie' (this was on the radio show)," said McCobb. "Casey was sort of fascinated [by it], because he called it 'longhair music.' It sounded classical to him, . . . because of all the chromatic handwork that's involved in that song." McCobb also specialized in "House Of Blue Lights," Chuck Miller's 1955 hit, and "Steel Guitar Rag."

Around spring 1955 the Lazy Ranch Boys cut a record for twenty-two-year-old Ray Gahan, who produced a sleeper hit in late 1954 with the Three Chuckles'"Runaround" on his Boulevard label. With visions of Gahan's luck rubbing off, Clark gathered Reynolds, Williams, Emmons, Hemminger, McCobb, and Bay into his Chevrolet limousine and took them to a local studio.

Gahan issued "Out Of The Darkness" backed with the instrumental "Chokin The Reeds." "Reeds" featured Reynolds playing harmonica. He recorded a version with the Brown County Revelers in 1938, which Vocalion didn't issue. The tune must have been a showstopper, with Reynolds frantically blowing his harp and the band rushing to keep up with him.

Mary Clark wrote "Out Of The Darkness" as a religious poem, which Williams recited. About halfway through the recording, the pitch faltered and made it sound as if the record slowed. This effect can be heard on 45-rpm and 78-rpm copies. "They might have had a drop in voltage, which would slow things down a little bit," said McCobb. "Something of high current may have [been] switched on, . . . and would cause a voltage drop in anything that was connected to the power at that time." The record sold well at personal appearances.

TWIN FIDDLES, TWIN GUITARS

Adron "Arkie" Childress, a fiddler from Knobel, Arkansas, joined the band. With twin fiddles, the Lazy Ranch Boys reached a new pinnacle of sound. The versatility of the Lazy Ranch Boys, its professional management, stage presence, and broadcast reach rivaled bands of the Midwest. Hemminger recalled playing live on WJR five days a week, "and every Sunday we did three shows at the hall on Mack Avenue for about one thousand eight hundred people per show. Our band backed up an *Opry* star or two on each show. The star would fly up to Detroit (without his band) and Casey could get them for a greatly reduced price," he said. "Buddy Emmons and I would find out who was coming each week, take his records out of Casey's record library, and memorize the tunes, keys, and tempos."[47]

With the band's geographical reach expanding, Clark purchased a bus from *Opry* star Ray Price. "It needed extensive work when he got it," said Evelyn Harlene. "He sent it back to the place in Ohio where they built it, and every nut and bolt on it was replaced."

"Almost every night, the band would pile into the flex bus, . . . and go into Canada and play various towns at ice arenas, for about one thousand people at each show," said Hemminger. "While I was there, we did close to one hundred recording sessions down at United Sound. Each session paid the sidemen forty-two dollars and fifty cents. I was gettin' paid from WJR radio, CKLW-TV, the record sessions, and two hundred fifty dollars a week salary from Casey. And during intermissions between the shows at Mack Avenue, we sidemen would make about a thirty dollar commission selling Casey's [souvenir books] to the audience. All together, I was makin' about five hundred to six hundred dollars a week! In 1955–57! I think the average factory wage then was sixty dollars a week. I blew it as fast as I made it."

STEEL AWAY

On Saturday, June 11, 1955, "Little" Jimmy Dickens and his band, along with pianist Del Wood and vocalist Okie Jones, played two shows with the Lazy

Ranch Boys in Detroit.[48] "We opened, as usual," said Emmons. "When Jimmy went on, I sat in the wings watching [steel guitarist] Walter Haynes and all the stuff he was doing pedal-wise with Little Jim. . . . After we got through with our opening the second time, Little Jim came up to me and said, 'My steel player isn't feeling well. He's out in the car. Would you mind doing the second show with me?' I said, 'Not at all.'"

"I had Walter Haynes playing steel for me," said Dickens, "and he left and went to Korea, in the army. When he came back, he worked with me for a while, and he said he should get off the road because his nerves were bad. You know, the Korean thing had messed him up a little bit. So I said, 'Will you find me a steel player?' He heard Buddy and said, 'I think I found you a steel player.'"

"After the show, I was packing up," said Emmons, "and [Dickens] said, 'Well, my steel player has just turned in his notice. I don't know if he's serious or not, but if he is, would you consider taking the job?' I was bowled over. I said, 'You bet! I'll be there.' He said, 'Well, you never know about musicians. . . . I don't know how he's feeling today, or how he'll be feeling next week, but if he's serious and he does leave, I'll get in touch with you.' About a week or so later, I got a telegram from him that said, 'Come to Nashville.' . . . Casey wasn't all that happy about it. [*laughs*] . . . He was just a little touchy about it."

"On the night Buddy Emmons left," said Don Rader, "Casey laid down his fiddle, walked over and picked up [one end of] Buddy's steel, and Buddy was on the other side just pickin' like crazy—and they walked right off the stage. They had that planned like that—that was really funny."

"Casey was [a favorite] source for musicians, because I knew he knew the best, and always had the best around him," said Dickens.

For the next several years, Emmons worked with Dickens, Ernest Tubb, Ray Price, and Roger Miller, to name a few. He earned a reputation as one of the most-recognized innovators of the steel guitar—not only in technique, but also in manufacturing when he teamed up with Shot Jackson in Nashville to produce the Sho-Bud steel guitar, as well as his own musical instruments with the Emmons Guitar Company during the 1960s. Emmons played sessions with country and pop music artists, cut jazz albums, and drew accolades from steel guitar fans worldwide.

BLUEGRASS MOVES FAST

By July, Emmons had moved to Nashville. In August, the Osborne Brothers left Jimmy Martin. "As it happened, it was the best move we ever made," said Bobby Osborne. "When we left there, I never looked back." About a year after leaving Detroit, M-G-M Records issued the Osborne Brothers' "Ruby Are You Mad." In October 1956, they joined the WWVA *World's Original Jamboree* as a featured act. Between 1958 and 1980, eighteen Osborne Brothers records climbed into the upper reaches of country music charts.

"[Bluegrass] was kind of a new thing to the people up there, but they accepted it pretty well," said Osborne. "A lot of people from the South were working in the car factories. And that's what made bluegrass big up there, 'cause all them folks love bluegrass."

Two days after the Osbornes left town, Martin recruited Earl Taylor (mandolin) and Sam Hutchins (banjo) to carry on as the Sunny Mountain Boys.

STARS OF TOMORROW

Steel guitarist Terry Bethel, another graduate of the Honolulu Conservatory of Flint, joined the band after Emmons' departure. Bethel, born in 1938 at Monette, Arkansas, grew up in Flint. At age eleven, he began taking lessons for steel guitar.

"My mother used to take me to a place called the Wagon Wheel on Richfield Road. . . . On Sunday afternoons they'd have a jam session and . . . they would let me get up there and play. Don Green was playing steel there, . . . with Sonny Sexton," he said.[49] Don "Sonny Boy" Sexton operated the Wagon Wheel for decades. He also led the house band, the Musical Westernaires.

Every Saturday at noon, the Honolulu Conservatory sponsored *Stars of Tomorrow*, hosted by Russ Waters, on WTAC radio Flint. "They would have different students play, and Chuck Rich, Don Rauch, and myself were the house band," said Bethel. "All three of us played . . . bass, rhythm [guitar] and steel. We would switch off every week, who would play steel. . . . [We played] 'Steel Guitar Rag' and things of that nature, a lot of Hawaiian tunes, because they were hot back then. . . . We even worked Moose clubs. And we worked a lot of functions, like car dealerships."

Bethel and Chuck Rich played western swing with bandleader Tommy Vaughn on Saturdays at WKNX, as well as gigs Vaughn lined up across mid-Michigan. Some weekends, Bethel and Rich played "twin steel guitars" for Vaughn.[50]

Bethel worked with the Lazy Ranch Boys until September, when he returned to high school. Clark brought in Jimmy Murrah, originally from Knoxville, Tennessee, who played western swing on a three-neck Fender steel in nightclubs around Detroit. Bob Crooks completed orders of Standel amplifiers for Murrah and Hemminger on September 30, 1955. "[Casey] always tried to have the best [equipment]," said Mary Clark, who confirmed her husband furnished Standel amplifiers for his musicians.

By early autumn 1955 Fairley Holden left the troupe. But when Jimmy Dickens returned to Detroit in October, he left behind a surprise.

ALL THEY HAD TO SAY WAS THE WORD

In late 1949 Okie Jones, a young singer from Fort Worth, Texas, made a guest appearance at the *Grand Ole Opry*. "Chet Atkins, . . . he had heard about me out in Texas, and got me to sing backstage; and they put me on the *Grand Ole Opry*. . . . Jimmy Dickens' manager hired me to go on the road that night."[51]

Before Elvis Presley and rockabilly music, most country entertainers stood still on stage as they delivered a song. A few exceptions included Ferlin Husky, Charline Arthur, Bill Carlisle, and Okie Jones. "Some people call it personality and I called it just kind of actin' silly," Jones said. "When I would do a song, I'd express things in it, you know. . . . It was a novelty back then to jump around, and it finally became the norm [*laughs*].

"I worked with 'Little' Jimmy Dickens 'til I went into the army in 1953," said Jones, who recorded for Columbia Records while in the service. Upon his discharge two years later, Jones rejoined Dickens' show. "I was with 'Little' Jimmy Dickens whenever we worked Detroit, and Casey offered me a job. . . . Casey was awful good to me.

"We used to do early morning radio at WJR," he said. "It was really hard to sing early in the morning [*laughs*]. . . . The Saturday show was the main thing. . . . On Friday nights, I think we did the television show. Other than that, we just, . . . during the week may go out and do one or two shows over in Canada. . . . I remember he used to say if they wanted us to stop in their new auditorium, or wherever, all they had to say was the word. And the word was 'money' [*laughs*]."

MOVERS AND SHAKEUPS

Carroll Smithers joined the Lazy Ranch Boys as a vocalist, pianist, bassist, guitarist, "and anything you wanted to hand him," said Evelyn Harlene. A younger brother of "Cowboy" Smithers, who Clark worked with at WKLX Lexington, Kentucky, Smithers introduced himself to Clark while still in the U.S. Air Force. "He came to the barn dance," said Harlene. "He liked it so much, he made his reservation in the band when he was here. . . . I was very fond of him. He was probably the closest thing to an older brother that I ever had."

After just a few weeks, Jimmy Murrah left the Lazy Ranch Boys, prompting another call to Flint.[52] Jim Baker, newly discharged from the army, returned for a couple of months, before he quit to concentrate on working in Flint. He taught at the Honolulu Conservatory and moonlighted in country bands. During the early months of 1956, Baker and his family moved to Alabama, where he operated music shops in Gadsden and Decatur, before moving to Knoxville, Tennessee. Sudie Mae and her sisters sang on radio for grocer and politician Caswell "Cas" Walker while Baker taught music lessons at his shop. "I'd go on the road with guys coming through there from the *Opry*, going in that direction; east and northeast," said Baker. In February 1963 the Bakers moved to Nashville, where Sudie Mae and her sisters worked independently for recording studios. A popular steel guitarist, Baker played radio, road, and studio gigs. "You hang around Tootsie's and see everybody," he said. "I worked with Clyde Beavers, . . . Lonzo and Oscar . . . Justin Tubb—all over Southeast Asia, and stayed in Vietnam quite a bit. Come back from that, and took two weeks down in Atlanta, Georgia, with Charlie Pride. . . . One night, Mel Tillis, Porter Wagoner, and [E. W.] 'Bud' Wendell, the manager, come in . . . to listen to Charlie. And they liked the band, so me and Mel got together, and I was the first Statesider—Mel's first bandleader. . . . I stayed with Mel for two years." Jim Baker worked four decades in Nashville before he passed away in 2008.

While Baker played with the Lazy Ranch Boys for the second time, Clark had professional photos of the band shot at the soundstage of his television show. These portraits appeared in a custom-printed 1956 *All Star Scrapbook*.

PERSONALITIES, PROMOTIONS

Steel guitarist Billy Cooper came to Detroit with Ferlin Husky in late 1955. Bandleader Eddie Jackson hired Cooper. When Baker left the Lazy Ranch Boys, Clark lured Cooper away from Jackson. "Billy Cooper used to leave his guitar at our house after they'd come home from a personal appearance," said Mary Clark. "[Cooper] would give our son Billy his guitar until the next time he needed to use it." After noting his son's dedication to his steel lessons, Clark purchased a Standel amplifier in Billy Clark's name in 1956.

In March 1956 *Billboard* reported the band worked every other Sunday in Flint. "Among recent guests with the Clark group were Jim Edward, Maxine and Bonnie Brown; Ernest Tubb, Grandpa Jones, Cousin Jody, Dusty Owens, Mac Wiseman, Jimmy and Johnny, Webb Pierce, and the Davis Sisters."[53] A quarter-page ad for the *Casey Clark Jamboree* graced the previous page. The next edition of *Billboard* listed featured artists Okie Jones, "Little Evelyn and Herb Williams, vocalists; Charlie and Honey; Lazy Ranch Rockers, harmony group; and Nat and Bill, comedy team."[54] The Lazy Ranch Rockers may have been a vocal quartet of performers in the band.

SAGE AND SAND

In April 1956, Lonnie Barron reported in the *Richmond Review* newspaper he cut a new record with the Lazy Ranch Boys in Detroit. "I'm using Casey Clark's eight-piece band on this record. This should be a big help," he said. "Speaking of Casey Clark, I was on his TV show last Friday night. We previewed one side of our new record."[55]

Ohio-based promoter Pat Nelson signed Barron to W. O. "Woodie" Fleener's Hollywood, California, record label Sage and Sand in 1955. In 1956 Nelson signed up Clark for four sides. Recordings took place at WXYZ studios in the Maccabees Building (on Woodward Avenue at Putnam). Personnel included Clark, Reynolds, Williams, Childress, Hemminger, Cooper, Bay, and McCobb. Three singles from the sessions, held April 29 and 30, were released in mid-May.[56] For Clark's record, Reynolds reprised the folk tune "Lost John," which he recorded with Eldon Baker's group eighteen years before. Just like the 1938 performance, Reynolds sang a fast-paced, rocking number. A vocal quartet of band members backed him up, and Hemminger played the blues, delivering one of the most twisted rockabilly guitar breaks ever. "He was a jazz guitarist trying to play like Scotty Moore," Clark said of the solo. Clark's fiddle was nowhere to be heard on "Lost John" but showed up on its flipside, "Pot Of Gold."

Jones recorded "Could You, Would You," a bopper that he and Dickens' bass player Joel Price wrote, along with Mary Clark's "How Could You." Barron cut two originals: "Don't Doubt My Love" and "Go On, It's OK."

Of the three records, Barron's fared best, showing up in regional country music playlists. "[Our] Sage and Sand records weren't produced in any great quantity," said Harlene.

Later that year, Jim Denny at Cedarwood Publishing Company in Nashville accepted a few of Mary Clark's songs. In 1955 Bobby Sykes moved to Music City from the Motor City. "He went to Cedarwood Publishing Company with ... three songs of mine," said Mary Clark. Mercury Records issued Mary Clark's "(All You've Given Me Is) Heartaches" recorded by George and

Earl that year, and "If I Didn't Have A Conscience" cut by Benny Martin in 1956. Bill Phillips recorded "How Could You" for Columbia Records in 1961.

DEPARTURES, DE-PARTNERINGS

Dick McCobb reported to the navy May 10, 1956. "Somewhere between May first and May tenth, I played for the last time with Casey," he said. "San Diego was my base. . . . I was with one of the navy bands." After his discharge in 1960, McCobb found employment at St. Rose Church in Lima, Ohio, where he played the church organ and taught music.

Around June 1956 Cooper left Clark to re-enter the Detroit nightclub circuit. At the same time, the Lazy Ranch Boys partnership changed. Williams left his Nebraskan wife and married Don Rader's sister. A little while after cutting the Sage and Sand session, Clark and Reynolds bought out Williams. Williams played nightclubs around Detroit for a few years before making his way back to Maryland, where he died in 1995.

On Saturday, June 23, the final listing for the WJR *Goodwill Jamboree* appeared in the *Detroit Free Press* radio schedule. The Lazy Ranch Boys carried on with the *Casey Clark Jamboree* television show, weekend barn dances at 12101 Mack, and personal appearances through a network of booking agents that Clark and his wife had established during the previous four years.

Another student of Russ Waters at the Flint Honolulu Conservatory, sixteen-year-old Chuck Rich, from Lapeer, Michigan, played a four-neck Fender steel guitar in Lonnie Barron's band. When Billy Cooper left the Lazy Ranch Boys, Clark hired Rich. "That was quite a thing for me, because my dad and grandfather farmed together, and my grandfather really liked country music. He used to listen to Casey and all that stuff," said Rich. "I worked with Casey on weekends and summers, until I graduated from high school [in 1957]." Terry Bethel played with Clark on weeknights.

Charlie and Honey Miller left the Lazy Ranch Boys in 1956. Mary Clark said, "The last contact we had with them, they were in [Las] Vegas" pursuing photographic arts.

ROCKIN' COUNTRY STYLE

Often at the expense of older, established artists, the media followed rock 'n' roll music, its young fans, and performers. Clark's daughter seemed to be in the right place at the right time—if not for her own career, then to boost the profile of the Lazy Ranch Boys. Since joining her father on stage when she was eight years old, Harlene had grown into an accomplished country and pop singer. Her voice resembled jazz singer Kay Starr's in elocution, timing, and sass.[57] In western-styled dresses, "Little Evelyn" sang country swing and tunes from the hit parade, including rock 'n' roll, with the heart and assurance of a seasoned performer.

Rockabilly singer Roy Moss worked Clark's shows, in 1956 and 1957. Born in Plainview, Arkansas, Moss had appeared with Jimmie Skinner in Cincinnati, Ohio, and on the KWKH *Louisiana Hayride* in Shreveport, Louisiana. Mercury Records issued two rockabilly singles by Moss around the time Elvis Presley's popularity exploded. Moss cut a rock 'n' roll single for the Detroit-based Fascination Records Company and worked local nightclubs with Cliff Allen, whose band backed him on his Detroit record.[58]

Another young lady, Joannie King, often appeared with the Lazy Ranch Boys. A Cody High School student and a distant relation to Roy Acuff, King was about the same age as Harlene. In 1957 she sang country-western in Detroit area hospitals with the Ralph Davis band. She cut a session for Sage (Sage and Sand shortened its name in 1957), resulting in a rockabilly single promoted in Detroit's *Teen Life* newspaper.[59]

BEFORE THE SUN GOES DOWN

In July 1956, banjo picker J. D. Crowe joined the Sunny Mountain Boys. The next year, Earl Taylor departed and Martin hired Paul Williams to play mandolin and sing tenor. In 1953, after working with the Lonesome Pine Fiddlers in Detroit, Williams enlisted. "I'd gotten out of the air force in October [1957]," said Williams. Martin hired him as soon as he could. "We worked a club up there in Pontiac for a long time. I think it was about three nights a week. . . . We'd pick there from about six or seven o'clock 'til about midnight," he said.[60]

TRAGEDY AND TRIALS

In May 1956, Lonnie Barron and Okie Jones drove to the Jimmie Rodgers Memorial Days in Meridian, Mississippi, with their new Sage and Sand records in hand. The festival was an annual country music tribute to the "Singing Brakeman," as Rodgers was known during his brief, influential career. Barron and Jones performed on stage, television, and radio.

Barron's career picked up steam that summer. He and Clark traveled to the South together on several occasions. In September, Clark helped Barron with a recording session in Nashville. "Please Blue Heart" featured Clark's fiddle and harmony vocal on the refrain. Issued by Sage Records in October, the song attracted spins and sales right away in Michigan, Indiana, and Ohio. During January 1957, Barron and Clark met with Columbia Records agents in Nashville, and Barron signed a recording contract.

Just days after returning to Michigan, Barron was murdered in his home near Richmond. The Clarks endured shock and disbelief as news outlets across the country reported a man had killed Barron for supposedly having an affair with his wife. "It really hurt us," said Mary Clark. "All that terrible publicity when he died was just sickening to me."

"I didn't know Lonnie real well. We were just pretty good friends in the music business," said Jones. "I never did see him with anybody. When he came to the shows, he was usually by himself. He was very interested in his music business, . . . and it was really a big thing with him."

A couple of weeks after Barron's death, the *Casey Clark Jamboree* ended. Clark found a new outlet at WXYZ-TV Channel Seven Detroit, where the band performed Friday nights following comedian Soupy Sales' "Soup's On" program. "The only place they had set up for us to do the show was in the parking garage," said Harlene. "And so, Soupy would come downstairs to get in his car and leave while we were working [*laughs*]."

IMPULSIVE EXIT

One cloudy April afternoon, Clark and company rode the flex bus to a booking in Canada without a lead guitarist and featured vocalist.

"Okie Jones and I decided we should go to Nashville. . . . So we up and left Detroit—without telling anybody," said Hemminger. "I sold a '50 Ford and we took Okie's '56 Oldsmobile 88. Before we left, we filled the trunk with about three hundred picture books that we used to sell [for Casey]. . . . I was twenty-two, and had never been married. Okie had been married for about two years, but was divorced. . . . We were debt-free and had an itch to explore the wonderful world."

"The reason I left Casey," said Jones, "we were working over in Canada, and [Hemminger] and I wanted to drive the car over there. We had some friends over there and we didn't want to come right back on the bus. Casey said, 'You either ride the bus, or there ain't no reason for you to show up.' . . . So that was the last time I ever saw Casey Clark [*laughs*]."

Hemminger and Jones undertook a few weeks of adventures, driving more than five thousand miles cross-country, barnstorming nightclubs along the way with impromptu performances, and selling Lazy Ranch Boys souvenir books for food and gas money. They drove to Nashville; wandered to Texas; cruised to Los Angeles, California, and up the West Coast, over to Montana. They ended their travels back in Fort Worth, Texas, where they formed the Sunset Starlighters and started a weekly dance. Just as the men started making a profit, Hemminger received his draft notice. The army sent him to Germany in late 1957.

Jones returned to Nashville in 1959, entertaining a little before landing a job with Marty Robbins in 1960. "I was gonna get back in the business," said Jones. "Then I found out I was real good with doin' things with my hands. I just kinda amazed people at things I could do, especially Marty. I could fix things. . . . He said, 'You ever drove a bus?' I said, 'I drove Casey's a little bit.' I tried out and he liked it, and I become his bus driver and I drove him for ten years. Then I quit to work with Hank Williams, Jr. Then I went back with Marty for another five years." During the 1980s, Jones retired to a ranch outside of Nashville.

During Hemminger's army years, he toured Europe playing guitar in a jazz sextet. He returned to Toledo, Ohio, where he taught lessons in a music store until 1975, when he moved to central Florida. Hemminger taught guitar and played jazz until his death in 2002.

I WANTA BE FREE

Clark's next guitarist, Glen Beeler, proved a valuable addition to the Lazy Ranch Boys with his vocals and songwriting skills. Born in 1933 in Maynardville, Tennessee, Beeler grew up in Toledo, Ohio. At age seventeen, Beeler worked with Tommy Lloyd and His Strollin' Cowboys on WTOD radio Toledo. Beeler had just returned from service in the army when Clark hired him. He sang solos, replaced William's voice in the trio, and took over the part of "Bill" in Clark's comedy duo Nat and Bill, the Kentucky Boys.

A short time after Beeler arrived, the band cut a session for Sage Records at United Sound Systems, including Beeler's fox-trot "Much Too Much" backed with a trio vocal of the Delmore Brothers' "Blues Stay Away From Me." Also from the session, Sage issued Evelyn Harlene's first solo record around June: Mary Clark's "I've Got The Blues" backed with Clark and Harlene's "I Wanta Be Free." With Harlene's hepcat vocals, Beeler's rocking guitar licks, slap bass, and snare drum, the band turned out one of the most romping rockabilly records in the Sage catalog.

During the first half of summer 1957, the Lazy Ranch Boys served as Pee Wee King's band on tour through the Midwest. "The day I graduated [high school], I drove to Detroit and got on the band bus," said Chuck Rich. After the tour, Clark returned to his television show and barn dances.

Ted Bay left, and Louie Dunn, who had played fiddle and drums with Jimmy Dickens, joined the group. As winter drew near, the barn dance at 12101 Mack Avenue ended. "We weren't getting the crowds that we'd had," said Harlene, "and Daddy couldn't afford to continue booking the hall."

The local and global economy headed for crisis, and operations of Detroit factories slowed. Layoffs resulted in widespread unemployment in the city, peaking at 20 percent. "The recession in Detroit in the late fifties hit the entertainment business hard," said Mary Clark.

"Those were lean days," said Harlene. "I remember we played a New Year's Eve show [1957–58] at the Michigan Light Guard Armory on Eight Mile Road, and hardly anybody showed up."

YANKTON PROPOSITION

In the southeast corner of South Dakota, the city of Yankton sits on the Missouri River as it flows east to feed the Mississippi River. From the 1920s, WNAX Yankton broadcast to a mostly rural audience across a territory that included parts of South Dakota, North Dakota, Minnesota, Iowa, and Nebraska. The station's CBS network affiliation provided momentum for pop bandleader Lawrence Welk's career before World War II. During the 1940s Herb Howard (who later worked for the WLS *National Barn Dance*) produced the WNAX *Missouri Valley Barn Dance* for several hours on Saturday nights. The program provided a welcome diversion for thousands of listeners until it ended in the mid-1950s.[61] In 1958 WNAX management invited the Lazy Ranch Boys to Yankton, to resurrect the *Missouri Valley Barn Dance*.

"I was right there with [Casey] until they drove the bus out the door and went to Yankton," said Chuck Rich. "I just didn't want to go there." Rich returned to Flint nightclubs. "I worked on weekends with bands while I learned to be an X-ray tech," he said. Through the 1960s, Rich played with Frankie Meadows at the Wayside Bowling Lounge in Hazel Park.

In 1966 Chuck Thompson, a guitarist Rich met when they worked with Lonnie Barron ten years before, got in touch from Cincinnati, Ohio, where his employer, Baldwin-Gretsch, was based. "He traveled around the country demonstrating their guitars," said Rich. Thompson told Rich the WLW *Midwestern Hayride* was looking for a steel guitarist. After an audition, Rich joined WLW as a staff musician.

"They had all this live programming. . . . And the *Hayride* was syndicated at that time," he said. "We were in one hundred and twenty markets around the country. . . . As being part of the music staff, we had to put in sixteen hours a week, live. . . . Every week we did the *Midwestern Hayride*. Then we did an early morning television show every Saturday."

After live music broadcasts ended in 1972, Rich made the rounds of Cincinnati recording studios. "From that period until about '84, there was a lot of recording done here—gospel recording, that kind of stuff, in Cincinnati," he said. "I worked for eight different studios and stayed busy. . . . In 1975 I played on one hundred and seventy albums. . . . That was my record."

MISSOURI VALLEY BARN DANCE

Rather than move to Yankton, Adron Childress settled down with his family in Detroit. Jimmy Martin and his group (J. D. Crowe, Paul Williams, and Billy Gill) moved to the KWKH *Louisiana Hayride*. Martin introduced evergreen songs during the next several years, including "Rock Hearts," "Night," "Sophroni," and "Widow Maker." An enthusiastic performer until his death in 2005, Martin became widely known as King of Bluegrass.

Terry Bethel re-joined the band, and in July 1958 the Lazy Ranch Boys bus pulled out of Detroit for the last time.

The inaugural revival of the *Missouri Valley Barn Dance* was the biggest production in which Clark had been involved. He booked the Sioux City Auditorium, largest venue in the WNAX listening area, for Saturday, September 13. The Everly Brothers, whose record "All I Have To Do Is Dream" reached number one in pop charts that summer, headlined, along with special guests Smiley Burnette and folk singer Bob Gibson. Both *Cash Box* magazine and a full-page ad for WNAX in *Broadcasting* magazine reported a record-breaking crowd of about four thousand five hundred in attendance and hundreds more turned away at the door.[62]

Clark and company went from advertising automobiles, industrial manufacturers, and department stores in the Motor City to farm equipment, livestock feed, and seed companies in Big Aggie Land. For a while, trading economic environs worked out well, and members of the band lived comfortably. Every Saturday they traveled to a different town within four hundred miles of Yankton to perform a three-hour barn dance, ninety minutes of which WNAX shared with listeners. *Cash Box* reported, "Clark does a disk show in the mornings, 3 live shows per day and 1½ hours on Sat. nite."[63]

"Every Saturday was a broadcast," said Bethel. "Then we'd play a dance after that. . . . We were doing three radio shows a day, six days a week. On Monday, we went in and taped the Monday night show and we taped the Tuesday morning show, and we did a noon show live every day. So on Friday, we would tape Monday morning's show. We were on . . . at six, noon, and six. They were twenty- or thirty-minute shows. The noon show was fifteen minutes. . . . We pre-recorded a bunch of stuff because when we got to working the barn dances, we wouldn't get back in time, some Mondays. They had a complete log of songs . . . with the intro's and everything on 'em," he said.

Harlene learned to play drums and sing at the same time. "I can remember us going to do a show at a school," said Harlene. "The population [of the town] was thirteen—this was in Nebraska. . . . We just kind of looked at each other. . . . And there was a hundred people there [for the show]. . . . It was nothing for them to drive a hundred miles to go to a show."

The band's first winter on the Great Plains was a real eye-opener, as severe weather caused delays and cancellations. "I remember one morning, my dad got up—he did a DJ show in the morning," said Harlene, "and he always called the tower before he went in. He asked what the temperature was, and they said, 'thirty-two.' He said, 'Okay.' He got ready to go to work, and went outside and the car wouldn't start. He came back in again and called the tower, and he said, 'By the way, it feels colder than thirty-two degrees out there.' And they said, 'Well yeah, Casey, it's thirty-two below [zero]' [*laughs*]."

Around December, Reynolds sold out his partnership and joined Ernie Lee in Tampa, Florida. Lee had just begun hosting the *Good Day Show* every morning at WTVT-TV during which he played music and told fishing stories. The program lasted until Lee's death in 1991. Reynolds passed away three years later.

From the WSAZ-TV *Saturday Night Jamboree* in Huntington, West Virginia, Gene McKnight joined the Lazy Ranch Boys in January 1959.

McKnight played rhythm guitar and sang. "After Brownie left, the band didn't work with a bass," said Harlene.

FOLK MUSIC SONGBIRD

The folk music trend of the late 1950s influenced the material Harlene chose for her 1959 Sage records. Her first single after moving to Yankton included Mary Clark's "I Was Number One" backed with "Goodbye Jimmy, Goodbye," written by WNAX program director Jack Vaughn. Sage issued the record in April, a couple of weeks after Kathy Linden's version of "Goodbye Jimmy, Goodbye" began riding up the charts, peaking just outside the top ten.

Harlene's next and final single for Sage was "My Oregon Home" backed with "Guilty One," issued later that year. Despite honey-smooth, flawless vocals, Harlene's lackluster record sales pointed to her record company's promotions (and lack thereof), her geographical circumstances, and her devotion to the Lazy Ranch Boys.

WELCOME TO THE CLUB

At the start of winter 1959, Clark gritted his teeth through more cancellations of weekend dances due to inclement weather. Audience numbers fell off. "At one time we was making it real good out there," said Bethel, "and then it just dropped to nothing. . . . There was something to do with the radio station, too. I think [Clark] went in and asked for a raise for everybody, and I don't think he got it. So he decided to move on."

"The day that we decided that we were going to have to cancel all of our shows and not do that anymore," said Harlene, "we had gotten up and got ready to go, and there was an ice storm. And that ice storm lasted for I can't tell you how long. We just realized that we couldn't get around well enough."

The band left WNAX and headed for an extended engagement at Club 500 in Sioux City, Iowa. It was the first time Clark himself had ever worked in a nightclub, but the rest of the band (except for Harlene)[64] had performed in bars. By 1959 the number of radio stations broadcasting live, local music had dropped precipitously across the nation. Clark depended on nightclub bookings for the rest of his career.

After six months in Sioux City, the band took a gig at Lucille's in Toledo, Ohio. "We went into that club for about two months and the business wasn't that good," said Bethel. "They switched to rock 'n' roll, because it was really hot at the time. We stayed there another week and I played drums. . . . God, what a long week! I'm no drummer to start with. . . . Then Casey went back to Detroit and I went out to Iowa."

After a year in Iowa, Bethel worked in the house band at the Flame Café in Minneapolis, Minnesota, for about four years. Then he hit the road with stars such as Ferlin Husky, Claude Gray, Mel Tillis, Billie Jo Spears, and Loretta Lynn, before settling in Branson, Missouri, working for Tillis. He designed his own steel guitar and authored instructional books for pedal steel. Through the years, Bethel earned a worldwide reputation as one of the instrument's foremost players.

From Ohio, Smithers returned to Kentucky. "In 1963, I ended up in Kansas for about six months," said Harlene. "I was walking down the street and I ran into him. He was working in a club, in a little place outside an army base. . . . Their drummer was going on vacation, . . . so I sat in and played with them for a couple of weeks. That's the only time I worked with him after we left South Dakota. I think he went back to Kentucky from there."

Beeler rejoined Tommy Lloyd's band in Toledo. Eventually he started his own group, Night People, named after a song he wrote. Beeler taught guitar lessons, sang, and played guitar around Toledo and Southeast Michigan until his death in 1997.

RETURN OF THE LAZY RANCH BOYS

Back in Detroit, Clark found disk jockey work at CHYR radio Leamington, Ontario, besides nightclub bookings. Through the 1960s, Clark held sway at clubs such as Tistle's Lounge (at Wyoming and Curtis) in Detroit.

Clark sent a collection of Lazy Ranch Boys and Lonnie Barron masters to Crown Records of California in 1963. The resulting album, "In Memorial to Lonnie Barron," featured a full-color painting of Barron and five of his Sage and Sand recordings on one side. The other side dished up memorable cuts by the Lazy Ranch Boys.

"One of the most fun things that I ever did, when it came to recording," said Harlene, "Pat [Nelson] came by and picked me up one day. We went back to United Sound. . . . And he had Rusty York there. So Rusty and I decided we were gonna try to sing together." Ohio musician Rusty York had a hit on Chess Records with "Sugaree" (1959). Detroiter Jody Payne, who later worked as guitarist for Merle Haggard and Willie Nelson, played banjo at the session.[65] The trio cut "Nine Pound Hammer" and "Barbara Allen," which Nelson issued on the Jewel label in 1961. "Of course, Pat never said anything about it being released [*laughs*]," said Harlene.

"I used to go with Pat down to where Rusty was working and sing with him," she said. "They played a couple of air force bases and things like that."

Music City News—Michigan Supplement reported on a mammoth jamboree Clark hosted at the Camelot Inn, Walled Lake, in December 1966. The cream of country entertainers from Detroit, Pontiac, and Flint, as well as Canada, performed from one o'clock in the afternoon to half past one in the morning. For several months, WEXL radio Royal Oak aired Clark and his band's performances six nights a week from the Camelot Inn, and Clark booked entertainers from Nashville. In 1967 guitarist Bill Merritt left the Lazy Ranch Boys when Johnny Paycheck hired him.[66]

By 1968, the Lazy Ranch Boys featured Harlene (drums and vocals), Clark (fiddle, bass, and vocals), Harlene's husband Mick Kreutzer (guitar), and Billy Clark (steel). In 1971 Mike Clark died unexpectedly. A talented musician who played in rock bands, Mike had also filled in as drummer in the new Lazy Ranch Boys.

In 1973 Kreutzer died, leaving Harlene to raise their children. Later that year, Clark was honored as the first living artist of the Michigan Country Music Hall of Fame during a celebration marking the premier of an annual country music festival near Saginaw. Headliner Ernest Tubb presented Clark with his award. Lonnie Barron and Gene Starr were given posthumous honors at the ceremony.

CASEY'S KIDS

In 1973 Clark hired guitarist and banjo player Gary McMullen to play bass. Steel guitarist Gary Morse gigged with them while Billy Clark played with Jimmy Dickens for several months. Clark changed the name of the band to Casey Clark and Casey's Kids. "When I first joined them, we were playing at the Caravan Gardens," said McMullen. "I remember helping Casey build [new] stages at a few bars he booked us in, he was so concerned about showmanship."[67]

In 1974 the group cut a record with guitarist Paul Sharpe, pressed on the Great Lakes label. "I was a friend of Fred Flowerday, Jr., whose dad owned Special Recordings on East Grand Boulevard," said McMullen. "Most of their business was voiceovers and commercials for radio and the auto companies. Since they didn't cut music regularly, they let us have some studio time." The band sounded electrified, yet traditional, on "Orange Blossom Special." On the flipside, Clark sang "Corrine, Corrina" to a funk groove. "It was an era of transition in country music," said McMullen. "Rock music was creeping in, and we had to do some songs of that style, but we mixed western swing, and bluegrass into the sets, too." Besides standards such as "San Antonio Rose," McMullen remembered playing tunes he learned from Asleep At The Wheel records, such as "Choo Choo Ch'Boogie" and "Bloodshot Eyes."

During 1975 and 1976, they toured overseas for the United Service Organizations Inc. (USO). "They went to the Caribbean first," said Mary Clark, "and then they went to Japan, Korea, the Philippines, and all the islands on the way back to Hawaii."

COUNTRY IN THE CITY

McMullen left the band in 1976, and Casey's Kids broke up soon after. Country music was well established in Detroit, and Clark worked steadily with different musicians. In 1980 Harlene married Dave Atkins, who led a band called Whisky River. In November 1977 Atkins quit his day job and started publishing *Country in the City News,* a monthly magazine about country music in Metro Detroit. Harlene and Mary Clark contributed to its production, which grew from a twelve-page newspaper to a fifty-six-page magazine. "It was a lot of work, but we loved doing it," said Harlene. Around 1986, Atkins ended *Country in the City News* and began a weekly newspaper for the city of Romulus, west of Detroit. He died in 1990, and Harlene carried on the business.[68]

In another tragic instance, Billy Clark died in 1978. He had played steel guitar, bass, and lead guitar, working with artists such as Eddie Jackson and Swanee Caldwell in Detroit. He also taught lessons at steel guitarist Freeman Cowgar's music store on Dix Road, south of Detroit. "Billy and I used to collect record albums by steel guitarists," said Gary McMullen. "I've heard the best, and in my opinion Billy Clark was as good as any of them."

During the late 1980s Clark reunited with Brownie Reynolds and Ernie Lee in Tampa, Florida. "I thought it was great," said Harlene, "to think of the three of them together again." Clark returned to Michigan around 1990. Many of his last performances took place at the Blissfield Theater in Blissfield, Michigan. Calling himself the "King of Northern Swing," Clark continued gigging through the early 1990s.

A series of health-related adventures led to Clark's passing in August 1999, at age eighty-one. More than two hundred people gathered to pay respects at his memorial service in Dearborn Heights, Michigan. Many more witnessed Clark's funeral in Soldier, Kentucky, where he was buried in the Clarke family cemetery. Mary Clark assisted her daughter with her newspaper, scribing the occasional feature or poem, and updating the "Sassy Seniors" events column. She passed away November 29, 2008, and was laid to rest beside her husband in Kentucky.

Figure 8. Roy Hall and Harvey "Flash" Griner visit friends at a table in the Dixie Belle, on West Vernor in Detroit. Hall is front and center; Griner is seated at far left; the mustached man third from right may be Tim Dale; the rest are unknown. Used by permission from Faye Griner Phillips.

Chapter 8

THE HOUND
Roy Hall

He was kinda hard to keep up with, you know. I mean, he'd run off a lot of times.
—BUD WHITE[1]

The Cohutta Mountain Boys, the group Roy Hall and Bud White assembled in Detroit, was among the top western swing makers in the city after World War II. Hall's bands mixed hillbilly music with pop, blues, and boogie-woogie, well before rock 'n' roll crashed the mainstream. The Cohutta Mountain Boys' 1949 jukebox hit "Dirty Boogie" heralded a stack of rocking music they cut for the Fortune and Citation labels in Detroit. After renting an apartment in Nashville in 1951, Hall swam with the big fish, playing piano for the likes of Webb Pierce and Red Foley. In 1955 he cut vanguard rockabilly for Decca Records. Hall was best remembered for his Decca rockers—particularly "Whole Lotta Shakin' Going On"—although one could argue his rocking-est music was made in Detroit.

James "Roy" Hall was born May 7, 1922, at Big Stone Gap, Virginia, between West Virginia and Tennessee. Hall took to the piano from a young age and learned to play by ear,[2] learning many songs from radio broadcasts.[3] He also learned from Smith Carson, an African American man who worked in a minstrel company.[4] In 1933 Hall played his first professional shows with *Grand Ole Opry* star Uncle Dave Macon.[5] Within a few years he was on his own, playing piano full-time in any café or bar he could talk his way into.

Hall's sometime musical partner Bud White, born July 26, 1926, in Dalton, Georgia, learned guitar from his father. A few years after inheriting an uncle's fiddle, White "got to where I played everything on it. . . . After I got into the public, I played it for a while, but not as much as my guitar, 'cause I was singin' all the time," he said.

White formed a vocal duo with his friend Geeter Coker singing lead, and they performed on WBLJ Dalton just after it opened in 1941. Working with Don Parsons and His Melody Range Riders, White and Coker played local schools, theaters, and barn dances.[6] "We started that [station] and were on it for . . . two or three years, with sponsors and everything," said White. After performing as guests at WNOX Knoxville, Tennessee, singer Archie Campbell hired Coker and White to join him on the *Midday Merry-Go-Round*.

"Lowell Blanchard [program director and host] used to bring us on with, 'Bud White and Geeter Coker: radio's most smoothest duet,'" said White. "We probably would have went on to the *Grand Ole Opry*, but I got a letter in the mail. . . . That's after Japan went crazy and bombed Pearl Harbor." White was drafted into service overseas, and Coker joined the Merchant Marines.

After the war, White and Coker performed with Smilin' Eddie Hill at WNOX, until Hill moved his band to WMPS Memphis, Tennessee, in 1946. White returned to Dalton and took a job at his brother's building supply store on the main drag downtown. During his lunch hour, White and a friend performed a lunchtime show at WBLJ. In 1949 he met Roy Hall, who had just finished a gig with Robert Lunn in Nashville.

"He just happened to drift down this way," said White. "He run into an attorney down here, Rue Barnes. . . . He was telling [Barnes] about how he played fine piano and . . . [they spoke] about this big hall down there . . . at the Coca-Cola place (it used to be the Ford Motor Company). . . . Right away, Rue rented the whole auditorium."

Hall walked into White's brother's store and asked to hang posters for his local booking.

> We had two big windows. I said, "Well, yeah. Who're you?" And he said, "I'm the piano player that's got the band for the shows Friday and Saturday night." I said, "I'm Bud White, and I got a noonday show up here on WBLJ. We'll be on from noon 'til one. You can come up and sit in with us." . . . He sat in with us, and I asked him, "Do you have a fiddle player to play the square dances?" He said, "Yeah, but I think I'll just fire him. I been wanting to, but I don't know no

other ones. I didn't know you played fiddle 'til now." So I laid the guitar down and played a hoedown every now and then, and for different swing tunes like "Sheik Of Araby" and all that hot stuff.

COHUTTA MOUNTAIN BOYS

With bass player Dub Brummett (also from Dalton) White and Hall played social halls, school auditoriums, and dances around the region. After a few weeks, a man who'd just visited Detroit told them Southern music was heating up in the Motor City, with a growing number of nightclubs hiring country-western entertainers. "Years later, we found out who started that," said White. "He came up from West Virginia: Luke Kelly. He got started at one club, had a band in it, and then this other club heard about it and they got started—then the whole town got started!"[7]

The trio headed north, first playing at the West Fort Tavern (West Fort Street at Scotten). "We got there just in time to open the Caravan Gardens [Woodrow Wilson at Davison]," said White. "All we done was, we went in there. They wanted to hear us and [know] where we was from; and we sang a few numbers on the microphone. That was before they ever opened up. It was a big place. It was one of the big ones there in Detroit." They rotated thirty-minute sets with Eddie Jackson's band for continuous entertainment.

Dub Brummett returned to Georgia after a few weeks. Hall lured bassist Harvey William "Flash" Griner away from a gig at the West Fort Tavern. Born March 28, 1921, at Oriskany, Virginia, Griner grew up in Clifton Forge (northeast of Covington), playing guitar, bass, and harmonica. With his Oklahoma Trailblazers, Griner played music in the Virginias from the mid-1930s. Around 1940 the band performed daily on WJLS Beckley, West Virginia, and made guest appearances at Renfro Valley. After serving in the army, Griner moved to Detroit in 1945. Gene Roe, the Melvindale-based columnist for *Country Song Roundup*, called Griner "Roy Acuff Junior" after his vocal affinity to the famous Acuff.[8]

At the Rose Club (West Vernor at Clark Street) White and Hall discovered fiddle player and singer Frankie Brumbalough, working with take-off guitarist Tommy Odom. Brumbalough was from Ellijay, Georgia, and

Odom from Paris, Tennessee.[9] They both joined Hall's band at the Caravan. "I think Frankie came over there first," said White. "He got into it with the guy that owned the Rose bar, and he quit. Oh, he drank like a fish. (Well, so did Tommy!) Right away he got to drinking over there and Joe Greenberg [an owner of Caravan Gardens] told Roy, 'You're gonna have to fire him, 'cause we can't put up with that.' Frankie was talking to some people at a table, and taking his pants off!"

When Hall, White, Griner, Brumbalough, and Odom performed together at Caravan Gardens, they made recordings for Fortune Records.[10] "Me and Roy went down there and talked to Mrs. [Dorothy] Brown and Jack [the owners of the label]," said White. "Of course, Roy shot 'em a pretty good line. She wanted us to cut some records for her, Mrs. Brown did. . . . I said, 'Well, I got one number I wrote that I would like to get on the label.' So I sang it to her, and boy, she really liked it.[11] Roy told 'em, 'We'll have to get all this set up in the mornings and the afternoon—real early, 'cause we have to go into work at night.'"

Fortune issued three 78-rpm records in 1949–50. The group's debut, "Dirty Boogie," was a knock-down, drag-out boogie with origins in Johnny Barfield's "Boogie Woogie" (1939) on Bluebird. Through his dung-eating grin, Brumbalough's deep, craggy vocals sounded joyfully obnoxious. In one verse Brumbalough spun a local reference into an old blues lyric: *I got a gal out on Schaefer Road / She made more money than Henry Ford when she done the dirty boogie.*[12]

Schaefer Road runs north and south along the western edge of the Ford Motor Company's River Rouge complex, in Dearborn. The flipside, "No Rose In San Antone," was an answer to Bob Wills'"San Antonio Rose." Fortune reissued "Dirty Boogie" a year later, backed with "Okee Doaks."

Fortune credited the band as Roy Hall and His Cohutta Mountain Boys. White said the region where he and Brumbalough grew up inspired the name. "Chatsworth [Georgia] is only twelve miles from Dalton, and that's going up to Cohutta Mountain, towards Ellijay. Up on the mountain, when you get to Ellijay, they call it Cohutta Mountains," said White. "Roy said, 'What would be a good name for us to put on these?' I said, 'Well, there's the Cohutta Mountain Boys.' And he said, 'OK, let's use that.'"

The Cohutta Mountain Boys' other Fortune records presented hillbilly ballads—"Five Years In Prison" sung by Brumbalough and "We Never Get Too Big To Cry" sung by White—and hot western swing—"My Freckle Face Gal" sung by White and "Never Marry A Tennessee Gal" sung by Brumbalough. The group played with relentless propulsion of the beat, and a looseness that made the records swing. Odom's guitar playing was as close to jazz as one could get away with in a cowboy band. Brumbalough's fiddle swung mightily, while his vocals shot life into the corny lyrics he sang. In contrast to Brumbalough's bodacious style, White's vocals sounded smooth as suede. Hall provided a bridge between the rhythm section with his left hand and the frantic take-off instrumentalists with his right. No matter how briefly the lineup lasted, the Cohutta Mountain Boys sounded as if they'd been together for years.

Bill Hayes, a musician and bandleader from Arkansas who lived in Detroit from 1944 to 1957, remembered Hall "played piano and he was a showman. . . . He could absolutely ignite a crowd. He played that action and did a lot of rock songs, even then [1949]."[13]

During the same year, Hall's group backed "Tennessee" Ernie Ford in Michigan. Ford recommended the band to a friend of his at Nashville's Bullet Records Company.[14] They recorded four sides for Bullet, with guitarist and singer Hal Clark, Odom, Brumbalough, White, and Griner at a session in Nashville. Brumbalough sang two songs for the first Bullet record: "Mule Boogie" backed with "Old Folks Jamboree." Their second featured Clark singing two originals: "Ain't You Afraid" and "Turn My Picture To The Wall." Clark played all lead guitar solos during the session. Odom picked solos in the background of "Turn My Picture," his only appearance on the Bullet sides. Again, the band was referred to as the Cohutta Mountain Boys.[15]

THE EAGLES

Tommy Odom and Frankie Brumbalough came in and out of the group, as needed. Odom and White said Brumbalough died before the end of the 1950s (they both blamed Brumbalough's alcoholism). In 1952 Odom sang the novelty "She Won't Turn Over For Me" for Floyd Compton's Western Troubadours on Fortune subsidiary label Renown. The last time Odom met Hall in Detroit was around 1961, when Hall was on tour with Webb Pierce.

Odom played guitar with country groups in Detroit bars until a stroke ruined coordination in his hands. One of the most recognized C&W guitarists of his generation in Detroit, Odom died in 2010.

Hall picked up the accordion for playing in nightclubs with no piano. In
May 1950 *Billboard* noted that Hall and the band broadcast from WCAR
Pontiac and performed nightly at Caravan Gardens.[16] That year, music publisher Louis Parker invited the band to record for his Citation record label,
which had offices in Detroit's Music Hall building (on Madison at Brush).
"[Parker] used to come out to the Caravan when we was there," said White.
"We knew him pretty well. . . . He was real liberal with his money, so he mus-
ta had quite a bit of it. Like when we'd go into clubs together, me and him
and Roy, . . . if there were any girls along, he wouldn't let us pay for nothing."

Parker hired the band to cut six sides. Hall, Griner, and White brought
in part of Bill Sova's Ranch Boys, musicians from Lansing who also played at
Caravan Gardens.[17] Dick Poulton and Dick Dixon played twin guitars (lead
and steel, respectively), and a banjo player strummed Dixieland jazz-styled
syncopation. Flash Griner made his vocal debut on record with a backwoods
ditty called "Wild Wild Man From Tennessee," the first Citation record by
the band. Hall, White, and Griner sang the flipside, "You Can't Come Back,"
in unison.[18]

Hall cut his premier solo vocal with a talking blues called "I'm The Boss
Around My House," which could have been written for "Little" Jimmy Dickens, who achieved major hits on Columbia Records with novelties at that
time. "Skinny Minnie From Texas City," with a vocal by Griner, appeared on
the flipside.

The group's third Citation record featured Griner on "You're Gonna
Be Sorry (For Slippin' Around)" backed with Bud White and the Gilbert
Sisters singing "You'll Still Be The Captain Of My Heart." The Gilbert
sisters—Boots, a bassist and comedian, and her older sister Dee, a rhythm
guitarist married to violinist Victor Cardis—entertained at Caravan Gardens as the Westernaires until they moved to Texas, later that year. While
in Detroit, Boots rented a room from Bud White and his wife Fran, and the
Cardises rented the flat above them.[19]

Although the band on the Citation records was called "The Eagles," ex-

cept for the first single, *Billboard* magazine mentioned the rest as by Dick
Poulton and Dick Dixon, whose names also appeared on the record labels.
Parker died a few years later.[20]

LEAVING DETROIT

When the Cohutta Mountain Boys toured the state of Michigan as part of
an International Harvester Company showcase in late 1950, Bill Sova's band
took over their gig at Caravan Gardens. White said talent scouts from the
Gus Sun Booking Agency offered them a contract after hearing them at the
Caravan one night.

> Ray Hock ... was emcee. He told a lot of jokes and played a real fine chromatic
> harmonica. Then there's Trixie McCormack. She did a western rope act, and she
> rode one of them unicycles. Then they had this other girl, Betty Boop, ... she
> turned flips on the stage. You didn't know if she would make it or not, rolling,
> you know. They had one elderly guy, ... him and his wife used to be in vaudeville
> in New York. .... We done our show for about thirty minutes. We'd also come
> back before the show was over. And we had to play [music] for all the acts.
>
> They had 'em booked a year ahead of time. .... [We played] different places
> every night. .... Then they wanted to send us to Oklahoma and do the tour out
> there. Roy asked 'em how long that tour was, and they said, "It's about seven or
> eight months." Roy had got tangled up with some girl and he didn't want to leave
> her. I reckon that's how him and Grace [Hall's wife] separated.

Hall rambled down to Nashville in 1951, to see what kind of work he
could scare up. A few weeks after Hall disappeared from Detroit, he surprised White with a phone call.

> He hadn't got into nothing. That's why he was calling me in Detroit. And he was
> talking to his wife, ... wanting her to come down. So he said, "I got us a job at
> the Andrew Jackson Hotel." There was some guy playing there, but Roy done
> talked that woman into hiring two pieces.

> Me and [Grace] left about twelve o'clock one night and we went down
> there. Me and Roy went to work that evening in the cocktail lounge of this
> hotel. . . . When I came down the stairs to go to the cocktail lounge, who was
> standing there? Eddy Arnold and Eddie Hill! [Hill] was emcee'n the *Opry* at
> that time. Eddie said, "Lordy have mercy! Where have you been?" He hadn't
> seen me since the *Midday Merry-Go-Round*. I said, "I'm going in here to play."
> [*laughs*]
>
> I think it was an eight-week contract. That gave us all kinds of time to look
> around. That's where we run into Billy Cox about the Knotty Pine Cocktail
> Lounge. His dad owned three clubs down there, and he owned three or four.
>
> We was there a pretty good while. It was just me and Roy entertaining. I was
> playing rhythm guitar and singing, and Roy playing piano and singing. . . . We
> did duets together.

The Knotty Pine Cocktail Lounge (this was White's name for the club,
which has also been referred to as the Music Box and Musician's Hideaway)
sat on Commerce Street, near the Ryman Auditorium, where WSM staged
the *Grand Ole Opry* Saturday nights. Musicians and headliners from the
Opry "would just cover up [the nightclub], when they wasn't on the road,"
said White. They'd drink, socialize, gamble, and take the stage for spontaneous performances.

The early 1950s were good years for musicians to shove their boots
through the swinging doors of song publishers' offices and recording studios.

In 1951, Del Wood had a country and pop hit with a honky-tonk piano instrumental called "Down Yonder" on Nashville's Tennessee label. By
playing sessions for other artists, Hall established himself in town, and he
cut four instrumental sides for Tennessee. "Golden Slippers" backed with
"Back Up And Push" (1952) and "John Henry" backed with "Put On Your
Old Gray Bonnet" (1952) followed the same formula as Wood's "Down
Yonder"—piano instrumentals of old standards. Hall's piano pounding in-
jected a modern beat into the proceedings. The addition of a drummer, bass,
and rhythm guitar helped turn the records into performances for a downtown dance hall, unlike Wood's parlor music.

BULL SHOOTERS

In December 1952 Casey Clark left the WJR *Big Barn Frolic* Saturday night barn dance. *Frolic* management hired the Lonesome Pine Fiddlers from West Virginia, but they couldn't start until January 1953, so Hall shoehorned his way onto the show after Clark's departure.[21] Hall, White, and Griner performed every Saturday night at the Dairy Workers Hall in Highland Park with the Davis Sisters (Betty Jack and Skeeter), May Hawks, Bob Quinn, Frankie Brumbalough, Boots Gilbert, and steel guitarist Chuck Hatfield, besides guest stars. After the Lonesome Pine Fiddlers arrived, Hall left the show.

While engaged with the *Frolic*, Hall helped the Davis Sisters cut their first studio recordings.[22] Hall may have played piano on the Davis Sisters' "Tomorrow I'll Cry," cut in a WJR studio. Fortune Records issued Roy Hall and the Davis Sisters' performance of Dorothy Brown's "Jealous Love" around December 1952. In a fortuitous circumstance, the band included members of Leon Benson's Rhythm Ramblers, from the St. Joseph/Benton Harbor area in Southwest Michigan. The Rhythm Ramblers had visited Detroit to cut a record at the Fortune studio ("Prison Cell No. 13" backed with "St. Joe Boogie").[23] Hall also sat in with Benson's group. White described the flipside of "Jealous Love," "Going Down The Road Feeling Bad," as an instrumental warm-up performance captured on tape.

While Hall and White split their time between Nashville and Michigan, they didn't always stick together. White married guitarist Fran Westfall in 1950 and played in clubs from Detroit to Flint, Bay City to Oscoda. White's wife played guitar and worked with a variety of C&W groups in town. She tended bar during the day, and White sometimes performed with her at night. After eleven months of marriage, they divorced.

In late 1953, Gene Roe noted in *Country Song Roundup* a bizarre act touring the Great Lakes region: Sharpshooter Montana Frank and animal trainer California Joe were traveling with Pinto, a horse from the Lone Ranger movies, along with El Toro, "the world's best-trained Hereford bull." Accompanying them were Roy Hall and His Mountain Boys.[24]

Hall's routine in Nashville developed into playing at his club by night and recording sessions by day. He played piano for Webb Pierce, Marty Robbins, and Hawkshaw Hawkins, and accordion on some of Red Foley's gospel records. In 1954 Foley left the *Grand Ole Opry* to host the *Ozark Jubilee* in Springfield, Missouri. After the first three weeks, ABC television syndicate picked it up. Hall played piano and accordion during the first month of the program.

Toward the end of 1954, Webb Pierce, the most successful country singer of the mid-1950s, hired Hall to play piano in his band. They first met in Detroit when the Cohutta Mountain Boys backed Pierce at a personal appearance. Hall appeared on Pierce's Decca recordings and worked in his band for about six years, sometimes driving touring vehicles. To boost his road show's profile, Pierce helped Hall sign a contract with Decca in 1955.

WHOLE LOTTA SHAKIN'

In September 1955, Roy Hall shuffled down to Owen Bradley's Quonset hut recording studio in Nashville for his first Decca session. With some of the city's top studio musicians—Hank Garland and Grady Martin (guitars), Floyd "Lightning" Chance (bass), and Buddy Harmon (drums)—Hall cut four sides: a cover of Fats Domino's "All By Myself"; his own "Offbeat Boogie"; "Move On," a tune by Crowley, Lousiana, producer J. D. Miller; and a song that Hall wrote on a fishing trip the year before, "Whole Lotta Shakin' Goin' On." Hall's piano wasn't prominent in the mix—bluesy guitar dominated "Whole Lotta Shakin'." Artist and repertoire agent Paul Cohen probably regarded Hall, close in age to Decca label-mate Bill Haley, who was topping pop charts with rock 'n' roll, as a contender in pop and country markets. Decca issued "All By Myself" backed with "Whole Lotta Shakin' Goin' On" in October.

Blues singer Big Maybelle premiered "Whole Lotta Shakin'" on Columbia's Okeh label in March, and Hall sang the same lyrics. Written with Dave Williams, a black musician, during a 1954 fishing trip to a lake in Georgia, Hall used the name Sunny David to claim co-authorship. A young Louisiana boogie-woogie pianist and singer named Jerry Lee Lewis learned the song when he worked Hall's Nashville nightclub for several weeks that year.

Most of Hall's Decca singles covered rock 'n' roll hits. The major labels often hired artists to record new versions of up-and-coming ditties issued by smaller record companies. For several years the majors held an advantage with their well-established distribution networks. Hall's second and third records covered songs by Bobby Charles and Carl Perkins. Hall cut Charles' "See You Later Alligator" for his second release, but the song hit when Bill Haley and His Comets remade it. Hall's version of Perkins' "Blue Suede Shoes" featured vocal accompaniment by the Old Hickory Singers quartet. None of Hall's covers topped the originals. But on his frantic rocker "Don't Stop Now," the B-side of "Alligator," Hall dished a dab of offbeat vocalizing.

Decca issued the last of Hall's four singles in September 1956. He wrote "Three Alley Cats" with Nashville songwriter Jimmy Rule. About three rockin' musicians from Georgia taking over a nightclub, the lyrics were as clever as any rock 'n' roll of the time. For the B-side, Hall remade Piano Red's 1951 R&B hit "Diggin' the Boogie." Both sides tore it up better than any of his previous Decca singles, but they failed to chart. By then, Decca sought the next Elvis Presley by signing young rockers such as Johnny Carroll and Buddy Holly.

Almost thirty years later, the 1950s rock revival in Europe and the United States brought to light several unreleased cuts from Hall's Decca sessions, including "Christine"; "You Ruined My Blue Suede Shoes," a mean-sounding answer to "Blue Suede Shoes"; and a blues called "My Girl And His Girl" in the country-pop style Owen Bradley was developing at his studio.

A woman who worked bookings with Hall's groups in Detroit probably inspired "Christine." Singer Don Rader said he and Christine worked with Hall in Detroit and Port Huron in 1958.[25] She played a cocktail drum with brushes. One of Hall's best originals, he produced a record of the song in 1956 with Nashville saxophonist Hank Crawford on the Rhythm and Range label, by Little Hank and the Rhythm Kings.[26]

SUN SET IN MEMPHIS

Around 1956, Fortune Records issued a single with two instrumentals by Roy Hall in their pop series. "Corrine Corrina" and "Ask Me No Questions

(I'll Tell You No Lies)" featured piano, bass, rhythm guitar, and a saxophone. Bud White remembered playing the tunes at the Fortune studio on Third Street. "We was just goofin' around and did that," he said.

Flash Griner continued singing and playing music with various bands in Detroit. For instance, he appeared as a guest vocalist on the WXYZ *Motor City Jamboree* around late 1953 or early 1954. Griner sang a rocking version of "Night Train To Memphis" before guest star George Morgan mounted the stage.

After working in Port Huron with Tommy Durden during 1957, Bud White left Detroit for Nashville and focused his attention on the Musicians Hideaway. Singer Bobby Sykes, who grew up in Detroit and moved to Nashville in 1955, frequently stopped in with Marty Robbins. "When we took intermission," White said, "[Robbins] would say, 'Bud, is it all right if I sing a few?' I said, 'Gosh, sing all you want to!' They'd give him a big hand and he'd stay up there for fifteen or twenty minutes."

In the summer of 1957, Jerry Lee Lewis hit the music charts with a fiery version of "Whole Lotta Shakin' Going On" for Sun Records of Memphis, Tennessee. White said Sun owner Sam Phillips and his brother Jud frequented his nightclub.

> Those two guys that owned Sun Records used to come down every week. . . . They would come up and see us while we was playing. We cut a big album with them, one time. Me and Roy, and Armand Hernandez (he was a real fine lead guitar player). We was supposed to have another session, . . . but I don't know what ever happened.

Discovered by researchers digging through old Sun session tapes, four songs from two recording dates in December 1957 were issued in recent years. With Memphis musicians providing rhythm, Hall, White, and Hernandez cut a fast version of "Christine" and stomping takes of "My Girl And His Girl," "Lost My Baby," and "Sweet Love On My Mind." Hall's Sun sessions made for decent demo recordings, but the results weren't ready for commercial release.

FORTUNES MADE AND LOST

During summer 1958, twenty-year-old Don Rader visited the Fortune Records building on Third Street in Detroit to see if he could make a record. Rader wound up playing rhythm guitar with Roy Hall that day. "The band was Roy Hall on piano, Glen Ball on guitar, Buddy Heller on drums, and a girl on the cocktail drum by the name of Christine," said Rader. "All I know we cut for sure was 'She Sure Can Rock Me.'" The song was a 1950 R&B hit for Piano Red, originally titled "Rockin' With Red." Christine played a driving beat while Hall's hands pumped boogie-woogie as if it were early in the morning at West Fort Tavern in 1949. Fortune issued the track as one side of a Strate-8 label record that erroneously listed Don Rader as pianist. It was also included on the album "The Original Skeets McDonald's Tattooed Lady And Others" (1961).

Rader joined Hall's band for a month-long engagement at Dutch's Log Cabin in Port Huron, the number one country bar at the southern end of Lake Huron. "Roy was wild," said Rader. "He used to line up shots of whiskey on top of the piano, and knock 'em all back before a set was over. We were living in a little cabin along the lake, . . . and I slept on a couch downstairs. We'd all drink beer and go swimming in [Lake Huron] after the bar closed." At the end of the contract, Rader moved to Chicago, while Hall headed for a gig in Indiana with Christine.

He received some royalties for "Whole Lotta Shakin' Goin' On," but Hall later said he sent most of it to the IRS and his ex-wife.[27]

During the first weeks of 1959, CKLW-TV Channel Nine, Windsor, Ontario, held auditions for a country music program. Billy Gill, a singer, and guitarist, went to Windsor to try out. Program directors rejected Gill's group because some of the musicians weren't members of the union. "We couldn't go audition," said Gill, "so they wound up with Roy Hall, the piano player. They gave him four weeks, but they didn't renew his contract after the four weeks."[28]

Around that time, Hall cut the wildest records of his career, issued on Fortune subsidiary Hi-Q. Credited to Roy Hall and His Jumping Cats, the distorted recordings recalled the craziness of the Cohutta Mountain Boys ten years before. During guitar solos, someone shouted like they'd been stabbed with a knife. Hall remade "Three Alley Cats" and "Diggin' the Boogie" (retitled by Fortune as "Dig Everybody Dig That Boogie") and cut a talking blues novelty called "Bed Spring Motel." Fortune paired "Dig That Boogie" with a remake of Chuck Berry's "Little Queenie." Playing with an aggressive, guitar-driven "twist" beat, the band on "Little Queenie" could be Hall's with a different vocalist—possibly the guitarist (Armand Hernandez?). A piano player sounding like Hall was buried in the mix behind guitar and saxophone.[29]

In 1960 a record by the Hunt Sisters and Mark appeared on Fortune, with backing by Roy Hall and His Boys. "Elvis Is Rocking Again," issued during the media frenzy that occurred when Presley returned to civilian life after two years in the army, represented the last gasp of 1950s-styled rockabilly on the label. Hall's honky-tonk piano was heard more prominently on "Teardrops," the B-side. A 1963 Fortune single by Esta Hunt credited Hall on piano.

Around 1960 Hall cut another pair of killer-dillers, this time for Webb Pierce's short-lived Pierce label. "Flood Of Love" backed with "One Monkey Can't Stop The Show" was credited to Roy "the Hound." Hall adapted "One Monkey" from a 1955 record by Big Maybelle (issued after "Whole Lotta Shakin'"). The guitar tone and style of picking on the Pierce sides was similar to that heard on Hall's Sun sessions—perhaps Armand Hernandez was at it again. It was a superb blues record, but the style was more 1955 than 1960.

COHUTTA MOUNTAIN BOYS REUNITED

In 1959 Flash Griner joined White and Hall in Nashville. For a few months, Griner made a go of playing music in Music City. Eventually he took a job at the Firestone/Bridgestone Corporation in Lavergne, Tennessee, where he settled, raised a family, and retired. In 1996, Griner and his wife of fifty years died in a fire at their home.

The Musicians Hideaway closed sometime around 1960. Bud White married again and moved close to Chattanooga, Tennessee. "I opened up another club on Lee Highway. . . . Named it the Caravan Club. I had thousands of members." Armand Hernandez followed White out there. White divorced his wife, who took ownership of the Chattanooga Caravan, and he returned to Detroit. The last time White met Hall was in Detroit during the 1960s. "I was over at the Dixie Belle and Roy came in," said White. "He was talking about going back to Nashville and doing something. I got him up and he played piano with us [for] a couple of sets." By the 1970s White had returned to Dalton.

THE PITCH, THE WINDUP

Besides playing piano in Nashville, Hall got involved in the promotions side of the music business. His job in Webb Pierce's band ended around 1961, after appearing with Pierce in the movie *Buffalo Guns*. In 1967 Hall moved to Dallas and opened a talent agency. He returned to Nashville in 1972 and continued working in artist promotions. He sobered up and helped restart Jud Phillips' Judd label, recording country and religious songs. He sold talking-book tapes of the Bible, played piano at parties, and published the *Nashville Enquirer*, a tabloid of music-related news.

Hall cut new albums of rockabilly and country that proved he hadn't forgotten his recipe for Southern-fried rhythm, before he collapsed in his Nashville apartment on March 2, 1984. A March 6 obituary in the *Tennessean* newspaper described Hall as a "rockabilly tunesmith" and pronounced his recordings for Decca and Fortune as foundations for the rock 'n' roll revolution of the mid-1950s.[30]

"Some [woman] had rented a room in his apartment," said White. "Grace told me that she was the one they thought killed him. Poisoned him. I reckon she got away with it. Took his car and everything." On the evening of March 2, Hall told the folks at his office he was going home to fix a supper so big that he wouldn't feel hungry for a week. "She had to put poison in it, Grace said, 'cause they rushed him to the hospital right after that meal," said White. "He was dead in just a short time."

Figure 9. May Hawks, 1953. Used by permission from Joy Carter.

Chapter 9

MEET ME DOWN IN NASHVILLE
May Hawks

I auditioned at WSM, . . . I'm singin'"The Waltz Of The Wind" and before I got through even one stanza, they said, "We'll take ya!" . . . Everything that's ever happened to me has been like an accident, just unplanned.

—MAY HAWKS[1]

While most female country singers in Detroit's nightclubs and radio of the 1940s and 1950s struggled against the male-dominated current of the industry, May Hawks fell into the drink and let it carry her upstream. Lucky to be widely appreciated for her singing and gracious personality, Hawks attracted people who helped her avoid the burden of promoting herself. For several years during the 1950s, she held one of the highest profiles among women in country music in Southeast Michigan. Her career blossomed almost effortlessly, taking her to the WSM *Grand Ole Opry* and back to the Motor City, where Hawks recorded records and performed on clear channel WJR radio.

Lily May Gibson was born June 16, 1921, her parents' sixth child, on a farm five miles west of Cookeville, Tennessee. Her mother Della played the organ, father Lee played harmonica, and sister Leona played ukulele. While Hawks attended grade school, one of her brothers moved to work in Detroit. A few months later, he returned for a visit with a gift: a new guitar for the household. "We had a musical family," she said. "Sunday was our big day. . . . Our friends always gathered at our house because my mother and dad were so gentle, and so kind, and so good to people. . . . And they taught us to play and to sing."

Hawks' first public performance occurred when she was about twelve years old, in a schoolhouse in nearby Algood, where she, Leona, and a friend made five dollars each. During the early 1940s, she performed her own program at WHUB Cookeville.

SAGINAW SONGBIRD

Leona married and moved to Troy, Michigan, a rural community north of Detroit. When she and her husband returned to Tennessee for a vacation, they brought a friend named Robert Hawks with them. "He was a good man. A nice looking man. Had a little mustache," said May Hawks. "He started writing me. Just wouldn't take 'no' for an answer. . . . He was a little bit older than me, but he was a wonderful man. He didn't drink and he didn't swear." They married and she moved to Michigan, where Robert Hawks worked the afternoon shift for Chrysler's Plymouth division. "He had a lot of seniority there, and never was late but one or two times in his life. He worked forty-three years there," said May Hawks.

In spring 1947 WKNX Saginaw opened. The station carried live performances by bands led by Casey Clark, Jimmy Dickens, and Tex Ferguson. During an era when stations didn't fill every available frequency on the AM band, the Hawks could dial in WKNX broadcasts from their home in Troy. Robert Hawks knew friends who farmed in Marlette, and he enjoyed hunting on their land. One Saturday, the Hawks went to Marlette with another couple, and someone suggested they attend the weekly country music show that Clark and Dickens hosted at a skating rink in Bad Axe.

> They said, "Let's go hear that. Maybe you could sing on it!" I said, "Ooooh!" I really didn't want to sing. . . . I didn't think I did. So we got there, and here was Casey Clark and "Little" Jimmy Dickens. . . . They said, "Well, come on and sing

us a song." And I did. . . . The next week, WKNX radio station sent me a letter and asked me if I'd like to have my own program. . . . That was a big thrill. I
drove all the way from my house to Saginaw—tried it two or three times, just
driving back and forth. It was such a joy to be on the radio. . . . "Uncle Don"
Andrews was mostly my announcer.[2]

For the next several months, Hawks hosted a radio show, and appeared
as a guest with the WKNX bands. Bob Cooley (guitar) and his brother
Dick (bass), members of Ferguson's band, traveled with Hawks to personal
appearances around the region. She rented a room in Saginaw during the
week and spent weekends with her husband in Troy. "I stayed [at WKNX]
until 'Little' Jimmy Dickens [left for Nashville]," said Hawks. "Roy Acuff got
him on the *Opry.*"

INTRODUCING LITTLE MISS
MARTHA WHITE

In 1948 Royal Flour Mills sponsored the *Martha White Biscuit and Cornbread Time* every morning on WSM Nashville, Tennessee. The mills
planned fiftieth-anniversary celebrations, including hiring a woman to sing
on the *Grand Ole Opry* for them.[3] "Martha White was looking for a 'girl
singer,'" said Dickens. "I knew Milton Estes real well. I worked some of his
programs at WSM before I formed a band. I told him I had a lady who I
thought would do a good job for them. So she came down and auditioned,
and got the job."[4]

"I [was] supposed to represent the little girl on the bag [of flour], you
know, Little Miss Martha White," said Hawks. "It was a wonderful sponsor
and a good product. So I had the opportunity to go there and work because
of Jimmy Dickens."

Despite this exciting development, Hawks felt rather settled, living with
her husband in their cozy home. "So I waited and waited," she said. "It was
about two weeks [later], my husband said, 'If you don't go, some day you

might wish you had. You go and try it, and if you like it, we'll move back there.' He took me down there and I auditioned." Before Hawks could finish singing "Waltz Of The Wind" she was hired.

Hawks appeared on the *Grand Ole Opry* at the Ryman Auditorium during segments sponsored by Royal Flour Mills, as well as on morning shows at WSM with Milton Estes, leader of the Musical Millers.[5] "I stayed in Nashville with my best girlfriend," said Hawks. "She lived right there on Main Street, out in Madison. . . . I'd [work] the program, then I'd go back to her house. . . . We'd make dresses and just have a good time, . . . cook and shop. My husband would come down on the weekends from Michigan. . . . It was a great experience and a great opportunity. They told me . . . that my possibilities were unlimited."

Incredibly, the singer's true name wasn't revealed to the public while she worked in Nashville. The contract Hawks signed with WSM and Royal Flour Mills forbade it. After nearly a year, Hawks assessed her situation. "When I seen the environment I was going to have to contend with, I said, 'This isn't for me,'" said Hawks. "I had to make a decision between [my husband's] work and my work. I didn't want to interfere with his retirement. He just kind of left it up to me. The time came where I said, 'I've got to make up my mind.' I was married, and I do believe in marrying once. . . . I was trying to do what was right. And I prayed very seriously about it.

"I went back to Michigan," she said. "And I hadn't hardly been back in town [when] they found out about me—I [joined] the barn dance show from WJR with Casey Clark."

THE *MAY HAWKS SHOW*

In March 1952 the *Big Barn Frolic* premiered at the Dairy Workers Hall in Highland Park. After some months performing on the show, Hawks was offered her own program on WJR. The *May Hawks Show* aired seven days a week. "I also had a Sunday morning hymn program," said Hawks. "Just me and my guitar. My theme song was 'Church In The Wildwood.' I got a lot of mail for that program, too."

As Hawks' popularity rose, she performed all over Michigan.

They started booking me through the Michigan Milk Producers Association. . . . The man's name was Norm Peterson. . . . Sometimes he would call
me and book me for, well, one time I remember twelve shows! I played for the
people who had the cows, who produced the milk, and for their banquets. I'd
play a thirty-minute program then we'd have food. They always invited me to
eat. You know me, I love to eat! Then we went to the haulers' meetings. . . . Even
in little churches, . . . sometimes in big church houses, . . . just any place where
they could get a group together.

Hawks began her association with Fortune Records in 1952. "I guess . . .
[Jack and Dorothy Brown] wanted me to record because I was on WJR," she
said. "They wanted me to record the song that the Davis Sisters first record-
ed ['Jealous Love']. I didn't like it. I didn't think it was for me." Nevertheless,
Hawks went to United Sound Systems on Second Avenue and cut the song.
Songwriter Dorothy Brown had intended "Jealous Love" for a pop singer.
The Browns commissioned recordings by Hawks and the Davis Sisters, and
they issued records of both versions.

Hawks sang a stanza that wasn't sung by the Davis Sisters, and she
achieved the harmony vocals of the refrain by overdubbing her voice.
Hawks' harmony was traditional, unlike Skeeter Davis' intuitive "high harmony."[6] Hawks said she recorded "Jealous Love" before the Davis Sisters,
which would place the session in late 1952. *Billboard* magazine noted the
release of the Davis Sisters' record in March 1953. *Billboard* noted Hawks'
record in July. It also received a mention in the January 1954 *Country Song
Roundup.*[7]

The record labels credited Lester Thomas and His Southern Pals, with
a pianist who sounded like Roy Hall. Hawks said Lester Thomas was raised
in Knoxville, Tennessee. "He was a rhythm [guitar] player, and they used
him on my [first] session. Then he got wanting to sing with me. He was from
around the Smokey Mountains, up where they do all these crafts. He had a
very talented hand for woodworking. . . . He did that inlay on my guitar. He
put my name on my guitar."

Nineteen fifty-four was a banner year for Hawks. Although the *Big Barn Frolic* ceased in June 1953, Hawks continued personal appearances and guest shots on the WJR *Goodwill Jamboree*, a half-hour broadcast of Casey Clark's barn dance that began in September 1953. She worked as a country music disk jockey at WJR, as well as the WJR "Goodwill Cavalcade" to New York City.[8] Casey Clark's Lazy Ranch Boys and the Make Way for Youth Choir, directed by Don Large, traveled to the Big Apple, where they performed at the Waldorf-Astoria hotel in Manhattan. "There was thirty-nine of us that went up there," said Hawks.

Jane Boice of Rochester, Michigan, established a May Hawks fan club and published the *Hawk-Eye News*. In 1954 *Cowboy Songs* magazine ran a feature on Hawks, where she listed her favorite color as green, and favorite food as Southern fried chicken and biscuits.[9]

Hawks recorded with Chuck Hatfield and the Treble-Aires for her next two records on Fortune. The Treble-Aires played the *Big Barn Frolic* in 1953. *Billboard* noted the release of Hawks' "Wasted Years" backed with "Meet Me Down In Nashville (At The Opry Tonight)," in September 1954. "Wasted Years" was a slow, romantic number. In "Meet Me Down In Nashville" Hawks belted out the refrain with the kind of enthusiasm only someone who had been backstage at the *Opry* could feel. More cute novelty songs followed in 1955 with "Straighten Up And Fly Right" (a vocal duet with Lester Thomas) backed with "Baby You're A Bygone Now." Hatfield's band provided solid backing for Hawks' sessions at United Sound.

'X' MARKS THE TUNE

Norman O'Neill, one of the organizers of the *Big Barn Frolic*, managed the Davis Sisters when they lived in Detroit. He also managed Hawks. "He was a builder," said Hawks, "and he liked country music. He once told me, 'If I ever hear of you being in a bar, I'll drop you like a hot potato!' [*laughs*] I said, 'You don't have to worry 'bout me 'cause I don't go in there, in the first place [*laughs*].'" Hawks told O'Neill about a couple of songs she wrote, and in 1954, before the WJR trip, she visited music publishers in New York City.

> Mr. O'Neill made arrangements for me to fly to New York, to [meet with music] publishers there. I'd never been to New York in my life. I'm a country girl. I didn't know where I was going, and I was alone. I flew in there. . . . I don't know how I got around, but I did. I went to see the publishers the next day after I got there, and this man, he listened to my audition. . . . And he wanted [the songs], right then.

Hawks most wished to record "Don't Let Them See My Face." RCA Records issued it on its subsidiary Label "X." Inspired by a dream about a friend who had developed cancer in her face, Hawks wrote lyrics that pushed the limits of subject matter typically heard in country music. *Billboard* noted its release in January 1955.[10] Country disk jockeys in Southeast Michigan played the record, but Hawks thought most programmers avoided it. "At that time, cancer was very rare," said Hawks, "and they wanted the world to think that it was something that could be cured. My story told about the lady dying and she advised her little girls to take care of their daddy because she had gone on to heaven. *Don't let them see my face. Leave a pleasant memory in my place.*

"I had it in the agreement that the two little girls would get the royalties off of this," she said. "I thought maybe it could help [the father] with the children."

During her trip to New York, Hawks also pitched "They Can't Take Your Love," which Kitty Wells recorded for Decca in 1956. "It's on her album 'After Dark.' I made some royalties off that," said Hawks. "Somebody said, 'Why don't you record your own song?' I said, 'Because she sells millions of records.' [*laughs*]"

NO SPRING CHICKEN, HAWKS FULL-GROWN THRUSH

Around 1954, Don Large produced a record with Hawks, issued on his Don Large Enterprises (DLE) Horizon label. Hawks' funny-bone tickler "I Ain't No Spring Chicken," based on the melody of Hawks' earlier "Straighten Up And Fly Right," included a riff from "Chicken Reel" to make sure the jazz guitarist sounded like corn. It was backed by "No Tears Little Darlin'," a waltz with vocal chorus and piano. The Spellbinders, a vocal group that originated in the Make Way For Youth Choir in 1951, provided backup vocals.[11]

Although her disk jockey program at WJR ended in 1955, Hawks continued performing at Masonic Lodges, Shriner functions, and the Detroit Yacht Club.

In 1956 the Coin label, based in North Hollywood, California, issued another Hawks-Thomas collaboration. The duo must have been satisfied with their formula, which they used again on the knee-slapping "Jealousy Vs. Bossy." Hawks wrote the other side, "Soft Lips And Poison Kisses," sung by Thomas with sweet harmony by Hawks.

In early 1958 a single by Hawks appeared in a Starday Records custom series. During the 1950s and 1960s, musicians could order a package where Starday pressed a few hundred records and distributed promotional copies in their home regions. "Talk A Little Louder" was the last duet Hawks recorded with Thomas. Her upbeat solo "Forever And A Day" appeared on the flipside.

HAWKS NEST EASY

After 1960 Hawks' bookings expanded into elementary schools. "Sometimes I'd play three shows a day," said Hawks. "I'd go for the early morning show, then on to another school for the noontime show, then I'd go to another show before they were closed in the evening. The little children were just lovely. They'd draw pictures of what I looked like, and I'd get them up on the stage and have them sing."

Hawks and her husband built a second home on their property in Troy and were blessed with a daughter. After Robert Hawks retired from Chrysler in 1970, the family moved to Cookeville. Hawks often visited her sister's family in Michigan, and she performed occasionally at local jamborees.

In 1997 May Hawks was elected to the Michigan Country Music Hall of Fame. When asked what kept the spring in her step, Hawks cited God and music. She died November 4, 2010.

Figure 10. The Westernaires, a.k.a. Treble-Aires, 1951. From left: Betty Lee "Boots" Gilbert, Vic Cardis, Dorothy "Dee" Cardis, and Chuck Hatfield. Cardis led the Westernaires and Hatfield led the Treble-Aires; both acts included the same personnel, at times. Used by permission from Trevon Hatfield.

Chapter 10

CHUCK HATFIELD AND
THE TREBLE-AIRES

> [Chuck Hatfield and Boots Gilbert] came in [to the Detroit country music scene], and all the rest of us were just sort of . . . bar musicians. They had had some training on the radio, . . . and they were smoother and more commercial, or more sophisticated, than we were. They'd do that Spade Cooley stuff.
>
> —BILL HAYES, MUSICIAN[1]

After the tone arm drops its stylus into the groove in the flipside of a Davis Sisters single issued by Fortune Records, a steel guitar fanfare announces the arrival over the speaker of one of the top C&W groups that worked in Detroit: Chuck Hatfield and the Treble-Aires. The instrumental that follows, titled "Steel Wool," jumps with improvisations on steel guitar, fiddle, and standard guitar. Led by husband-and-wife team Chuck Hatfield (steel) and Boots Gilbert (bass), the Treble-Aires entertained in Detroit during the 1950s. Gilbert's sister Dee Cardis played rhythm guitar, and her husband Vic swung the fiddle. Guitarist Al Allen appeared on "Steel Wool," too. "If they were going to a studio," said Allen, "they'd call me."[2]

A gifted steel guitarist with a slick and punchy style influenced by innovators such as Jerry Byrd, Noel Boggs, and Earl Joaquin Murphey Jr., Hatfield led the Treble-Aires on a stack of records on the Fortune label in Detroit. They backed the Davis Sisters, May Hawks, the York Brothers, and other celebrated entertainers at engagements across Southeast Michigan. They starred in programs at WJR radio and WWJ-TV Channel Four. Singer Danny Richards remembered Hatfield "could play a steel guitar and turn your head—and you'd think it was Merle Travis on the guitar. Brother, he was good."[3]

CHUCK HATFIELD

Charles E. Hatfield was born August 24, 1930, in Flint to Mr. and Mrs. Herman K. Hatfield, who came to Michigan from Missouri by way of eastern Kentucky (yes, those Hatfields). A 1952 clipping from the *Flint Journal* gave an account of Hatfield's childhood, noting he taught himself to play mandolin, ukulele, guitar, piano, and organ by age six.[4] Three years later, "he went professional as a 'trick' yodeler" with the Rio Grande Cowboys in Flint. During the same year, he fell from the upper level of a barn and injured his back. While recuperating in bed, Hatfield practiced his music. Contrary to the *Flint Journal,* he completed at least one course at the Honolulu Conservatory of Music, in downtown Flint.[5] At age seventeen, he chose to concentrate on steel guitar.

Singer Dusty Owens said he met Hatfield in 1947 when they worked together with Bud Davis and His OK Ranch Boys at WWOK Flint. Owens learned accordion at the Honolulu Conservatory.[6] In the early months of 1948, Owens joined Tex Ferguson and His Drifting Pioneers at Saginaw's WKNX radio. Ferguson's band performed alongside groups led by Jimmy Dickens and Casey Clark. In September Chuck Hatfield began playing steel for Ferguson.

Just as Hatfield settled into his role as a Drifting Pioneer, Ferguson moved to KFEQ St. Joseph, Missouri. About the same time Ferguson left Saginaw, Casey Clark took a job at a radio station in Fort Madison, Iowa. Clark may have worked with Bob Manning, a bandleader at the station. Hatfield may have traveled with Clark to Iowa, because he wound up playing in Manning's group, the Riders of the Silver Sage.

Born in 1912 in Sherman, Texas, Manning spent his first eight years in the Lone Star State before his family moved to California. During the late 1930s he led the Bob Manning Trio, singing and yodeling in Bakersfield. Manning settled in Dallas, Texas, after World War II. In 1947 he organized a band that played barn dances, dance halls, nightclubs, and the Texas State Fair in Dallas.[7]

They made recordings for Jim Beck at his Dallas studio, and Beck issued two singles on his Dude label before the group disbanded and Manning moved to Fort Madison in 1948.[8] Manning regrouped with Billy Gray (vocals, guitar) from Paris, Texas, Robert Lawrence "Texas Blackie" Crawford (take-off guitarist), James "Pee Wee" Reid (bass), and Hatfield (who also sang tenor in the group). Right away, Manning had the new band cut music for Beck. They remade Ted Daffan's 1940 hit "I'm A Fool To Care" backed with "I'm Reading Your Letter With Tears In My Eyes." Nashville's Bullet Records leased the sides and earned respectable sales (sheet music with Manning's portrait for "I'm A Fool To Care" appeared that year). Another Dude label single featured "Lola Lee" backed with "Old Folks Boogie." A third record presented a cover of Hank Thompson's "Green Light" backed with "I Left My Heart In Texas." Manning sang "I'm A Fool To Care" and "Lola Lee," and Gray sang the rest.

With a bare-bones sound, the Riders played in the style of postwar honky-tonk. Hatfield's playing was good but did not tug the ear as his later recordings would. Hatfield favored steel guitarist Jerry Byrd's style.[9]

The band recorded without Manning as the Texas Rhythm Riders for the Royalty label, based in Paris, Texas. Royalty hired unknown musicians to cut hit songs, pressed records with inexpensive plastic, and sold the disks at a discount. The group cut around eight sides, covering country and pop hits of the day, including "Then I Turned And Walked Slowly Away," "Tennessee Saturday Night," and "Red Sails In The Sunset." With the addition of a fiddle player, the performances felt more relaxed and swinging compared to previous sessions.

Crawford left the band in 1948. With Manning in and out of the picture, the group renamed themselves the Sons of Texas and played nightclubs and dance halls in the Dallas/Fort Worth area. Vocalist Frank Larry joined the group by February 1949, when they appeared on the *National Hayloft Jamboree* in Springfield, Missouri. A few weeks later, the act performed daily over KSEL Lubbock, while they played the Cotton Club ballroom every Wednesday night through the spring.

Astor movies filmed a short feature of the Sons of Texas called *The Talented Tramps* in Dallas that year. Billy Gray and Frank Larry sang one song each. Hatfield's performance in the movie revealed he had come into his own. He laid into his solos like a hot knife through butter, skillfully using knobs on his double-neck steel to control tone and volume. At ease on screen with a smile, Hatfield's swing timing was perfect, his solos clean and playful, as he pushed the beat.

In 1948–49, singer Hank Thompson met and worked with the band. Thompson grew up near Waco, Texas, and began performing on radio while a teen-ager. His earliest recordings sold well for small labels, and Thompson signed with Capitol Records in 1946. After achieving hits with "Humpty Dumpty Heart" and "Green Light," Thompson moved to Dallas.

> I'd booked some dates for a tour, about ten days or somethin' like that, all around, through Texas. I needed a band, and there was a band called Bob Manning and the Riders of the Silver Sage. Chuck Hatfield played steel in that band. And Billy Gray was the guitarist. In fact, I hired practically the whole band later on—everybody except Jody Shook, who was a lead guitar player. I hired Chuck Hatfield on steel, Pee Wee Reid on bass, Wayne Foster on drums, Billy Gray on guitar, and—I don't believe they had a fiddle at that time.
>
> They'd been up in Iowa. . . . They came to Texas, and they were all livin' around there at the time. Bob was kind of a singer. He was the front man. He was the one who handled the bookings.
>
> Seems to me like I met them before—maybe at the *Big 'D' Jamboree* or something like that. We worked this tour together and we all got well acquainted.[10]

In 1949 Manning moved to Flint, Michigan, where he worked as an announcer, disk jockey, and agricultural news editor at WWOK Flint.[11] In early 1950 the Sons of Texas played the Round Up Club No. 1 in Dallas.[12] Billy Gray led the band seven days a week, backing guest artists such as Jimmie and Leon Short, the Delmore Brothers, and Hank Thompson.

In 1949 Thompson accepted an offer to join the *Opry*, but after just a week he decided to return to Texas and its numerous dance halls.

> When I decided that I wanted to get together a western swing band, Billy Gray helped me put it together. . . . At that time, the Southwest was *full* of dance halls. Every town had some place you'd have a dance. We were working something like twenty, twenty-five days a month.
>
> We did a tour with Tennessee Ernie [Ford], and Ernie had just had the hit record "Mule Train." So we backed him on a tour. The two of us kind of co-

starred on the band[stand]. We worked about a two-week tour, all through Texas, Oklahoma, New Mexico, Louisiana. And Chuck was playing steel at that time.... He never did record with me. I didn't make any records during the time that he was working with my band.... He was there with us for several months. I don't remember exactly how long. But that had to be about the latter [part of] '50.[13]

Thompson and his new band, the Brazos Valley Boys, moved to Oklahoma City after Bob Wills and His Texas Playboys relocated from there to Dallas. In June *Billboard* magazine reported personnel included Gray (guitar), Hatfield (steel), Wade Wood (fiddle), and Billy Stewart (bass).[14]

A few years later in Detroit, Hatfield told bandleader Eddie Jackson how he left the Brazos Valley Boys, and Thompson verified the tale. Thompson's manager booked the band out to California, and one night in San Diego, Thompson stopped Hatfield and another musician (probably Wade Wood) from leaving their hotel to visit Mexico. Hatfield and his buddy gave their two-week notice, intending to leave the band. Thompson replied, "You've been with me for more than two weeks and I ain't noticed you yet."[15]

The *Billboard* reported in November, "Thompson's regular steel man, Lefty Nason, has returned, with Chuck Hatfield leaving to go with the Rowe Brothers at their Bridgeport Club, Dallas. Thompson has replaced fiddler Wade Wood with Red Hayes."[16]

The Seven Rowe Brothers, who held an interest in the Bridgeport Club, grew up playing Texas swing during the 1930s and worked with cowboy star Tex Ritter before the war. In late 1950 or early 1951, a member (or members) of the Rowe Brothers band may have been called out to California, because Hatfield participated in a Tex Ritter tour.

In May 1951 steel guitarist Harold Lee "Curly" Chalker joined the Brazos Valley Boys in Oklahoma City. Chalker had been working with Blackie Crawford's band, the Western Cherokees, in Dallas. In September 1951 Chalker played on Thompson's recording "The Wild Side Of Life." Chalker later earned a reputation for playing pedal steel. Hatfield told his son that Chalker learned some licks from him. However, "Dad looked down on guys who played pedal steel," said Trevon Hatfield. "He thought they should know how to bend notes without pedals."[17] A steel guitarist uses a fretting bar on the strings of the instrument to achieve a chord or note. The player of a standard (non-pedal) steel must slant the bar to make certain chords, which arguably demands more skill to achieve without pedals or levers.

During the same month Chalker joined the Brazos Valley Boys, twenty-one-year-old Chuck Hatfield was married in Oklahoma City.

THE GILBERT SISTERS

In 1929 grocery store owner Orton Caswell "Cas" Walker began sponsoring a radio program at WROL Knoxville, Tennessee. Featuring local folk and country music acts, Walker's *Farm and Home Hour* appealed to laborers, farmers, and their families. One group that worked on Walker's program through the 1930s and 1940s was the Young Gilbert Sisters with Pappy, from nearby Clinton. "Pappy" Basil Gilbert and wife Pearl Ella had three girls, all of whom participated in the show: Dorothy Evelyn (born 1924), Betty Lee (born 1926), and Willa Mae (born 1928).

"Betty Lee, or 'Boots' as we called her, played some fiddle, mandolin and bass. She also did comedy. Willa Mae, or 'Wink,' played bass as she stood on a box," said Dorothy (Gilbert) Cardis, known as "Dot" back then. "Daddy played country fiddle and five string banjo. Our mother didn't play anything. She just supported us in whatever we did."[18]

Cardis played rhythm guitar using a technique of barre chords and sock rhythm strokes, playing a new chord on every beat. "I took [lessons] from Henry Farrell, who was a teacher there in Knoxville. He taught Homer and Jethro, . . . Aytchie Burns," said Cardis. In 1936 Aytchie Burns worked with Henry Haynes in the Stringdusters band on the WNOX *Midday Merry-Go-Round.* Burns' younger brother Jethro (mandolin) and Haynes (rhythm guitar) teamed up during Stringdusters performances, lampooning popular songs with farcical backwoods delivery as "Junior and Dude," until one day program director Lowell Blanchard forgot their names and introduced them as "Homer and Jethro."

"I took lessons, . . . and I didn't take very many," said Cardis. "When you get enough to make a few chords, you say, 'Well, that's enough [*laughs*].' Because it cost a dollar a lesson, back then. And times were hard."

Pappy and his two oldest daughters started working for Cas Walker's radio program around 1934, when they first met Roy Acuff, with whom the Gilberts played a few medicine shows. They appeared as guests on Blanchard's *Midday Merry-Go-Round* as well as his *Tennessee Barn Dance* on Saturday nights at the Old Lyric Theater.

Around 1944 the family moved to Tampa, Florida, where Pappy booked the act into restaurants and theaters. "We played at the Victory Theater in Tampa. And we played around the state. Boots, she did a little comedy," said Cardis. "There was the Hi Hat Club in Tampa, . . . [where] we did a country act, with daddy playing the fiddle and the banjo, and my sister coming out with her teeth [blackened] and a big bow on her toe. . . . Just a short little thing, in-between more sophisticated acts like adagio dancers, . . . back when they had floorshows. We were just a comedy break. . . . [We'd] come out and play country fiddle and sing." Most patrons of the High Hat were U.S. soldiers.

In the decade leading up to the United States' entrance into World War II, the federal government invested heavily in Florida, building military training grounds and factories. Two shipbuilding operations emerged in Tampa, as well as MacDill Air Field. "During the war," said Cardis, "we were working a theater—a show place here, and this musician came in with his band. That was Hal Black. He was a drummer." Black and Wink Gilbert started dating, and in 1946 they tied the knot. "They were married for thirty-nine years," said Cardis.

Ches Davis, a veteran minstrel performer who had worked as an advance man for John Lair's Renfro Valley traveling tent shows out of Kentucky, hired the Gilberts in 1945 for a tour he booked in theaters across the Deep South, called the All-American Barn Dance.[19] Among the troupe was steel guitarist Tommy Durden, from Jacksonville, Florida. Drawn to the Gilberts by their happy-go-lucky attitudes, Durden enjoyed sitting in with their act. "We all worked one job in Tallahassee, and that's where Boots met Tommy," said Cardis. A romance between the two began.

Pappy Gilbert retired from the road after Davis' tour ended in New Orleans, Louisiana. The Gilbert Sisters formed a group called the Westernaires with Hal Black, Durden, and violinist Vic Cardis.[20]

"Vic was Hungarian," said Dee Cardis. "His real name was Victor Kardos [pronounced "KAR-doash"], but he had an American spelling and an

American pronunciation for it. His mother was Romanian and his father was Hungarian, and they were born right on the border." Born 1913 in Trenton, New Jersey, Vic Cardis grew into a talented violinist, mastering jazz, pop, classical, country, and traditional Hungarian folk music. "We played the St. Charles Theatre, and [Vic] was playing at the old Barn [Theater], in New Orleans," she said. "He came backstage after our show and we got acquainted. We kept in touch after that."

The Westernaires toured with Dub "Cannonball" Taylor, a western movie star, comedian, and musician, winding up in Galveston, Texas. Then for several months they worked a circuit of T. D. Kemp's grind houses (Southern theaters in which Kemp paired C&W acts with western movies), supporting headliners such as Hank Locklin, Webb Pierce, and Hank Williams. When the tour ended in New Orleans (probably May 1947), the Westernaires split up. The Blacks headed to Mississippi, the Cardises married and moved to Galveston, and Durden and Gilbert, who married in April 1947, returned to Florida.

It wasn't long before Irving Yates, Dub Taylor's manager in California, called Durden to book the Westernaires for Texas dates with movie star Bob Steele. Steele's movie career began during the 1920s, and he was one of the first singing cowboys on film (in Amity/Tiffany movies), 1930–31. He appeared as Tucson Smith in Republic Pictures' Three Mesquiteers series, 1940–43.

During Steele's 1948 tour, he sang cowboy songs and performed rope tricks. The Durdens and the Cardises backed Steele up to four times a day. Theater shows included the movie *The Navajo Kid*, and appearances by cowboy actor Jack O'Shea (the "Man You Love to Hate") and Max Terhune, who played Mesquiteer "Lullaby" Joslin, with his cowboy puppet Elmer. *Billboard* reported in May, "Bob Steele is currently engaged in successful personal appearance tour of its Western-type program. Unit opened in Houston April 29, will follow with three or four stands at Galveston, Austin, Waco, Dallas, and San Antonio."[21]

The tour wrapped up nine months later, at the end of which the Westernaires landed in Galveston. Then Yates called with an offer to back Woodward Maurice "Tex" Ritter on the road. A star of screen and records, Ritter had been in show business since 1928 when he moved to New York City from his native Texas to work on stage and radio. In 1933 he made his first recordings for the American Record Company. In 1936 he moved to Los Angeles to star in western movies, appearing in dozens of cowboy musicals through 1945. Between 1944 and 1950, Ritter's top sellers on Capitol Records included "I'm Wastin' My Tears On You," "There's A New Moon Over My Shoulder," "You Two Timed Me One Time Too Often," "Rye Whiskey," "Deck Of Cards," and "Pecos Bill."

Durden said Ritter was a joy to work with. In 1948–49 the Westernaires brought in Alan "Spud" Goodale (guitar) and Myrl "Rusty" McDonald (banjo, fiddle), when Vic and Dee couldn't make a tour. Every day included two to seven programs, and sometimes these occurred in different towns. They played theaters, parks, halls, and fairs.[22] The press noticed the Westernaires, and Boots Gilbert for her comedy. In 1948 the *Washington Post* reported, "The hero of all those westerns brought along his horse, 'White Flash,' his guitar, some gags, and a lively Tennessee lass who's unbilled but who pleased yesterday's customers."[23]

Vic Cardis played with a variety of acts in Dallas and Fort Worth, including Lefty Frizzell's band.[24] "We were living in Dallas and worked on the radio station there," said Cardis.

In 1949 Skeeter Elkin, who played piano in Bob Wills' Texas Playboys, worked with the Westernaires at the Top of the Hill Club at Grantham Lake, near Shreveport, Louisiana. Jazz saxophonist Pud Brown also played in the band. The core of the group included the Blacks, Cardises, and Durdens.[25] Durden said a furniture company sponsored daily fifteen-minute programs on KWKH radio. Dee Cardis remembered working radio shows in Yazoo City, too. Boots Gilbert and Durden divorced in Shreveport but maintained a professional relationship. Then Yates called them to work a Ritter tour through the Midwest and East.

WESTERNAIRES

Musician Bud White, who worked with pianist Roy Hall, recalled meeting Tex Ritter in 1949, at Dalton, Georgia. White and Hall's group opened Ritter's show. "Roy knew him," said White. "I never met him [before]. Roy said he could really drink that white lightning." White said he and Hall chatted with Ritter over some moonshine that evening.[26]

White and Hall moved to Detroit in 1949, just in time to land the opening gig at the Caravan Gardens nightclub at Woodrow Wilson and Davison. A few weeks later, they met Ritter and the Westernaires again, when Ritter played the Michigan State Fair.

> We wanted to know if they wanted to come down and see us that night. They said, "What, you playing in Detroit?" And I said, "Yeah!" And so I told 'em where to come. And I got Boots up [on the bandstand] and she did a few jokes and sang. . . . So then they talked with Joe Greenberg and Morrie Baker [who operated Caravan Gardens] and they booked 'em in there.

Ritter's tour ended in Philadelphia a week later. The Cardises and Boots Gilbert returned to Detroit and played out the winter at the Caravan Gardens. They also joined White and Hall in cutting a song for Lou Parker's Citation label. "You'll Still Be The Captain Of My Heart" was credited to The Eagles, with vocals by Bud White and the Gilbert Sisters.

In 1950 the Westernaires moved to Houston, Texas. Vic Cardis and the Westernaires cut a record for Four Star Records. They also helped Tommy Durden with a record for the Houston-based Freedom label.[27] Durden invited his ex to join him at KTXL-TV San Angelo, which she did for several weeks.

In early 1951 "Tex Ritter called," said Cardis, "and Boots and I went out to California. They had hired Chuck Hatfield, and she met him on that tour. And then they were married."

Within weeks, the Cardises and the Hatfields assembled as the Westernaires at Teve's Tavern in Duluth, Minnesota.[28] The band performed a mix of pop, country, and comedy (by Boots Gilbert). Of their booking at Teve's, a local newspaper noted, "Some of the 'western' airs the Westernaires air well are 'How High The Moon' and 'Stormy Weather.'"[29]

After playing in Chicago for the McConkey Artists Corporation, a talent agency with offices in seven major cities, the Westernaires split up. The Cardises moved south, while Gilbert and Hatfield settled with his parents in Flint. Hatfield played with bands around Flint and Detroit. The couple had a baby girl, and then Hatfield joined the U.S. Marine Corps.

"My uncle Gilbert [Hatfield] was one of the first soldiers to land at Normandy during the D-Day invasion," said Trevon Hatfield. "My dad had some envy for his older brother, and that influenced his decision to join up." Hatfield shipped out to California for training. However, his childhood back injury returned to haunt him, and he spent some weeks in the hospital before receiving a medical discharge in summer 1952. Back in Michigan, Hatfield and Gilbert collaborated with a mustached guitarist named Tim Dale as the Midwestern Trio in Detroit nightclubs.

TREBLE-AIRES

In March 1952, WJR began broadcasting the *Big Barn Frolic*, a barn dance held in the Dairy Workers Hall of Highland Park. The cast included Casey Clark's Lazy Ranch Boys and vocalists May Hawks, the Davis Sisters (Betty Jack and Skeeter), and Bob Quinn. Rusty McDonald, an old friend of Gilbert's from Tex Ritter tours, played fiddle on the *Frolic*. By November, Clark left to start his own barn dance across town, and Quinn brought in pianist Roy Hall and His Cohutta Mountain Boys. Hatfield and Gilbert joined the show before the start of 1953, when Hall left the program.

From West Virginia, the Lonesome Pine Fiddlers joined the *Frolic* in January 1953. "Curly" Ray Cline of the group recommended his cousin's husband, Al Allen, to play electric guitar on the show. Allen was soon working with Hatfield in nightclubs and recording studios.

During the week, the Hatfields played at the Dixie Belle on West Vernor, a nightclub well known for country music. When Tim Dale left the scene, Hatfield brought in vocalist Bobby Sykes and they worked as the Treble-Aires.

"The Treble-Aires played at the Dixie Belle . . . for a long time. Then they moved to the 3-J's [3-JJJ] bar," said singer Arizona Weston. "Chuck [and his wife] used to stay at our house [north of Pontiac] every once in a while, instead of going home to Flint. They'd drive from Detroit to Flint every night—back and forth, seven nights a week, to play music. [Chuck] used to talk about driving up Dixie Highway at ninety miles an hour."[30]

Weston's wife Margueritte Breeding described Gilbert's performance of Johnny Ray's "Cry." "She wore a wig of floor-length hair bundled inside a tall hat. And when she sang the line 'Let your hair down, baby, and cry,' Boots pulled off the hat and all of the hair from her wig tumbled over her face, down to the floor," she said.[31]

AUDIO EXCELLENCE

After their first record, "Jealous Love," when the Davis Sisters recorded at Fortune Records in Detroit the Treble-Aires played with them. The band included Chuck Hatfield, Boots Gilbert, Al Allen, Curly Ray Cline, Charlie Cline, and Vic and Dee Cardis. Recordings included Dorothy Brown's "Heartbreak Ahead," Hank Williams' "Kaw-Liga," and Davis Sisters originals "Sorrow And Pain" and "You're Gone."[32]

Fortune issued "Heartbreak Ahead" in mid-1953 backed with the Treble-Aires' "Steel Wool" instrumental, which defined the sound of western swing combos in Detroit. Hatfield played rollicking solos with jazzy blue notes. A master of volume, tone, and timing, he supported vocalists with tasteful fills. Hatfield's musical phrasing displayed incredible control, sensitivity, and knowledge of his instrument. He was probably the finest steel guitarist in Detroit during the 1950s. "Chuck was so modest about his playing," said Margueritte Breeding. "He didn't know how to take a compliment. He said things like, 'Yeah, I know I'm good,' which may have come off as a little conceited."

During spring 1953, the *Big Barn Frolic* expanded to one hour. The cast of the *Frolic* also made personal appearances outside the Saturday night broadcasts, including a show with George Morgan at the I.M.A. Auditorium in Flint. In a poll published in June by *Billboard,* the *Frolic* ranked second most popular Saturday night radio program in Detroit—which made its disappearance from WJR the following week all the more surprising.[33] "I seem to recall it might have had something to do with them not being able to pay the musicians," said Al Allen. "I remember loaning Bob Quinn twenty-five dollars to pay someone, and I never did get it back [*laughs*]."[34]

MICHIGAN BARN DANCE

In March 1954, musician and comedian Phil Girard organized a country music variety program for WWJ-TV Detroit, Channel Four. Called the *Michigan Barn Dance*, the half-hour show aired at eleven o'clock Saturday nights. Girard hired Dee and Vic Cardis, Bobby Sykes, Eddie Jackson, May Hawks, Chuck Hatfield, Boots Gilbert, and Smilin' Max Henderson, a bandleader and radio broadcaster from Flint, as emcee. A promotional photograph included accordionist Tony Dannon and an unidentified fiddle player. The show premiered with guest Johnny Maddox from Tennessee, who was a year away from making his million-seller "The Crazy Otto Medley" for Dot Records. The pianist was booked at the Roosevelt Lounge on Mack Avenue.[35]

Vic and Dee Cardis worked as the Westernaires at the Dixie Belle and Scenic Inn, hosting artists such as Skeets McDonald. Dee Cardis remembered an occasion when her husband worked in Lansing with Bill Sova's Ranch Boys while she remained in Detroit, leading a band at the Dixie Belle. Vic and Dee also worked a supper club at Dix and Vernor for a while. They played pop standards and Eastern European folk music, while her sister and brother-in-law performed down the road at the 3-JJJ bar.

> A Greek man, Jimmy Manteros, owned that place.... He had two places.... He had a country place, and Boots and Chuck worked there. And Vic and I were working at his place where . . . he had different [themes], . . . Armenian night, and all kinds of stuff like that. We worked with a piano player and just played pop. . . . It was a place called the Stockade. . . . There were cattle somewhere in back of the area. [The location was called] "Five Points" in Detroit, and we worked there, and lived over the club.

Fortune pressed several records by the Treble-Aires in 1954, including three vocal duets by Gilbert and Sykes. "Take It Or Leave It" backed with "Man! Turn Me Loose" included Charlie Cline shouting, "Whattaya want?" in the middle of Gilbert's refrain: "Man! [Whattaya want?] Turn me loose." Their next record, "Fickle Heart" backed with "Please, Mr. Bartender," departed from novelty. Compared to other country acts on Fortune, the musicians on "Fickle Heart" presented one of the most polished performances on the label. Sykes and Boots' harmonies and enunciation melded perfectly, as the band maintained a driving beat.

Billboard noted the release of "Fickle Heart" in September.[36] Justin Tubb (Ernest's son) and Goldie Hill, whose duet of "Looking Back To See" was a hit for Decca that year, covered "Fickle Heart" with an arrangement copied from the Treble-Aires.

The band's final single, "When Senorita Comes To Hear The Senor Play," issued mid-1955, featured a rhumba beat with a vocal by Sykes, backed with another smooth Gilbert-Sykes duet on Dorothy Brown's "You Can't Stop Me From Loving You." In September 1955 *Billboard* reviewed another pressing of the record, which substituted "You Can't Stop Me" for "Sadie And The Cop," a novelty sung by Boots Gilbert.

The last *Michigan Barn Dance* TV broadcast aired December 1954. In 1955 Bobby Sykes moved to Nashville, where he performed in nightclubs and radio, worked as a recording artist and songwriter, and partnered with Marty Robbins on stage and in business. He died in 1994.

WESTERN AIRS

Hatfield and Gilbert's last recording for Fortune, cut around 1955–56, featured jazz piano and drums. She cut "He's A Mighty Good Man," a novelty song with lyrics built upon double entendres.

Gilbert's ex-husband Tommy Durden wrote Elvis Presley's hit "Heartbreak Hotel" and spent most of 1956–57 living off royalties earned from sales of Presley's record. In 1957 he moved to Port Huron, Michigan. During 1957–58, Vic and Dee Cardis reunited with Durden, playing daily radio shows at WDOG Marine City and nights at Dutch's Log Cabin in Port Huron. In 1959 the Cardises moved to Florida, and Durden moved north to Houghton Lake, Michigan.

When the economic recession of 1957–58 devastated the entertainment industry in Detroit, the Hatfields moved to Santa Clara, California. While battling the bottle, Hatfield sought work with local C&W acts and began learning the business of real estate. He ordered a custom-built steel guitar with four conjoined necks in a four-octave spread—without pedals—designed by Gene Fields, a product developer for Leo Fender. Hatfield worked nightclubs and variety shows such as *Cal's Corral,* a Los Angeles television program sponsored by used car salesman Calvin Coolidge "Cal" Worthington.

Hatfield and Gilbert had more children, before divorcing in 1962. Vic and Dee Cardis moved to California to be close to Gilbert, then moved to Las Vegas, Nevada. In 1965 the Cardises persuaded Gilbert to move to Las Vegas, where she attended beauty school. She raised her children, remarried, and worked in show productions through the 1990s, styling the manes of celebrities such as Merv Griffin. Betty Lee Gilbert passed away in December 2005.

During the late 1960s, the Cardises worked and lived in Elko, Nevada, supporting acts that toured the Las Vegas/Reno/Elko triangle. They toured with Tex Ritter again, before he died in 1974. The couple moved to the west side of Florida and played pop standards and Hungarian music at local events and restaurants. Vic Cardis set down his violin for the last time in 1998. With her partner gone, Dee Cardis retired from public performances.[37]

After his ex-wife's move to Las Vegas, Chuck Hatfield remarried and quit the music business.

"I ran into Chuck out in California, some years later," said Hank Thompson. "We were playing a fair out there. . . . It seemed like to me it was somewhere around Long Beach. . . . Chuck came out and visited with me. Said he was living there. That was the first time I'd seen him in a long time. And I'm pretty sure that was the last time I saw him. That was back in the early seventies."

In 1988 Chuck Hatfield passed away from cancer. "I think something in my parents died when they moved to California," said Trevon Hatfield. "Music really was their life, until then."

Figure 11. Eddie Jackson hosted the first jamboree ever held at Ted's 10-Hi on East Jefferson Avenue, ca. 1950. Back row, from left: unknown, Dewey "Smitty" Smith, Eddie Jackson, Al Wilson, Eddie Roberts, unknown, and Newton "Curley" Baggett. Second row (seated), from left: Tracey White, George Blevins, unknown, Dwight Harris, Johnny Clem, Ted Faith, and Smokey Stover (with glasses). Seated in front, from left: unknown woman, Don "Lucky Lee" Larsh, and Jack Dowdy. Used by permission from William Jackson.

Chapter 11

MUSIC WITH A WESTERN BEAT
Eddie Jackson

> When I was a kid, I'd sneak out of the house to play baseball, and my brother
> would drag me back to play music with him. One day, I came home and
> found him on the porch playing his banjo, surrounded by a bunch of girls.
> From that moment on, I knew that music was for me!
>
> —EDDIE JACKSON[1]

After finishing his second set of the night, Eddie Jackson lit a cigarette, stepped carefully down from the bandstand at Caravan Gardens, and surveyed the bar. One of Detroit's larger nightclubs featuring country music, the Caravan, as most people referred to it, was filled with friends and music fans tonight. Many had stopped in for a nightcap after seeing a show of country-western stars downtown at Ford Auditorium.

Ferlin Husky, who performed at Ford Auditorium that evening, stood with his steel guitarist, Billy Cooper, and chatted with patrons. Jackson smiled and greeted everyone who caught his eye as he strolled to the bar for his usual shot of brandy and a beer chaser. After joking with Husky and sharing a toast, Jackson asked if he'd like to join him on stage during the next set. "You got it, hoss," said Husky. "It'll be my pleasure!" Twenty minutes later, Cooper and Husky took the stage with Jackson's band, which included drums, piano, steel guitar, and Jackson playing rhythm guitar.

Jackson introduced Husky's alter ego, the buffoon Simon Crum, and Husky proceeded to rip through parodies of several hit country and pop songs to uproarious effect. After Husky scooted off stage, Cooper finished the set with Jackson's band. Then he asked for a job. "See, my wife's pregnant and she wants me to get off the road," said Cooper. "Sure," exclaimed Jackson. "But how does Ferlin feel about it?" Cooper disappeared into the crowd, in search of Husky.

Jackson hadn't even reached the bar when Husky stormed over, pressing his face into Jackson's personal space, teeth gritted and shoulders arched in a menacing posture. "So you're takin' my steel player!" he breathed. Jackson coolly took three steps to the bar, asked the bartender for a fresh bottle of Husky's favorite drink, and returned, holding the bottle by the neck like a club. With his free hand Jackson reached for Husky's. As they shook hands, Jackson slipped the bottle into Husky's coat pocket, stuck out his chin and grinned. Husky lost it, bursting into spasms of laughter as Jackson did the same.

During the next dozen years, Husky—and other traveling artists— visited Caravan Gardens because they knew Jackson led good bands, and the reputation of his character and hospitality drifted all the way to Nashville. Too successful to leave Detroit, Jackson played in local nightclubs through five decades.

James Edward Jackson, born March 3, 1926, in Cookeville, Tennessee, arrived in Detroit at age seven. Eventually his parents settled in a north-central neighborhood of Detroit, near Grand Boulevard and Woodward Avenue. Jackson's earliest experience playing guitar was sitting on the front porch of his family's home to accompany his older brother's banjo picking. Jackson sometimes took his guitar to his friend Bill Callihan's house after school. "Bill was crippled. He had a room lined with shelves filled with 78s and a record player. Played a steel guitar Hawaiian-style," said Jackson. "We practiced along with records by Jimmie Rodgers, Milton Brown, Hank Penny's Radio Cowboys, Roy Acuff, Ernest Tubb, and all those early country stars. I learned hundreds of songs by listening to his records.[2]

"A little restaurant on Bethune off of Woodward had a jukebox filled with Bob Wills 78s, and I used to stop there after I finished my paper route," he said. "I wanted to sing like Tommy Duncan [in Bob Wills' band]. I wanted to play western swing, so I learned all the chords I could on the guitar."

Another early memory conjured the vision of a café that Jackson's parents operated on Mound Road. "Our family lived in the back of the building, and my folks hired black musicians to play jazz and pop music at night. Some nights I'd huddle beside the drummer and ask him to hit a wood block on his [drum] kit. I loved the sound of that block, and the beat of the band," he said.

Jackson first performed for a public audience at radio station WHUB Cookeville, Tennessee, during summer 1940. In 1943 Jackson played his first paying gig at the Wayside Bowling Lounge, strumming rhythm guitar for Eveline Haire's band. Haire played bass and led a western swing band that mixed hot blues and cowboy songs.[3]

Jackson was soon working with Paul Perry and His Ramblers on WCAR Pontiac every week. "The boys and I'd ride a bus from Detroit to Pontiac carrying our instruments. We'd be dressed in our cowboy shirts, and hats. People on the bus gave us funny looks," said Jackson. "Paul played bass. We also had a lead guitar player. We followed Mountain Red with our show." Perry's band was a popular act at the Calumet Bar (on Calumet at Third Street in Detroit) during the mid-1940s.

During World War II, Jackson joined the navy and saw action in the Pacific theater. While his ship was in dry dock, Jackson was first in line at the Palomar dance hall in Stockton, California, to see Bob Wills and His Texas Playboys. "I stood next to the stage, at Tiny Moore's feet. He was playing lead guitar that night. The band played western and pop songs equally well," said Jackson. Between sets, he met his idol Tommy Duncan in front of the mirror in the men's restroom. "I told him that when I got out of the navy, I was going to make a living playing music," said Jackson. "He wished me luck and thanked me for stopping by the club."

MAKING A LIVING

In 1947, on his way home in Detroit, Jackson paused at the Deauville Bar (on Second Avenue at Brainard Street) to catch Paul Perry's act. "Paul invited me to sing a couple of numbers," said Jackson, "and after I stepped off stage, the owner of the place asked me if I wanted a job. I said, 'Doing what? Sweeping the floor?' He said, 'No, playing music here.' I was on my way home, . . . I didn't even have a band. He said, 'Just don't worry about that. You show up tomorrow night, and I'll have a band for you.'"

In the beginning, the bands were small—usually three pieces: Jackson on rhythm guitar, steel or electric guitarists to carry the melody, and an upright bass player. When possible, Jackson filled out the sound of the group with friends on accordion, fiddle, and, after 1950, drums. "I always wanted to have a full band with twin fiddles and everything," he said. "But in those days, I liked to starve with a big band! If musicians showed up in the audience, I'd usually get them up on the bandstand to join me for a few songs." Before he turned twenty-one, Jackson worked east side clubs. His bands performed country and western, pop tunes from the hit parade, polka, and Hawaiian music nightly.

"I'd set envelopes on tables with cards to fill out song requests," said Jackson, "and folks would write on them and drop 'em in our 'kitty'—a wood box shaped like a cat with blinking red lights for eyes. . . . On breaks, I would circulate through the audience, and say hello to everyone in the club."

Jackson helped open the Caravan Gardens in 1949. "The club was at Woodrow Wilson and Davison," said Jackson. "I thought I was their only act, but when I showed up for my first night, Roy Hall was playing piano on the bandstand. . . . I played seven nights a week and my band rotated sets with Roy Hall's band. We were the first [country] acts to rotate sets like that, in Detroit."

Guitarist Hal Clark and bassist Bob Norton worked with Jackson at Caravan Gardens. Jackson credited Clark and Norton for teaching him guitar techniques so he could sit in with any musicians. Originally from Alabama, Norton led western bands in Detroit from before the war, including the Silver Sage Buckaroos, who recorded a single for the Mellow label in 1941. Clark, who grew up in Columbus, Indiana, wrote songs and cut records for the Arden and Fortune labels in Detroit. Prior to working with Jackson, Clark and Norton played with Eddie Sosby's Radio Rangers at KFAB Lincoln, Nebraska. In 1951 Clark left Detroit for Southern California, where he changed his name to Hal Southern, joined a cowboy trio called the Frontiersmen, and wrote "I Dreamed Of A Hillbilly Heaven," a hit for cowboy singer Eddie Dean in 1955.

In 1949 Drake's Record Shop on East Jefferson Avenue sponsored Hank Williams at the cavernous Convention Hall on Woodward Avenue. Jackson was invited to open the show. "It was a big deal for me," he said. "I bought a new maroon western suit and yellow boots at the Arizona Saddlery on Woodward Avenue. . . . After our set, Hank asked to hire my bass man for his shows. While we talked, he noticed a fifth of Seven Crown I had stashed in my locker. I offered him a taste of it, and he drank half the bottle. . . . Then he put on one of the best damn shows I ever saw." Drake's hired Jackson for a Cowboy Copas appearance the same year.

Around the same time, Jackson hosted one of Detroit's first jamborees at Ted's 10-Hi Bar on East Jefferson Avenue near Fairview. "I offered free champagne to all musicians who showed up, and we had a huge turnout," he said. During his first contract at Ted's 10-Hi, Jackson's band alternated thirty-minute sets with the York Brothers. "This was right after they left the *Grand Ole Opry* [in 1950]," he said.

By 1952 Jackson fronted a trio called the Cowboy Swingsters featuring Dewey "Smitty" Smith on bass and Tracey White on lead guitar. Jackson played rhythm on a Gibson L-5 guitar with an electronic pickup. "Tracey and I grew up in the same neighborhood in Detroit," said Jackson. "We spent so much time playing music together, he could play things to clue me in as to what was coming up next in a song, so I could get the right chords in there."

In 1953 Ted's 10-Hi sponsored Jackson for six weeks of fifteen-minute performances on WMLN-FM Mount Clemens.[4] Two programs survived on reel tape and acetate disks. Jackson, White, and Smith performed pop instrumentals such as "In The Mood" (program theme), "Crazy Rhythm," and "Meet Mr. Callaghan," as well as country boogies (Hank Thompson's "Cryin' In The Deep Blue Sea") that approached a rockabilly sound. Jackson provided a solid backbeat with his rhythm guitar. "Ballads were hot, but I liked fast songs," he said. "Even when we did slow numbers, I liked to give them a little kick, so that the people dancing always had a reason to stay out on the floor.

"I love bluegrass music, but I couldn't stay in business playing it," he said.

"If someone came into the club where I was playing—like Jimmy Martin did, one time—they'd start playing bluegrass, and the dancers would leave the floor." Jackson's fans danced the jitterbug, two-step, waltz, and polka.[5]

Although Jackson worked full-time in Detroit's country nightclubs, he tried on Nashville for a few weeks, years before the city grew into a music industry metropolis. "Ricky Riddle moved down there. He had a hit record called 'Second Hand Heart.' I'd known him since grade school in Detroit, and he had a voice like Rex Allen," said Jackson. "I went down there to visit one time, and he took me to a studio where I watched Red Foley cut 'Chattanoogie Shoe Shine Boy.'[6]

"Ricky offered me a job at a nightclub that he managed. So I set up my wife and kids with my mother-in-law and went down there. After a couple of weeks playing for small crowds, I came back," he said.

EARLY MILESTONES

In late 1949 Jackson cut a record for Jack and Dorothy Brown of Fortune Records at a studio in Detroit's Music Hall. "I'm Willing To Forget" was the first song Jackson ever wrote. Penned after the demise of his first marriage,[7] the band performed with bass, take-off guitar, steel, rhythm guitar, and accordion. The flipside featured Hal Clark singing his "New Set Of Blues." The band on the label was credited as the Melody Riders.

Jackson changed the band name to the Swingsters by 1953. Without "Cowboy" in the name, he booked himself into nightclubs where country music wasn't usually programmed. Among Detroit area venues where Jackson entertained were Union Bar, Rose Club, Dixie Belle, West Fort Tavern, Crest Lounge, Haig's Lounge, Webb Wood Inn, Connor Show Bar, Roosevelt Lounge, and the Roxy. "The sound system at the Roxy was great," said Jackson. "Although they didn't have a dance floor, the place was always packed. The stage was raised behind the bar. When people requested a song, they'd toss quarters, half dollars up to me, and I'd catch 'em in the sound hole of my flattop guitar."[8]

Jackson played at Caravan Gardens on and off for twenty years and three moves to different locations. "We backed up Smokey Robinson for a couple of shows his manager booked there," said Jackson. "When the Caravan was at McNichols and Davison in the late 1950s and 1960s, I had an understanding with the owners. When stars from Nashville came to town, I'd invite them to stop by the club. We'd give them all the food and drinks they wanted. Boy, did we pack 'em at the Caravan. We played every night plus Sunday afternoons, and we'd have people like Webb Pierce and Jean Shepard on stage with us. One time I had Charlie Walker, Bill Anderson, Red Foley and Lefty Frizzell all sitting at the same table. The bartender always tore up my tab at the end of the night.

"Webb Pierce came for three days of shows," he said. "He let me take his '62 Bonneville for the weekend, and I drove it around town, parked it in front of the Caravan." Nudie the Taylor customized Pierce's car with silver dollars, elaborate leather upholstery, and chromed cowboy guns for door handles. Years later, Nashville's Country Music Hall of Fame placed the vehicle on display in its museum.

In March 1954 Jackson joined the cast of the *Michigan Barn Dance,* a country variety show broadcast from the studios of WWJ-TV Channel Four. The show, which featured local musicians and square dancers organized by musician Phil Girard, lasted through the end of the year. Steel guitarist Chuck Hatfield, bass player and comedian Boots Gilbert, and Bobby Sykes, among others, shared the spotlight every week. "Chuck could play the fire out of the steel guitar," said Jackson. "Boots played a blond bass that was taller than her. She could spin it around, and do tricks without missing a beat."

ROCK AND ROLL BABY

When Elvis Presley's rock 'n' roll flipped the nation's lid in 1956, Jackson was playing at Dutch's Log Cabin in Port Huron, the Blue Water region's largest country music nightclub. Many of Jackson's peers got out of the music business that year because they didn't want to—or felt they couldn't learn to—play rock 'n' roll. He quickly adapted by finding musicians who could play the big beat, and Jack Brown of Fortune Records invited Jackson to cut a rock 'n' roll record. Brown recorded the band in a studio behind his record shop on Third Street in Detroit. "My accordion player gave me the rhythm, and I wrote lyrics around it," said Jackson. "It didn't take long for me to figure out people just wanted to hear the beat."

The Swingsters cut a jumping number called "Rock And Roll Baby," featuring saxophone player Armand Grenada, borrowed from a local jazz group. "I got acquainted with Armand when he was playing at the Brass Rail downtown," said Jackson. "He played sax on a few of my records." A mix of western swing and jump blues, the tune rocked like Bill Haley's Comets.[9]

The Shelby Record Company in Detroit served songwriters as a custom recording service. Owner Joe Guinan approached Jackson to record songs for his customers, issuing three 45-rpm singles. Sessions were cut at United Sound Systems on Second Avenue. The only Shelby record featuring Eddie Jackson singing both sides was "Baby Doll" backed with "Please Don't Cry" (ca. 1958). "Baby Doll," a song Jackson learned from Hal Clark and Bob Norton, revealed the Swingsters' rocking style had matured. The flipside, "Please Don't Cry," was a slow heart song written by Jackson. Jimmy Murrah played solos on standard and steel guitar. The band included "Uncle" Jimmy Knuckles on piano and Herb Ivey on drums.[10]

Other songs included "I'm All Thru Being Lonesome," and "The Bug Song." The band backed pop vocalists on the flipsides of those records, which featured Armand Grenada playing saxophone. Jackson's friendships with jazz musicians around Detroit were well known among his fans. The Bobby Stevenson Trio's guitarist Bob Mitchell sometimes sat in with the Swingsters, because Jackson mixed jazz standards into his sets.

INDUSTRY INSIDERS

Along with autoworkers, Detroit during the 1950s attracted country musicians to work in its teeming nightclub scene. Bandleaders such as Jackson could often hire sidemen as needed.

In 1955, Ferlin Husky lost steel guitarist Billy Cooper to the Swingsters.

"Billy Cooper worked with me for a few years, before he moved back south," said Jackson.

By the late 1950s, Jackson hosted a disk jockey program at WEXL Royal Oak, spinning records and interviewing regional and national artists. During the mid-1960s, the *Eddie Jackson Show* featured evening performances by Jackson and his band live from Caravan Gardens, Monday through Friday, at eight o'clock. In 1967 a similar program was taped at Tistle's Lounge and broadcast three nights a week.

"I was the first guy in town to interview Buck Owens [on the radio]," said Jackson. "For several years back then, I was going to Nashville's [annual] disk jockey conventions. It was a good chance to visit with [his friend] Bobby Sykes and catch up with the guys I knew down there."[11]

While he worked at Caravan Gardens through the 1960s, Jackson's popularity kept the club jumping. "He was the only guy who could work the Caravan and have a crowd," said singer Danny Richards. "I don't care if you got Gene Autry and [his horse] Trigger in there, you wouldn't have a crowd unless Eddie Jackson was there."[12]

THE HIT RECORD

"One night I played a private party for my boss, Joe Greenberg, at the Caravan, and I did 'I'm Learning,'" said Jackson. "He loved it and wanted me to record it right away. So Richard Nick, Greenberg and I put together Caravan Records." In 1963, Jackson and the Swingsters cut Harlan Howard's "I'm Learning" backed with Jackson's "Blues I Can't Hide" for Caravan Gardens' new record label, Caravan Recording Company. Jackson ordered his records through a Columbia Records office located in the Fisher Building.

Jackson knew "I'm Learning" from an Epic Records single Bobby Sykes made in 1960. Jackson revised the music with a more sophisticated chord progression and a beat similar to Santo and Johnny's "Sleepwalk." Tracey White and Jim Knuckles traded leads back and forth, framing Jackson's vocals. While the slow side got all the radio spins, the flipside was a rocker. "I wrote 'Blues I Can't Hide' after watching [singer] Patti Lynn looking out a window and saying, 'I'm in the same old room, lookin' out the same old window.' She was referring to her husband at the time," he said.[13]

"I'm Learning" hit the charts at WEXL and climbed all the way to number two. Buck Owens' "Act Naturally" kept it from reaching number one. "I sold hundreds of my records from the bandstand, from the trunk of my car, and through Carl Thom and his Harmony House record store," said Jackson.[14] "Everywhere I went, people wanted me to sing the song. I almost got sick of it. [laughs] . . . I made enough money to buy myself a diamond ring and a new car. . . . I wore out the car, but I still have the ring."

For his next Caravan single Jackson remade Ricky Riddle's "Ain't You Ashamed" backed with Hank Thompson's "Make Room In Your Heart For A Memory." Jackson taped the "I'm Learning" and "Ain't You Ashamed" sessions at Special Recordings, an independent studio downtown.[15]

Jackson cut two more singles in Nashville, without his band. "House Full Of Heartache" backed with "When You Love And Lose" revealed no obvious references to the swinging style of Jackson's previous records. Ray Pennington, who led a western swing band in Cincinnati, Ohio, during the 1950s, produced the session. Pennington and Jackson kept the arrangements up-to-date, especially on the Bobby Sykes composition "House Full of Heartache," with vocal chorus and a walking bass.

By the mid-1960s, Jackson regularly shared the stage with *Grand Ole Opry* artists at Cobo Arena downtown. Reporters and disk jockeys began referring to blond-headed Jackson as the "Golden Boy of Country Music." His stage routine included jokes, announcements, song requests, and a version of Bill Carlisle's famous leap (straight up with legs kicking). "I showed my jump to Bill one time, when he was at Cobo. He was astounded at how high I could go," said Jackson.

In November 1966 *Music City News—Michigan Supplement* reported Caravan Gardens began a series of Monday night showcases of Nashville stars with Jean Shepard.[16] In a parade of snapshots from the era, Jackson stood at the bar grinning with Henry "Homer" Haynes (of Homer and Jethro), Red Foley, and Jimmy Dickens.

Everett "Swanee" Caldwell, a mainstay of the Detroit country scene from the 1950s, sang at many of the same shows with Jackson.[17] In late 1966 Jackson split a session with Caldwell at a studio in Nashville. Jackson cut Bobby Sykes' "World Wide Distributor (Of Loneliness)" and "You Put It There," an original that proved popular in Detroit.

Sound Incorporated, a full-service sound studio in New Haven, Michigan, mastered Jackson's and Caldwell's records.[18] "As far as the money went, it didn't have anything to do with the earlier Caravan label. I paid for it," said Jackson. "The guys at Sound Inc. pressed and distributed the records.[19] They told me that both of 'em were selling well in jukeboxes all over the Midwest, but I never saw any money from it. When I asked to get the master tapes back, they told me they lost the tapes. After that, I didn't care to cut another record."

Jimmy Knuckles, who provided a key element of the band's sound, died around 1970. Jackson purchased an auto parts store from a WEXL disk jockey, but he couldn't withdraw completely from entertaining. While appearing at the 3-Star Bar on Eight Mile Road with Caldwell during the 1970s, Jackson met guitarist Marvin Weyer.[20] Weyer and Caldwell hosted Jackson a few nights a week through the 1980s. He also participated in jamborees and benefit events.

In 1996 Weyer helped Jackson assemble another version of the Swingsters.[21] At the height of the 1990s swing music trend, Jackson was an underground sensation in Detroit. Health problems silenced his singing voice in 2000, and he passed away January 14, 2002. The Michigan Country Music Hall of Fame inducted Jackson posthumously, but he was informed of his award a few days before he died.

Figure 12. Fran Mitchell and friends in front of the Jefferson Inn on East Jefferson Avenue, ca. mid-1940s. From left: Doyle Starnes, Mitchell, and Taft "Rosebud" Blevins. Jonnie Lavender kneels in front. Used by permission from William Jackson.

Chapter 12

GUITARS, BARS, AND BARRE CHORDS

Fran Mitchell

> Roy Hall told me last time I seen him, he wanted to take me on the road with him. He wanted to hire me, and I said, "Roy, I can't do that. . . . I got a daughter in school and I'm not gonna drag her all over the country."
>
> —FRAN MITCHELL[1]

Around 1942, Fran Mitchell arrived in Detroit with her first husband and baby daughter. Though her marriage didn't last, her skills on the guitar helped her find work in Detroit country-western nightclubs, beginning with a trio that included herself, Bob Norton, and Duke Medley. Mitchell worked with a variety of bands through the early 1950s, before she decided she could make more money by tending bar than by playing guitar.

She was born Frances Westfall in Ridgeley, West Virginia, across the Potomac River from Cumberland, Maryland. Railroad companies provided most of the jobs for Ridgeley residents. When her father lost his during the Great Depression, the Westfall family moved to Toledo, Ohio. "I was raised in Toledo, . . . and my brother Bob taught me how to play the ukelele. . . . When I was ten, I could play a uke a lot better than [radio and TV host] Arthur Godfrey ever thought he could."

SWINGTIME COWGIRLS

Around 1943, Mitchell joined the Swingtime Cowgirls. Led by vocalist Eveline Haire, and probably named for Patsy Montana's "Swingtime Cowgirl" (1940), the band cut four sides for Edward Kiely's Mellow label (also issued on Hot Wax) in 1942. The records featured cowboy swing ("Prairie Sweetheart") and hillbilly blues ("Triflin' Woman") performed by a female quartet of guitar, bass, accordion, and fiddle.[2]

"Eveline was a good entertainer," said Mitchell. "She played bass and sang real good. . . . We worked at the Wayside [Bowling Lounge, in Hazel Park], and all over. . . . We had Irene Wright on fiddle—she could play—and Jeannie Lutes [on accordion], she was real good, too." The band performed at WKMH Dearborn and in John's bar on Grand River. Since WKMH opened in December 1946, Mitchell probably worked on and off with Haire during the 1940s.

GUITAR GAL

Mitchell befriended local guitar players Chuck Oakes, Tommy Odom, and Cliff Gilbert (Gilbert worked as a Fender guitars representative in the 1950s and 1960s). Gilbert and Mitchell gigged with Oklahoma and the Westerners, as well as Tommy Whisman, who led groups around Detroit and on WEXL Royal Oak during the 1940s and early 1950s.

In 1950 Mitchell married musician Bud White, who arrived in Detroit with piano player Roy Hall the year before. Their marriage lasted eleven months, but the couple parted on good terms. By the mid-1950s, Hall and White moved to Nashville, Tennessee, but returned frequently to Detroit. During one visit, Hall offered Mitchell a job on the road with him. She promptly turned it down. "I couldn't do it," she said, "but I appreciated it. . . . Kirk [McGee] came to my house with some of the musicians once, and he said, 'Fran, I can get you a job with WSM, . . . the USO shows.' I said, 'Thank you, but I can't drag my daughter around the country.'"[3]

Mitchell started tending bar during the day.[4] She enjoyed the company of musicians, and they appreciated her, letting Mitchell sit in whenever she felt the urge to play.

BOB MITCHELL

Mitchell raised her daughter to adulthood before reconnecting with Detroit jazz guitarist Bob Mitchell, who lived in Detroit during the 1940s and 1950s. Working mainly with pianist Bobby Stevenson, his picking influenced a generation of local country guitarists, with whom he often jammed. "We had known each other since we were both twenty-two," she said. They married in Phoenix, Arizona, where Bob Mitchell had retired.

Bob Mitchell probably worked with Bobby Stevenson during the early 1940s, before Stevenson joined the air force.[5] After Stevenson returned to Detroit in 1946, Bob Mitchell's main gig was in the pianist's trio, which included bassist Bob Foster, at the Wyoming Show Bar in northwest Detroit.

They cut records for the Detroit-based Trophy label around 1946. One disk included hot instrumentals of popular C&W numbers. "Wabash Cannonball" highlighted Stevenson riffing through a mix of honky-tonk and jazz piano, while Bob Mitchell displayed speedy, sophisticated picking on "Steel Guitar Rag." Stevenson's trio also worked with the WXYZ radio orchestra ca. 1949–51. A couple of years later, they performed together on the television talent show *Chance Of A Lifetime* in New York City. "Bobby Stevenson played piano, so he got the five thousand-dollar [prize]. . . . Bob [Mitchell] played beautiful," said Mitchell.

By then the trio had moved, first to Cleveland, then New York City.[6] In October 1955, RCA subsidiary Label "X" issued an album comprised of old and new recordings. Titled "Patterns In Purple," the disk featured Bob

Mitchell at his best, supporting arrangements highlighting Stevenson's scintillating style. The men moved to Las Vegas, Nevada, but within a few years parted ways.

"[Bob] went to work . . . with a movie star named Mary Beth Hughes," said Mitchell. "She got up a singing group, and Bob was in it with three other musicians."

Despite his cult-like status among Detroit's country musicians, Bob Mitchell may have been his own worst enemy. Guitarist Al Allen admitted he was a fan. "Bob Mitchell could have been a star," said Allen, shaking his head, "if he'd laid off the booze."[7]

GOOD TIMES AND FRIENDS

Other friends in town included bandleader Eddie Jackson and vocalist Bobby Sykes, who played steel guitar when Mitchell first met him during the 1940s. "Bob Sykes was a good singer. He sounded more like Red Foley than anybody I ever heard," she said.

> I remember Roy Justis was in Toledo (and his brother Johnny). I used to drive down to the Crow's Nest from Detroit every Sunday afternoon and I'd go square dancing, . . . sit in with the band, and had a ball. I'm glad I read that [Justis] was a pallbearer at Chick Stripling's funeral. That made me feel real good, 'cause Chick was one of my best friends. He was the funniest man I ever seen. I was down with Eveline Haire . . . to the Masonic Temple . . . the first day I met him.[8] [Haire] used to know Jimmy Riddle [who] used to play the harmonica with the *Grand Ole Opry*.[9] Bill Monroe and his band was there, and Chick looked around and said, "There's the girl I want to meet," and pointed at me. Ever since then we were such good friends.

Through the years Mitchell played local jamborees, benefits, and in the bars where she worked. She died in 2004. No matter how well she tended bar, Fran Mitchell was better remembered as one of the finest western swing guitarists in town.

Figure 13. Joyce Singo, a.k.a. Joyce Songer, 1952. Used by permission from Mimia F. Singo Songer.

Chapter 13

ROCKY ROAD RAMBLING
Joyce Singo

> I got tickled at [guitarist Tommy Odom] one time. We had a little contest in
> a little bar down there on Vernor Highway. . . . The song that we were to play
> was "Steel Guitar Rag." Well, he played it and he just ate that guitar up. And I
> played it my plain ol' simple way, and I won [laughs]. Boy, he just did not like
> that at all!
>
> —JOYCE SINGO[1]

Earl Songer and his wife Joyce, who grew up playing music in West Virginia and east Tennessee respectively, spearheaded the evolution of Appalachian string band music to electrified honky-tonk and boogie-woogie that
swept the country after World War II. Although many country bands in
Detroit during the postwar boom played western swing, and despite the few
years they worked together as a professional team (1949–55), Earl and Joyce
Songer's update of old-time music with Joyce's electric guitar made for a successful and unique style in Detroit. After their divorce, Joyce Songer (a.k.a.
Joyce Singo) played guitar in nightclubs and theaters, and on records with
her own bands, and with local musicians such as Jimmy Kelly, Casey Clark,
and Rufus Shoffner, before returning to Tennessee in 1967.

SMILING THROUGH THE YEARS

Earl Songer was born in 1916, in Ruth, West Virginia, on his father's farm in
Kanawha County. Just a hop, skip, and jump northeast, WCHS Charleston

(originally launched in 1927 as WOBU when Songer was eleven years old) featured live music, including West Virginia's early country star Bill Cox, the "Dixie Songbird." With a rack harmonica and a guitar, Cox cut more than one hundred performances for record companies through the 1930s (many with guitarist Cliff Hobbs, who contributed tenor vocals), populariz-ing country songs such as "Filipino Baby" and "Sparkling Brown Eyes," while remaining in Charleston for most of his career.[2] Songer's dad, close to the same age as Cox, also played harmonica and guitar. Around age seven, Earl Songer began learning how to make music in similar fashion.

Songer's parents divorced when he was young, and he lived with his mother until he moved to Detroit during the late 1930s.[3] Unable to find a steady radio gig in the Motor City, Songer hired into the Ford Motor Com-pany and settled on the west side of town, playing music for friends and co-workers after his shift ended.

The gregarious Songer first met Singo at a picnic event for Ford employ-ees around 1940. A recent arrival to the Ford rolls and Dearborn, Michigan, Singo was born February 22, 1924, in Ducktown, Tennessee. Surrounded by the Chattahoochee National Forest, Ducktown sits close to the borders of northwest Georgia and southwest North Carolina, at the center of an Appalachian valley called the Copper Basin. Her parents, Charles and Lula Goode, raised fifteen children, as Charles worked at the Burra Burra Mine for the Tennessee Copper Company. During the Great Depression, her fa-ther moved the family to Knoxville, where he found employment with the Works Progress Administration.

Singo's parents played five-string banjo and sang, performing in church and at family events. She began learning guitar and eagerly befriended oth-ers who played. Her memories of Knoxville included jam sessions with legendary guitarist Chet Atkins, the same age as Singo. "We used to meet under the Henley Street Bridge and pick the guitar," she said. "Have you ever heard him play that 'Spanish Fire Bells'? Well, at the time, under that bridge, I could beat him playing that on guitar [laughs]. He showed me, didn't he? [laughs]"[4] Singo's story suggests Atkins had been working on finger-picking techniques before he left Knoxville in 1936. Singo's inspirations included Roy Acuff and His Crazy Tennesseans, who broadcast on Knoxville radio stations, Charlie and Bill Monroe, church music, and songs in the Goode family repertoire.

In Michigan, Songer and Singo developed a friendship based on their musical interests. Songer and a friend performed a show on WCAR Pontiac until Songer was called up for military service around 1944. While stationed at Camp Beale, California, he entertained in hospitals and for the Red Cross. He received a medical discharge in 1945 and returned to Detroit, where he and Singo married.

After work, the couple often played music late into the night at home. Making the rounds of local nightclubs, they checked out acts such as the York Brothers and Forest Rye and his Sagebrush Ranch Boys. "[Rye] was a fiddle player and a bandleader," said Singo. "I remember when we helped him build his house in Taylor." Rye, who recorded for Detroit's Mellow (1942) and Fortune (1953) record companies, often invited the Songers to sit in with his band. In 1955, Rye moved back home to Erin, Tennessee, northwest of Nashville. He worked with WSM radio as an entertainer and talent agent, and managed his own music publishing company through the 1960s.

Singo's archtop guitar with an electric amplifier brought a modern sound to Songer's vintage repertoire. Songer worked up songs from his youth, learned the latest country hits (by Roy Acuff, Eddy Arnold, and Hank Williams), and wrote a few himself. Singo's brother Chester Goode (bass) and Elton Adams (fiddle) joined the duo. During the 1940s, Adams recorded for Vargo (based in Owosso, Michigan) and Arcadia (of Detroit) with a band called the Blue Ridge Mountaineers. Described by Singo as an older gentleman, Adams probably worked with Charlie Jones and His Kentucky Corn Crackers at WMBC Detroit and WKMH Dearborn during the 1930s and 1940s.[5]

By 1949 Songer and Singo joined the American Federation of Musicians. Some of the band's earliest bookings occurred at Pete's Bar on Grand River and Vandewall's on Woodbridge, downtown. At Vandewall's, the Songers rotated sets with Chuck Oakes' band. In late 1949, Jack Brown of Fortune Records asked to record Songer. The group cut four songs, including a loose copy of West Virginia entertainer Buddy Starcher's "The Fire In My Heart (Will Be Drowned In Tears)." Starcher had spent most of the 1930s on

Charleston radio, and Songer may have been familiar with the song through Starcher's broadcasts.[6]

"The Fire In My Heart" landed in the top twenty on Nelson King's *Hillbilly Jamboree* radio show at WCKY Cincinnati, Ohio, for several weeks in early 1950. Songer sang hard, but with deep feeling, and Singo's harmony blended closely. The flipside, "Honky Tonkin' Blues," a vocal solo by Songer, turned the ears of listeners with a bridge that modulated into a minor key. Sales of the record led Songer and Singo to quit their jobs at Ford and play music full-time.

Neither of the songs on the first single featured Earl Songer's harmonica, but the next record found him blowing a hair-raising performance of the traditional "Fox Chase." Songer brayed like a bloodhound as he alternated music and barks through his harp. Adams' fiddle imitated several hounds' calls (the rest of the pack behind Songer's lead dog) while Singo's quick picking accentuated the fast pace of the hunt. From the first note, it felt like an exciting chase and sold well in Detroit. Songer may have derived the flipside, "Will There Be Any Flowers On Your Grave," from Bill Cox's "Will There Be Any Flowers" (1940). Singo's brother, slapping the string bass, gave the religious song a percussive, swinging treatment.

In mid-1950, Songer signed another contract with Fortune. Following the success of their first two records, the duo supported Hank Williams at the Detroit Convention Hall on October 15.[7] They played three shows to crowds of four thousand people.[8] Songer purchased a 1950 Studebaker, mounted a roof rack for musical instruments, and hired a painter to decorate the car's sides with "Earl Songer and His 'Rocky Road' Ramblers" in white letters.

Polished and energetic performances highlighted the next recording session, where the engineer managed a more consistent balance of bass, rhythm guitar, electric guitar, fiddle, and mandolin. Their third single, issued during late 1950, included a novelty lyric called "My Wife And Sweetheart Too," which hearkened back to Bill Cox's "My Wife And Sweetheart" (1937), a tongue-in-cheek tale of a man who claimed he loved both his wife and girlfriend with all his heart. Songer also mined a humorous vein on the B-side, "Mother-In-Law Boogie." The band's rapid tempo and volume tore up the boogie-woogie concept as no hillbilly band before, landing just this side of rock 'n' roll.

"Spanish Fire Bells," an instrumental that appeared on their next single in December 1950,[9] showcased Singo's finger-picking style, along with ringing mandolin and fiddle solos. Songer and Singo harmonized on the record's rhythmic flipside, "Whose Naughty Baby Are You?"

Although Fortune pressed three more singles in 1951, the public didn't repeat its reception of the first two records. Fortune issued "West Virginia Waltz" backed with "In A Broken Heart No Love Is Found" in early 1951, followed by "I Won't Confess I'm Sorry" with "Blue Mountain Girl" in spring, and "Dissatisfied" with "Someone To Call My Own" later that year. The act's territory expanded to communities downriver from Detroit, as well as Toledo, Sandusky, and Cleveland, Ohio. After Decca Records representatives witnessed a show, Songer signed a contract with Coral, a subsidiary label.

In December 1951, Songer's Rocky Road Ramblers helped revive a barn dance in the Hollywood Theater, located on the west side of Detroit, with the George Sikes Trio and "Slim" Hagerman. *Billboard* reported WKMH Dearborn broadcast the jamborees for four weeks, although it may have lasted longer.[10]

On December 6, Songer and Singo went to a Detroit studio and cut "We're Satisfied" and "Smiling Through The Years," which Coral issued in April 1952. Both sides presented a lively mix of honky-tonk and mountain swing with fiddle and piano. Disk jockeys in Michigan supported it, and the group made radio appearances in Michigan, West Virginia, and Tennessee.

Singo purchased a new Fender guitar in 1952, and Songer's fan club president, J.C. "Dude" Towler, dubbed her "Queen of the Guitar." They hired local musicians such as Ray Taylor (fiddle) and the George Sikes Trio to join the Rocky Road Ramblers, as needed. The Sikes Trio included George (bass), and his sons "Lucky" and "Junior" (mandolin and guitar). Specializing in cowboy trio vocals, they had recorded with the Kentucky Corn Crackers for Vargo in 1948.[11] When Coral invited the Songers to cut a four-song session in Nashville, Tennessee, the Sikes Trio went with them.

In October 1952 *Billboard* noted, "Earl Songer (Coral) reports that he has just returned from a Canadian tour and will tour the South for two weeks and then play a Detroit nitery for a month."[12] While on tour, the band met producer Owen Bradley at Castle Studio in the Hotel Tulane—a popular space before larger studios opened a couple of years later. "Chet Atkins was there, but he didn't record," said Singo. "Tommy Jackson played the fiddle; and a left-handed guitarist." The lefty was probably Jack Shook, who often played rhythm guitar at Castle sessions.

The high-quality recordings featured strong performances from Jackson, an unknown piano player, and Singo. Songer probably wrote "Sansoo" in response to the Korean War, telling a story similar to Bill Cox's "Filipino Baby," in which a soldier falls in love with a woman overseas. The band joined Songer during refrains of the waltz-time "Who Will I Send Your Picture To," the sad "Unwelcome Bride," and the up-tempo "Too Free With Your Love." They played the WSM *Ernest Tubb Midnight Jamboree* while in Nashville.

Before Coral issued Songer's first single, the group toured the Great Lakes region for International Harvester. During previous years the Gus Sun Booking Agency hired country music acts for tours of Michigan, sponsored by the agricultural machinery company. (Roy Hall and His Cohutta Mountain Boys worked a similar gig in 1950.) In January 1953 the Rocky Road Ramblers joined a professional contortionist and a juggler for a jaunt that ended in April. In February *Billboard* reported the three-act show had already performed for twenty thousand people.[13]

Around April 1953, Coral issued "Sansoo" backed with "Who Will I Send Your Picture To." In September, Coral issued the other two songs. Both records received good reviews in *Billboard*.[14]

The May 1954 edition of *Country Song Roundup* featured Singo's face in a full-page spread titled "Hillbilly Queens." Her image appeared above a brief text that described her "among the country's top female steel guitarists." "I don't know why they said that," said Singo, who never dabbled in steel guitar.[15]

Coming off his contract with Coral, Songer signed an agreement for two singles with Imperial Records of California. Better remembered for rock 'n' roll artists such as Fats Domino and Rick Nelson, Imperial issued a series of country records during the 1950s, Slim Whitman being the label's best-selling country singer. Songer and Singo drove to Dallas, Texas, for the session, promoting their act with visits to radio stations along the way. They probably recorded at Jim Beck's studio, because Singo remembered collaborating with a pianist (Madge Suttee) and a steel player who had worked with Lefty Frizzell. "Sonny James played fiddle," she said. Imperial issued "Whoopie" backed with "It's A Cold, Cold Love" around June 1954. The up-tempo "Whoopie" had an antique lyrical structure and a catchy guitar lick, while the flipside was pure honky-tonk, complete with hard-hearted beat.

Around March 1955, Imperial issued Songer's last record, "I Want Your Love" backed with "Let's Try Again," which featured a jazz guitarist—a departure from the sound of the Rocky Road Ramblers. Although he sang with volume, Songer's vocals seemed tired, even with Singo's harmony support. Songer's increasing unreliability caused the couple to split up later that year. Singo recruited two of her brothers and booked her first solo gig as Joyce Songer and the High Jumpers at Spattafiore's, on North Cass Avenue in Pontiac, where Jimmy Martin and Arizona Weston had worked extended engagements before her.

Songer drifted in and out of the music business, dabbling in real estate and used auto sales in Detroit, while struggling to live up to encouragements he received from friends, including his fan club president, Dude Towler. In January 1964 *Billboard* announced Towler had created the Earl of Dude Record Company, based at Jamboree Studios, at Towler's home address near Ypsilanti, Michigan. "Firm expects to issue its initial release, a pair by Earl Songer, late this month," said the article.[16] Nothing came of it. A few years later, Songer moved back to West Virginia, where he died in 1971.

GOT ANYTHING GOOD, YOU BETTER SAVE IT

From the 1920s through the 1950s, Monroe, Michigan, famous as a former home of Lieutenant Colonel George Armstrong Custer, attracted hundreds of workers from the South to its small city of factories (e.g., Ford Motor Company and Monroe Shock Absorbers) and paper mills. Situated between Detroit and Toledo on the western shore of Lake Erie, some residents worked jobs in Toledo and others found them on the west side of Detroit. Significant numbers arrived from Tazewell, Tennessee, including Charles Rufus Shoffner, a.k.a. Rufus Shoffner, whose siblings preceded his move to Michigan during the 1930s and 1940s. Born in 1916, Shoffner left home in 1932, riding freight trains around the country with guitar in hand. In 1939 he led a band called the Blue Yodel Boys on WROL Knoxville, Tennessee. In 1950 Shoffner settled in Monroe, in an apartment above the twenty-four-hour Rainbow Grill on West Front Street. A generous soul, Shoffner befriended musicians who performed in the You & I Bar across the street from the restaurant.

Before he and Singo began collaborating, Shoffner had written and recorded the hilarious "Shotgun Wedding" (1952) issued on Fortune subsidiary label Renown and the suggestive "Got Anything Good" (1954) for the Country Side label of Lexington, Kentucky. Shoffner's friend Speedy Rogers said the latter was recorded in Lexington.[17]

In 1954 Shoffner got to know Jimmy Martin and the Osborne Brothers, who had moved to Michigan to work with Casey Clark's stage, radio, and television programs. "We visited [Shoffner] sometimes for jam sessions," said Bobby Osborne.[18] In November of that year, Shoffner accompanied Martin and the Osbornes to Nashville, where they recorded "Got Anything Good" as "Save It! Save It!" at their first session for RCA-Victor Records. Nashville act George and Earl covered the tune as "(If You) Got Anything Good" for Mercury Records.

In Monroe, Shoffner operated a coin machine servicing company, maintaining jukeboxes, pinball, and other amusement games. Speedy Rogers, born in 1931 in Knott County, Tennessee, came to Michigan in 1954. A Korean War veteran, Rogers worked in a foundry before he met Shoffner and joined him in his vending business. Besides playing music with Shoffner, Rogers played bass in Buster Turner's Pinnacle Mountain Boys. A fan of Earl Songer's "Sansoo," Rogers was pleasantly surprised to meet Joyce Singo.

Singo worked in clubs from Detroit to Toledo with her own group, and with others including Shoffner and pianist Jimmy Kelly. In 1958 Rogers and Shoffner opened the Cadillac Club in Toledo, where Singo often joined them onstage.

Around 1959 Shoffner, Singo, Rogers, and Freddie Bach (piano) cut a session at Fortune Records on Third Street in Detroit, yielding a single on Fortune subsidiary label Hi-Q, credited to Rufus Shoffner and Joyce Songer. Two Shoffner originals, "Every Little Teardrop," an up-tempo blues, and "It Always Happens To Me," a witty lyric about bad luck, sold well from the bandstand of the Cadillac Club. A second Hi-Q single with banjo substituted for piano included Rogers' "Hillbilly Wedding Bells" backed with Singo's "Lovelight." Singo sang harmony with Shoffner, and Rogers' voice joined them on his song. The single was credited to Rufus Shoffner and Speedy Rogers.

During the early 1960s, Singo led a group called Joyce Songer and the Country Three at Caravan Gardens, alternating sets with Eddie Jackson's band. The Country Three sometimes included Rogers, Shoffner, and banjoist Ford Nix. At the time, the Caravan had a reputation for attracting famous artists who came to Detroit to perform at Cobo Arena. "I didn't play with him, but Webb Pierce was there," said Singo. "And George Jones was there. It was my job to go to the convention center and invite them over to the Caravan."

Shoffner started his own record label, American Artist Records, around 1963. He shared credit with Singo (as Joyce Songer) on his best-known record, "Orbit Twist" backed with "East And West Border." They cut another novelty, "Topless Bathing Suit," backed with "Raindrops" (a rewrite of "Every Little Raindrop"), credited to Kelly Rogers and Joyce Singo. Shoffner also issued records by Herb Davis and the Southerneers, the True Gospel Trio, and the Country Sounds. During the 1960s Shoffner spent a couple of years playing music in Nashville. Around 1968 he returned to Michigan, working with Roy McGinnis and the Sunnysiders, then went back on the road with Jimmy Martin during the 1970s. He passed away in 1993.

Singo remarried in 1964. Within a few years she left the nightclubs and settled down. In 1967 she moved to Tennessee, where she began a second career, performing with a group of women known as the Ladies of Bluegrass. Singo's supportive vocals and amplified Appalachian guitar boosted both Earl Songer's and Rufus Shoffner's musical ambitions, besides establishing her own legacy as one of the first women in the country to play modern, electrified country guitar on stage and records.

Figure 14. Jimmy Work, ca. 1955. Used by permission from Jimmy Work.

Chapter 14

WHAT MAKES THE JUKEBOX PLAY
Jimmy Work

> Detroit, Michigan, was a good place, a good country music town. They helped
> me a lot with my music. That's where it all got started.
>
> —JIMMY WORK[1]

Looking through a country music fan's music collection, one song that's
sure to be there, by one artist or another, is Jimmy Work's "Making Believe."
Trained as a millwright in Detroit during World War II, Work wrote songs
and sang them on radio as a hobby. In 1948 Work recorded his "Tennessee
Border" for a Detroit jukebox label. The resulting C&W hit distinguished
itself by breaking from the double-entendre novelty songs that local jukebox
companies preferred to carry during the 1940s. In 1955, he recorded "Making
Believe" and "That's What Makes The Jukebox Play," which grew so successful he left his skilled trade for several years to make music. Work could have
cut his next sessions with the best musicians at any studio in the country,
but he returned to Detroit time and again to record with Casey Clark's Lazy
Ranch Boys, until he moved to California in early 1957.

Work's life began in Akron, Ohio, on March 29, 1924. Some forty miles
south of Cleveland, Akron was a boomtown during the 1920s, with four major tire and rubber manufacturers based in the city. As happened in Detroit,
most of Akron's new residents arrived from Eastern Europe and the South-

ern United States. Work's parents had moved from Kentucky. Around 1926, they settled on a farm near Dukedom, Kentucky, straddling the Kentucky-Tennessee border.

Work listened to records by the Carter Family, Roy Acuff, and Gene Autry played on his grandmother's Victrola. He enjoyed hearing country music on late-night radio broadcasts pulled in from distant stations. "Years ago, [when] I was going to school, . . . my dad gave me about eight-tenths of an acre. I had to grow tobacco," said Work. He saved his earnings to purchase a battery-powered radio and marveled at midnight western swing broadcasts from Texas.

After discovering he could coax music from an old banjo, Work's parents bought him a Gene Autry guitar from a Sears-Roebuck mail-order catalog. He didn't take music lessons regularly, but sitting in with neighbors inspired him to keep picking. "In this part of the country, they had a lot of good musicians," he said. "I had a schoolteacher by the name of Miss Katy Barnes, and she was real good on the piano. I would chord and follow her, while she played." Work began writing songs when he reached his teen-age years. "I like to write. It's like inventing something," he said.

YOU'RE GONE, I WON'T FORGET

Around 1940 the young man left Kentucky and moved to Detroit, when Southeast Michigan retooled in support of the nation's preparations for war. "Back years ago, everybody around here [Dukedom], they went north," said Work. "They either went to Akron, or they went to Detroit . . . for a job.

"The first job I received in Detroit, I worked at the Willow Run Bomber Plant . . . as a millwright. I served an apprenticeship [there]," he said.

Shortly after his arrival, Work met the York Brothers, George and Leslie, at a tavern on Harper, near the Kentucky Pool Hall at Harper and Helen, where many Southerners gathered on weekends. "The York Brothers would have me to sing a song or two wherever they were playing. We were good friends," he said.

Eventually he auditioned at WCAR Pontiac, and he performed a radio show every week. "I have a book of songs that M. M. Cole [Publishing Company] published back when I was going to high school, [of] the songs I wrote," said Work. He sold copies of the book during his program.

"My hobby was, . . . I'd work up there and make a little money, . . . get some musicians together, and we'd make [recordings]," he said. Around 1945 Work cut four songs from his book for the Trophy label, based in the Penobscot Building, downtown. Work led the session at United Sound Systems on Second Avenue in Detroit. Guitarist Dorris Woodruff, also from Dukedom, imitated Jimmy Short of Ernest Tubb's band, while Work strummed rhythm guitar, yodeled, and sang "Those Kentucky Bluegrass Hills," "You're Gone I Won't Forget," "Rainy Rainy Blues," and "Hear That Steamboat Whistle Blow."

Modest sales of the Trophy records kept him writing. Work updated his style for his next record, which proved the breakthrough he was looking for.

TENNESSEE BORDER

In October 1941 Work married Ruth Coletharp of Dukedom. Several years later, their courtship inspired his first hit. "That song 'Tennessee Border,' it's a true song," he said. "Me and the wife, we got married [in Dukedom]. She lived on the Tennessee side, and I lived on the Kentucky side. My dad had an old truck—well, he had a new truck—1940 pickup truck, Chevrolet."

In 1948 Work visited the O-Kay Vending Company at an office on Selden near Woodward Avenue. The company operated hundreds of jukeboxes in Detroit. He asked owner Ben Okum his advice in getting a recording contract with a major label. Okum sent Work to a recording studio downtown and advised him to mail copies of his music (on acetate disks) to record companies. "If no one offers you a contract," said Okum, "pick the best two songs and we'll press a record."

After doing as Okum suggested, Work's inquiries received little interest. In keeping his word, Okum combined his first name with his business partner Al Smith's, to create the Alben record label. Okum pressed a couple thousand copies of "Tennessee Border" backed with "Jealous Heart Is Broken" around autumn 1948.[2] Credited to Jimmy Work and His Border Boys, the recordings featured two acoustic guitars and one electric, plus bass. The colorful story and swinging performance of "Tennessee Border" resulted in a very commercial record.

Vargo, Inc., a record company and manufacturer based in Owosso, Michigan, pressed Okum's records. Elected vice president of the Michigan Automatic Phonograph Owners' Association in 1948,[3] Okum traveled to St. Louis and New York City to secure distribution for his new label.[4] No doubt the combination of Work's musical abilities and Okum's business acumen led to the song's widespread acceptance. Drake's Record Shop on East Jefferson Avenue, which specialized in selling country-western records, also played a part. "I took some over to Drake's Record Shop," said Work, "and asked how many he might order. He listened to it and said, 'Give me all you got.' He was selling them to jukebox operators in Ohio and other states. It really took off. He sold thousands of 'em, through the mail, until Decca covered it."

While he still worked a day job, Work promoted the record in Detroit nightclubs, sitting in with other bands, as well as working movie theaters with the York Brothers, performing between movie screenings.

The record received a positive review in music industry magazine *Cash Box*, which noted "Tennessee Border" attracting spins around the country.[5] Several weeks after its release, C&W artists began covering the song. Versions by Jimmie Skinner (Radio Artist Records), Bob Atcher (Columbia), and Tennessee Ernie Ford (Capitol) landed in top twenty sales charts across the United States. Red Foley's interpretation (Decca) reached number three in 1949.[6]

Some say a work of art hasn't received its due until it is satirized. "Tennessee Border" received its ultimate accolade in Homer and Jethro's "Tennessee Border No. 2" for RCA-Victor in 1950. The team of Red Foley and Ernest Tubb covered the parody and took it into the top of the charts for Decca in 1950–51.

BLUE GRASS TICKLING MY FEET

Noting Foley's sales with Work's song, Decca Records' artists and repertoire agent Paul Cohen signed Work to a recording contract in 1949. Work placed his compositions with Hill & Range Songs, Inc., a music publisher that managed tunes by popular country artists such as Bob Wills, Eddy Arnold, and Hank Snow.

In April, Work entered Nashville's Castle Studio in the Hotel Tulane for his first Decca session. He probably sent Cohen titles of the songs he intended to record ahead of time, because someone got the idea from "Blue Grass Tickling My Feet" that Work needed bluegrass musicians. "When I went to record in Nashville, why, they had a bluegrass band," he said. "I told 'em, I said, 'I'm not bluegrass.' So we tried to make it that way, but it didn't work out. We had to change the musicians around." The first band was replaced by Grady Martin, guitar; Tommy "Butterball" Paige, steel; Ernie Newton, bass; and an unknown mandolin player (perhaps the leader of the dismissed band, retained to placate the musicians union). Due to lost time from the personnel shuffle, Work completed just two songs: "Blue Grass Tickling My Feet," a song about working in a city to purchase a Kentucky farm, along with a commendable cover of George Morgan's Columbia hit "Please Don't Let Me Love You." Decca issued the two songs, and *Billboard* gave "Blue Grass" a decent review in June.[7]

Prior to that, in May, Work appeared on the *Grand Ole Opry*. "The first time I was on there, . . . that was [to sing] 'Tennessee Border,'" said Work. "I played on the Prince Albert [Tobacco] program, . . . with Red Foley." The NBC radio network syndicated Foley's portion of the show across North America. Hank Williams made his *Opry* debut the same night during a non-syndicated segment hosted by Ernest Tubb. Work made his first appearance on the WSM *Ernest Tubb Midnight Jamboree* a short time later. "I also performed an afternoon [radio] show that Tubb had," said Work.

In August, Work cut another session for Decca at E. T. "Bucky" Herzog's studio in Cincinnati, Ohio, with members of the String Dusters, a band that included former members of Red Foley's Cumberland Valley Boys. Work wrote only one of the four numbers cut that day: "Surrounded By Water And Bars," about the end of a convict's love life as he adjusted to a cell on Alcatraz Island, home of the notorious prison in San Francisco Bay. Cohen attempted to market Work as another Red Foley, by choosing light novelty songs such as "I Would Send Roses (But They Cost Too Much)," "Smokey Mountain Moon," and "Who's Been Here Since I've Been Gone." Work and the studio band performed well, but the records didn't catch on.

By early 1950, Work signed a contract with Bullet Records in Nashville. He also gigged regularly with Shorty Sullivan's band at WVOK radio Birmingham, Alabama. "That was a good country station, down there. . . . Shorty Sullivan had a good band. I made a lot of personal appearances down through Alabama," he said.

In April *Billboard* reported Work had cut four sides for Bullet,[8] but he saw just one release: "Mr. And Mrs. Cloud" backed with "Hospitality." Hill & Range printed sheet music for "Tennessee Border" with Work's photo accompanied by the words, "Recorded by Jimmy Work for Bullet Records." "I recorded it, but they didn't put it out because too many people had it out already," said Work.[9]

At his next recording session, Work cut just his own compositions— except for one, a promising set of lyrics he found on his kitchen table one night, written by his wife.

LET'S LIVE A LITTLE

After some weeks in Alabama, Work returned to Detroit, working millwright jobs and performing around town on weekends. Construction and manufacturing sectors in Detroit continued to grow, attracting more workers from the South. The city's population reached its peak at almost two million in 1950.

Work signed with the London record label, which had offices in Chicago, Illinois. In late 1950, he traveled to the Windy City to cut a session with a dazzling, but unknown, group of musicians he could only remember as the record company's studio band. With piano, bass, rhythm guitar, take-off guitar, and steel, Work cut four songs.[10] London coupled "Pickup Truck" with "Do Your Honky Tonkin' At Home" around the turn of the year.

His second London record, issued around February 1951, included "Southern Fried Chicken," an ode to scrumptious food served on the Illinois Central railroad, which ran from Chicago to New Orleans, backed with "Let's Live A Little," about a soldier's farewell to his wife or girlfriend. A news story inspired Work's wife to pen the lyrics. "I came home one night, and she had this wrote down," said Work. "I said, 'Oh! That's good!' But you know, I had trouble singing that song. Because she wrote it, somehow it didn't fit my style. I don't think I done it justice on the record."

Peer Music Company sent the song to Carl Smith, who had recently begun making records for Columbia. Around May Columbia issued Smith's version of "Let's Live A Little." By July it reached the top five nationwide—resulting in Smith's first hit. Western vocal duo Margaret Whiting and Jimmy Wakely covered the song for Capitol Records, which, about a year later, signed Work.

In October 1952, Work returned to Cincinnati for a four-song session. "That's where Jerry Byrd played with me," said Work, referring to the famous steel guitarist. Capitol issued "If I Should Lose You" backed with "Don't Play With My Heart" in the early weeks of 1953. Another session of four tunes followed in April 1953. Although no hits materialized, the quality performances resembled the honky-tonk style of Lefty Frizzell.

Work made an appearance in Chicago at the annual convention of Music Operators of America (the jukebox industry) in May. In August he appeared at the WWVA *World's Original Jamboree* in Wheeling, West Virginia. Capitol issued two more singles before letting Work's contract lapse.[11]

He traveled to the WLS *National Barn Dance* in Chicago, Illinois, the KWKH *Louisiana Hayride* in Shreveport, Louisiana, and WFAA-TV *Saturday Night Shindig* in Dallas, Texas.[12] Back in Detroit, Work often sat in with bandleader Danny Richards at the Roosevelt Lounge, located a few blocks north of Work's house on the east side. "He's a good friend of mine," said Work. "Al Allen [Richards' guitar player], he was a good guitar player. . . . Years ago he played a lot of this rock 'n' roll stuff, but he could play it all. He's a good musician. Danny Richards had a [good] band there, at the Roosevelt Lounge."[13]

During autumn 1953, Work visited Casey Clark at WJR radio in Detroit, where Clark spun country music every weekday morning. As Work gave Clark a copy of his latest Capitol disk, he asked Clark if he and his band, the Lazy Ranch Boys, would make recordings for hire. Clark said yes and gave Work his phone number.

JUST LIKE DOWNTOWN

Work left Hill & Range Songs and joined the Acuff-Rose Music roster. "There are a lot of good publishers, but I like them people because they seem to try to help their artists," he said.

> Acuff-Rose, they're good people. . . . They got me the contract with Randy Wood of Dot Records. . . . It was a new company. . . . Dot had a lot of good pop stuff—Billy Vaughn and Pat Boone. . . . Some good country—Jimmy Newman and Mac Wiseman.
>
> I told [Fred Rose] that I was going to record . . . four songs I had. He said, "Now Jimmy, don't rush out there and do something. This time, just take your time."

During the summer of 1954, Work practiced with Casey Clark's band at Clark's house before recording their first session together at United Sound Systems on Second Avenue.

Work recorded "Making Believe," "That's What Makes The Juke Box Play," "Just Like Downtown," and "Don't Give Me A Reason To Wonder

Why" with Clark playing fiddle; Brownie Reynolds, bass; Chuck Carroll, electric guitar; and Buddy Emmons, steel guitar. Clark's group supported Work with a special attention to his songs that hadn't been paid since the last time he made recordings in Detroit. No one soloed behind the vocals or pushed Work in musical directions where he wasn't comfortable. Rather, Clark, Emmons, and Carroll played refrains and turnarounds, taking turns and letting Work's voice and the ideas behind the lyrics shine brightest.

> When you walk into a studio with a bunch of new musicians, you don't know each other, you know? One time their staff musicians is there, . . . and the next time there's some other musicians. . . . If you've got a little style of some kind, why, it just sometimes don't work out. But Casey and us, we done good!
>
> Some of those songs, we'd go in there, and we'd have no trouble recording. That "Making Believe," we recorded it twice, and we went back and took the first recording.

Randy Wood issued Work's first Dot single, "Making Believe" backed with "Just Like Downtown," at the start of October. By January 1955, "Making Believe" was on its way to number eleven nationwide. Decca issued a cover by Kitty Wells in February, and public response pushed hers swiftly up to number two.[14]

In March he appeared on Pee Wee King's television show in Chicago, as well as the KRLD *Big 'D' Jamboree* in Dallas. In April, he made a triumphant return to the Prince Albert segment of the *Grand Ole Opry*, this time hosted by Ernest Tubb. Just a couple of weeks before, he toured with singers Betty Amos and Elvis Presley.[15] Bob Neal, Presley's manager at the time, set up the schedule. "Bob Neal was also a disk jockey, there in Memphis," said Work. "So he called me in Detroit, and wanted me to go on tour. . . . We went down to the [Gulf] Coast and several different places."

Work considered himself strictly country, but after touring with Presley he admired his style, too. "He could sell a song. He made every song sound good," said Work. Neal gave him boxes of Presley's Sun singles to promote in Detroit, and Work visited jukebox vending companies and their suppliers, as well as country radio disk jockeys. "Actually, [Presley] came in the back door," said Work. "Most of the time, you start from the radio station, down. But the boxes, man, the jukebox operators, they really bought his records." Work credited the jukebox industry for promoting Presley before his music found its way to pop radio.

MY OLD STOMPING GROUND

Work's second single for Dot, "That's What Makes The Juke Box Play" backed with "Don't Give Me A Reason To Wonder Why," spent spring and summer 1955 in top ten country music playlists. "That's What Makes The Juke Box Play," a perfect cry-in-your-beer honky-tonk song, secured Work's reputation as a songwriter.

In Detroit, Work had time to track down musicians who suited him. By trial and error he learned how to produce his own sessions, and, for the most part, he chose the songs he recorded. A *Cash Box* magazine poll placed Work within the top five Most Promising Male Country Vocalists for 1955. That summer, Work spent a few weeks touring parks in Pennsylvania and New York. He scheduled more time to record with the Lazy Ranch Boys around July.

Clark reprised the instrumental lineup from the last session, but with a couple of new musicians: Terry Bethel, steel, and Don Hemminger, guitar. Work cut three originals, plus "Let 'Em Talk," written by his friend, Houston disk jockey Biff Collie. Backed with "Don't Knock, Just Come On In," "Let 'Em Talk" sold well during late 1955. "My Old Stomping Ground," also from the session, appeared with "Hands Away From My Heart," a song from Work's session in autumn.

Work's next recordings with the Lazy Ranch Boys included the same personnel as the last two sessions, except Jimmy Murrah probably played steel. Work's fourth single included "There's Only One You" backed with

"When She Said You All," issued in November 1955. Dot issued "My Old Stomping Ground" in early 1956. "It was getting in the top ten in a lot of places, but rock and roll got so strong. . . . Back then, it had a rough way to go," said Work.

Elvis Presley's popularity overwhelmed country music that year. When Work covered "Rock Island Line," a folk tune made popular by Lonnie Donegan's skiffle group, Clark helped update Work's sound.

> I had no intentions of recording "Rock Island Line," . . . and Randy Wood, . . . he said, "Jimmy, why don't you record it?" I said, "Well, it's out. Everybody's got it out." But he said, "I don't have it out." So . . . We sold a lot of records! It surprised me.

Probably cut in February at United Sound, "Rock Island Line" featured rocking solos by pianist Dick McCobb and guitarist Don Hemminger. Clark probably played bass and drummer Ted Bay played a snare with brushes. Work's "That's The Way It's Gonna Be," a country bopper in the style of Carl Perkins, graced the flipside.

DIGGIN' MY OWN GRAVE

A couple of months later, Work met Clark at United Sound for his last Dot session. Billy Cooper probably played steel, along with Clark, Reynolds, and Hemminger. Work performed pure country music during an era when rock 'n' roll seemed to have buried all other styles. Dot issued "Blind Heart" backed with "You've Got A Heart Like A Merry-Go-Round" that summer. He also cut the toe-tapping "Diggin' My Own Grave" and "That Cold, Cold Look In Your Eye," issued together in September 1956.[16]

His Dot contract lapsed, and in May *Billboard* reported Work had moved to Whittier, California, launching Work Music Publishing Company.[17] Randy Wood sold Dot Records to Paramount Pictures later that year.

LET'S BE ALONE TONIGHT

While living in Whittier, Work produced three singles on his own record label, All. In November 1958 Work issued "Pretty Penny" backed with "The Big Baboon," a pop record by New Jersey group the Cameos.[18]

The following spring, Work cut a rocking version of "Tennessee Border" and introduced the stroller "Let's Be Alone Tonight." Skeets McDonald, a musician Work knew in Detroit during the 1940s, played an upright bass, and country jazz great Roy Lanham picked electric guitar. Instead of using drums, someone smacked a wooden block.

"A guy by the name of Shorty Bacon, he had a band, and he played some for me, too, on those All records," said Work. Around March 1961, Work issued his final single. The style of "I Dreamed Last Night" and "I Never Thought I Have The Blues" [sic] borrowed from the sound of Southern California, with Bakersfield-style vocal harmonies and beat. Despite the quality of Work's last records, the pop-country sound of Nashville on radio drowned out his hit-making honky-tonk.

Work understood how good a run he'd had, and appreciated his past success with a level head. "I got tired," he said. "I don't like travel, . . . [to] go around and play. I'd rather write." Work moved back to Dukedom. He took a millwright job at the Goodyear plant in nearby Union City, Tennessee, and maintained a long-distance relationship with Acuff-Rose.

Although Work's recordings went out of print,[19] his timeless songs attracted new interpretations by country music artists. In 1977 Emmylou Harris sent "Making Believe" into the top ten country charts. A year later, Moe Bandy's version of "That's What Makes The Juke Box Play" hit number eleven. "You go back through the years, and it doesn't seem like a lot of time, . . . but it has been," said Work. "I've got quite a few song awards from BMI."

Work retired from Goodyear in 1982. He tracked down the pickup truck he sang of in "Tennessee Border" and restored it. "It seems like we're more busy now, than before I retired," said Work. "I have to go to Nashville, about my songs, occasionally."

In 2004 Work made a rare public performance at the Michigan Country Music Hall of Fame annual ceremony. "I feel I'm lucky to have some of my songs still going. . . . And people like 'em," he said. "I still think I could write a hit song."

LONNIE BARRON BARN DANCE
Every Sat.-9P.M.White Eagle Hall
10758 Gratiot Ave.(U.S.25)
Richmond,Michigan.

SAGE and SAND RECORDING ARTIST
Daily Feature of WDOG Radio
Marine City,Michigan.

Figure 15. Lonnie Barron's last promotional portrait, 1956. Used by permission from Jim Barron.

Chapter 15

THE MISSISSIPPI FARM BOY
Lonnie Barron

> I've been doing a lot of cross-country traveling, meeting a lot of new people and seeing some of my old friends. This show business is sure a rough racket, but when you add up the friends that can be made through it, it's worth the trouble.
>
> —LONNIE BARRON, 1956[1]

Arriving home late on a frost-filled night, the young singer spied a familiar car parked on the frozen dirt of his driveway. He quietly pulled up his station wagon and noticed the storm door at his front porch sagging open on its hinges, and a light glowing through a window nearby. Lonnie Barron's modest two-room cottage, and a hall in which he hosted weekend dances, sat on ten acres surrounded by sheep farms, on a main road between Port Huron and Detroit. Rather than alert police, Barron quietly exited the wagon and started around the side of the house.

He burned as if the Mississippi sun of his youth shined on him constantly, since signing the biggest deal of his career a few days before. The midnight mystery before him appeared as a dream while his mind concentrated on his future.

Barron seized an old pitchfork leaning near the back door, which he kept unlocked, and entered a small room half filled with cardboard boxes of mail from the radio stations. The smell of liquor wafted through the hallway as he stepped toward its source in the front room. He spied a man seated in shadow, cradling an empty pint bottle. As Barron called a warning, another man swung around the corner, grabbing for the pitchfork. When the singer recognized him, he yanked back the tool, and set it aside. Then he and his friend sat down to the last conversation one of them ever had.

Lonnie Clanceal Barron was the first of four sons born to Alma and Archie Barron July 1, 1931, in Forest, Louisiana. The family lived and worked as sharecroppers on a cotton farm during the Great Depression. Around 1940 the Barrons purchased twenty-five acres in Richton, Mississippi, through the Works Progress Administration. The family shared music and singing in their limited leisure. At age twelve, Barron spent his savings to purchase a guitar from a Sears-Roebuck catalog.

"Lonnie was always very interested in everything and everybody," said brother Jim Barron. "He was very close to Mother, but had some trouble getting along with Dad. I suspect that he was ahead of Dad, intellectually."[2] In a column he wrote for the *Richmond Review*, Barron revealed his mother encouraged him to sing while his dad discouraged it.[3] "No place could sustain his mental curiosity," said his brother. "While he carried his guitar with him everywhere, and he made straight A's in school, Lonnie remained restless with ambition."

STAIRWAY TO THE STARS

When he turned sixteen, Barron's parents allowed him to join the U.S. Air Force. Following basic training in Wichita Falls, Texas, he was sent to an airfield in Illinois. Then Barron transferred to Selfridge Air National Guard Base near Mount Clemens, Michigan, where he worked as a supply sergeant. During his free time, Barron worked odd jobs, hitchhiking to country music shows in Detroit.

In 1951, he participated in *Stairway to the Stars*, an amateur talent show on a Detroit television station. He followed that by winning the *Ted Mack Amateur Hour* three times. Barron's term of military service ended in 1952.

In November he began hosting a radio program over WSDC Marine City, seven days a week. Barron performed song requests with his guitar, spun records, interviewed local musicians, and read listeners' letters. "He used to have a show at noon, called *Lunch With Lonnie,*" said bandleader Jimmy Williams. "He'd come on with his guitar, strumming and singing."[4] Barron called himself the Mississippi Farm Boy and always closed his broadcasts with a hymn and theme song, "Where The Old Red River Flows."

Although determined to make a living as an entertainer, Barron took on sales jobs around Mount Clemens, where he rented a room for seven dollars a week. However, by autumn he maintained his radio show and a weekend gig at the Fair Haven roller-skating rink while living in his 1949 Ford.

GO ON, IT'S OK

George and Mary Dragneth, the owners of Dutch's Log Cabin nightclub in Port Huron, listened to Barron's radio show regularly. After noticing he had missed a few days of broadcasts, Mary Dragneth searched through Mount Clemens and found Barron in his car with the flu. The Dragneths took him into their home and nursed him back to health. Once Barron recovered, the Dragneths told him to return to his rented room in Mount Clemens and offered him fifteen dollars to perform at Dutch's every Monday night.

When Barron returned to the gig in Fair Haven, he discovered that his band had fired him. He rounded up a new group of musicians, rented a hall in New Haven, and built up his audience by promoting his weekend dances on radio.

Banjo picker Ford Nix first met Barron at May's Barn in Troy (Sixteen Mile and Rochester Road), just before Nix enlisted in the air force in January 1953. Nix introduced Barron to bandleader Casey Clark.[5] Barron's talent and his friendly and ambitious nature appealed to Clark, who invited him to appear at his weekend barn dances in Detroit. As a gesture of sincere fellowship, Clark purchased a suit of western stage clothes for Barron.

WHITE EAGLE HALL

When Barron had to move his dance to another hall, he searched for a permanent base of operations. New Haven ironworker Paul Starkey, a friend and fan, sold tickets for Barron's weekend dances. With Starkey's help, Barron found the White Eagle Hall on Gratiot Road in Muttonville, a tiny farming community north of Richmond. The owners, Polish immigrants, wanted twenty thousand dollars for the hall, ten acres of land, and a small cottage next door. Starkey mortgaged his home and loaned Barron five thousand dollars for a down payment.

At Barron's weekend barn dances, the band performed a stage show, played music for round and square dances, hosted guest stars, and maintained a family-friendly, all-ages scenario. No alcohol was allowed on the premises. "He was very strict," said steel guitarist Terry Bethel. "You didn't smoke, . . . or even drink water on the bandstand."[6]

Musicians who worked with Barron included guitarists Buck Gully, Al Allen, Chuck Thompson, and Dave Larsh; steel guitarists Delbert "Bert" McNally, Chuck Rich, and Terry Bethel; fiddle player Al Wilson; and bassist and accordionist William "Rockey" VanGieson. Featured vocalists included Ella Mae Ware, Tommy Cantrell, and Joannie King.[7] Starkey's family sold tickets and operated a concessions stand.

WSDC call letters changed to WDOG in early 1954. Barron also broadcast from WHLS radio Port Huron for a while. When they traveled with their senior high school class to Washington, D.C., Barron's brothers Jim and Tom struck out for Michigan. The boys hitchhiked, walked, and rode buses to Mount Clemens, where they rented a room in the same house where their older brother lived. By the end of summer, the three Barron brothers moved into the cottage next to White Eagle Hall.

Jim and Tom helped schedule their older brother's appearances around Southeast Michigan and Southwest Ontario. In Canada, Barron appeared in Sombra, Forest, Wallaceburg, Petrolia, and a vacation retreat called Kinwick-on-the-Lake. As bookings increased, Barron purchased a 1954 Buick station wagon. Jeanne Kerr of Sparlingville (west of Port Huron) took over the Lonnie Barron Fan Club, started by Bert McNally's wife the previous year. Friends helped construct a new bandstand in the hall, painting it with Barron's favorite colors of red and yellow. Jeanne Kerr's brother Roger Fetting, a carpenter from Lexington Heights, constructed an outdoor dance floor.

In November *Billboard* magazine reported Barron celebrated his second anniversary at WDOG with a party at White Eagle Hall that attracted five hundred fans. Guests included Lazy Ranch Boys Herb Williams and Buddy Emmons, singer Bobby Sykes, and Sage and Sand Records producer Pat Nelson. WDOG broadcast a portion of Barron's Saturday night dance live.[8]

A MEMORY OR TWO

In autumn 1954, Barron and Jimmy Minor, a Flint musician and broadcaster, cut a session with the Farm Boys at WDOG studio for Les Emery's Western Chuck-Wagon label. The owner of the Western Chuck-Wagon restaurant in Flint, Emery issued Barron's toe-tapper "I Better Go," backed with "A Memory Or Two," a slow heart song.[9]

Soon after, Pat Nelson, an Ohio-based booking agent, and promoter, signed Barron to a contract with Sage and Sand Records of California. According to a January 20, 1955, front-page feature in the *New Haven Herald*, Nelson and Barron planned a road trip to WCKY Cincinnati, Ohio; KWTO *RadiOzark* Springfield, Missouri; Oklahoma City, Oklahoma; the KRLD *Big 'D' Jamboree* in Dallas, Texas; and finally to California.[10]

Released in March, Barron's first record for Sage and Sand offered two originals recorded on the West Coast. "You're Not the First Girl" was a mid-tempo number complete with fiddle and steel guitar breaks. On "Sentimental Me, Sentimental She" Barron sang the refrain with a Faron Young–inspired yodel. The Sparton label of London, Ontario, pressed a single for sales in Canada.

Barron's records sold well in Michigan and Ohio. As his fame spread, he appeared on shows with Johnnie and Jack, Kitty Wells, Webb Pierce, Faron Young, and Jim Reeves. Barron performed on the WSM *Ernest Tubb Midnight Jamboree* in Nashville and hosted an episode of the half-hour *Mr. D-J U.S.A.* on the same station.

LONNIE'S COUNTRY CORNER

Barron pursued audiences through print, radio, and television. He visited Red Foley's *Ozark Jubilee* in Springfield, Missouri; the WRVA *Old Do-*

minion Barn Dance in Richmond, Virginia; the WWVA *World's Original Jamboree* in Wheeling, West Virginia; and Pee Wee King's television show in Chicago, Illinois.[11] Barron's portrait, song lyrics, and brief testimonials about the music business appeared in *Country Song Roundup* magazine, from 1954 through 1956.[12] From January through May 1956, Barron wrote "Lonnie's Country Corner" for the *Richmond Review* newspaper, in which he shared stories about local events, his upbringing, and country music. He also plugged local businesses, his records, and personal appearances. Most columns ended with a saying he often used on his radio show: "The only way to have friends is to be a friend yourself."

By the start of 1956, Barron's career seemed on track for success. He wrote his own songs; he studied the music industry; he played shows across the Midwest, Mid-South, and Southwest Ontario; and he cultivated friendships with fellow entertainers. In Richmond, Barron strove to be a good neighbor by joining the Richmond Chamber of Commerce; by organizing seasonal and holiday-themed dances; and by performing for charitable causes.

Johnny Powers, who played in Jimmy Williams' band before striking out on his own, said, "I used to listen to him on the radio. When I was learning to play guitar, I'd hear him on WDOG, and I'd be driving everybody nuts trying to play along with Lonnie Barron. When he was with Casey Clark, I thought, 'Oh man, this guy is something else!'"[13]

RECORD TWO REACHES NUMBER ONE

Barron made his second Sage and Sand record with Casey Clark at WXYZ studios in the Maccabees Building on Woodward Avenue in Detroit. Although the label credits the Farm Boys, Clark's Lazy Ranch Boys backed Barron. They held two sessions, April 29 and 30, 1956, with the musicians cutting additional songs by Clark's band and singer Okie Jones.[14] Barron's single included the romping "Go On, It's OK," about a young man's efforts to overcome his shyness in calling a girl on the phone. Clark's hot fiddle complemented twin guitar leads by Don Hemminger (guitar) and Billy Cooper (steel). The flipside was a catchy fox-trot called "Don't Doubt My Love."

In *Folk and Country Songs* magazine, Otsego, Michigan, disk jockey Sally

Massey rated "Don't Doubt My Love" the number one country record in the Detroit area. Massey also noted a sponsor had brought Barron to perform a radio show at WABJ Adrian, Michigan.[15]

MERIDIAN MEMORIES

In a May 17 newspaper column Barron wrote about his experiences at the first three Jimmie Rodgers Memorial Days in Meridian, Mississippi. Started in 1953 on the anniversary of Rodgers' death, the annual celebration attracted country music stars and fans. "The first year I was a spectator," wrote Barron. "The second year, I was on the show. (They have dozens.) Then, last year, I was on all the shows, both radio and TV. This year they have listed me among the name guests, it sure is a thrill for me."[16]

The Barron brothers caught Elvis Presley's act at the 1955 Jimmie Rodgers festival. In his May 10 column Barron mentioned Presley: "This rock and roll business is sure putting a thorn in good music. On dance jobs, seems all the kids ask for is 'Blue Suede Shoes,' and similar stuff. I'm not 'real gone' or 'hep,' I guess, 'cause I don't 'dig' this jive. I still go for the pretty ballad music."[17] Barron mentioned Presley's name a few weeks later. Although he seemed fascinated by the singer's rise to fame, Barron probably wasn't a fan. In both columns he misspelled Presley's first name "Elvin."

CONFLICTS

Tom Barron left Michigan in 1955 to attend college in South Carolina. After a year and a half of steady success, Jim Barron began to have conflicts (his word) with his older brother in early 1956. One heated conversation concerned the wife of Roger Fetting. Barron had received an amorous letter from her at his WDOG mailbox. "I said, 'You know what you have to do, because that can be real trouble. If you get involved with her, you could lose everything here. Because it'll affect your fans, and that'll affect your career.' He agreed with me, and the subject never arose between us again," said Jim Barron.

When he wasn't working for his brother or a Richmond grocery store, Jim

Barron enjoyed attending church services. One night in May, he received Jesus Christ into his heart. Soon after, he also enrolled in college in South Carolina.

Barron carried on his Saturday night dances. Casey Clark booked Barron on every show he could, including Clark's television programs in Windsor and Detroit. Barron placed an ad in *Billboard*, advertising his latest Sage and Sand release and himself: "Fast rising, young and thoroughly experienced Country and Western Artist now available for new personal management connection. . . . Available for personal appearances or permanent spot on Saturday night show."[18]

A report in *Billboard* provided a snapshot of Barron's career at this point. Between WDOG and WABJ, he produced thirteen radio shows a week. In October he performed at the Circle Theater Jamboree in Cleveland, Ohio, and the *WWVA Jamboree* radio barn dance in Wheeling, West Virginia.[19]

Toward the end of 1956, as the country music business adapted to a tsunami of rock 'n' roll, major labels signed dozens of young rockers, while managers and record companies cajoled established entertainers into making a go of it. Barron got into the game with his next record, "Teenage Queen," a hot rock-a-billy with swinging steel guitar, recorded September 21 and 22 in Nashville, Tennessee. Marion Sykes (wife of Bobby Sykes) wrote the A-side, "Please Blue Heart," which, upon the record's release in October, immediately attracted disk jockey spins in the Midwest.

Casey Clark played fiddle and sang harmony on "Please Blue Heart." Barron's record was issued on the Sage label on October 10.[20] Clark also accompanied Barron to the *WWVA Jamboree*.

Around that time, Roger Fetting found and opened a letter to Barron that his wife forgot to mail. Jim Barron said his brother told him during a telephone call that Fetting was "gunning for him." Some of Barron's musician friends also heard rumors of Fetting's bold talk, but Barron brushed off the subject with a casualness that led them to believe nothing would come of it.

FROM TOP SONG TO TOP STORY

Singer Don Rader recalled a visit to his family's home in Hazel Park by Barron and Casey Clark before they traveled to Nashville in early January 1957.

"He had a 78 of his latest record, 'Teenage Queen' backed with 'Please Blue Heart,' and we played it over and over on the hi-fi," said Rader.[21]

Johnny Powers remembered hearing "Please Blue Heart" on Detroit radio. "It was on its way to becoming a big record for him," said Powers. In the April 1957 issue of *Cowboy Songs* (probably for sale on newsstands in late 1956), Tex Clarke, a promoter for the Circle Theater Jamboree, wrote, "Lonnie Barron's new release, 'Please Blue Heart,' is getting excellent ratings on many charts throughout the country."[22]

On Tuesday, January 8, Roger Fetting drove to Barron's cottage. Certain that the singer was back in town, Fetting broke into the empty house and waited for Barron, who returned late that evening

When Paul Starkey got off work the next day, his wife informed him Barron missed his radio broadcast. Starkey drove to Barron's house around five o'clock in the afternoon and found the front door open and Barron dead in the back room. He jumped into his car and drove to the Richmond Police, who called the Michigan State Police. A few hours later, Starkey watched as a photographer for the Associated Press spilled boxes of mail around Barron's corpse to stage a photograph that appeared on the front page of the *Detroit Times*. Barron's parents in Mississippi learned of their son's murder from a CBS radio news report the following day.

The *Detroit Times* reported Barron was shot twice—once in his left arm, between the elbow and shoulder, and once in the head. Neighbors told police two men asked them about Barron during the daylight hours of January 8, and noticed lights in different windows of the cottage going on and off around half past eleven. Another neighbor saw an automobile careen wildly out of the cottage driveway and head south on Gratiot around half past five in the morning of January 9. However, Fetting lived north of the cottage in Lexington Heights.[23]

CONFESSION CONFUSION

Devastated by the news, Casey Clark's wife Mary blamed herself for contributing to the drama of the photo that appeared in the *Detroit Times*. "[The Lazy Ranch Boys] had a mailing list that was probably thirty thousand. Okie Jones' wife did our typing, and every time we were going to have a big show, we'd send out fliers," she said. "Lonnie was talking to me about it, and he was [building] an outdoor dance floor. He wished he could send out mail about it. I said, 'You get your fan mail at the [radio] station, don't you? Well, take it home. Keep it long enough so that you can get enough money [to] hire somebody to type up the names and addresses for you. Then you can get rid of the mail and save the file card. Whenever you are going to do a big show or an outdoor dance, and you want a big crowd, send 'em a flier.' And that's how come he had all those boxes of mail. It was just heartbreaking to me, that they'd do a thing like that."

Barron's sometime steel guitarist Chuck Rich was taken by surprise, as were many of Barron's associates. "I'd been around there, and I never saw anything 'shady' going on," he said.[24]

The *Detroit Free Press* published excerpts from a survey of the letters found in Barron's home. They reproduced lines written by women expressing admiration for Barron's singing and friendly personality. "He was the life of the party" wherever he appeared, said Jeanne Kerr, who told the *Detroit Free Press* that she was shutting down Barron's fan club immediately. She also stated Barron copied Elvis Presley's style, except for the "bumps and grinds" stage moves.[25]

Fetting confessed to broadcaster and *Detroit Times* correspondent William Saunders of WHLS Port Huron that, in a fit of jealous rage, he killed Barron. It took two visits from Saunders for Fetting to admit committing the murder. However, Fetting recanted after Saunders made the confession public. His lawyer, R. Gerald Barr of Port Huron, advised him to keep a tight lip until his arraignment and hearing scheduled for later that month.

As the investigation continued, State Police Detective Lynford Smith said he was not convinced that Fetting acted without an accomplice.[26] The *Detroit Free Press* reported, "Fetting said he couldn't remember what he had done with the gun or where he went before he went home."[27]

Police found steel guitarist Terry Bethel's things in the second bedroom of the cottage, and they called him in for questioning. Bethel worked in the Farm Boys during the summer of 1956, until his parents moved the family from Flint to Paragould, Arkansas. Chuck Rich took Bethel's seat but left in

December to join Casey Clark's group. Barron convinced Bethel to return to Michigan, and he moved into the cottage two weeks before Barron's death. Bethel contacted police from his aunt's home in Flint, where he had gone after playing Barron's dance the previous Saturday night.

"Terry and I had double-dated with two girls, and Terry was staying with me in Lapeer the night Lonnie was killed," said Rich. "When we came back in, my mother said it had been on the news that Lonnie had been murdered. . . . At that point, [Bethel] was a suspect. . . . It didn't take long to get that cleared up."

WDOG owner Jerry Coughlin issued a statement that echoed the views of many of Barron's friends.

> Lonnie has had daily association with our Radio Station WDOG, Marine City, for four and a half years. During this period we have come to know him for a fine young man of refreshing sincerity and honesty. To us, he typified the clean-living American youth and, certainly, he was genuinely liked by all with whom he came into contact.
>
> Never once, during his association with us, did we hear or receive a single complaint regarding his conduct. On the contrary, the thousands of comments reaching us at WDOG indicated that Lonnie Barron was extremely well regarded throughout the area covered by our station.[28]

REVELATIONS, RESOLUTIONS

Barron's brothers returned to Michigan to settle affairs and organize a one-night visitation in Port Huron. The *Detroit Times* estimated more than three thousand people paid their respects at the Robert Hartley Funeral Home on January 11. The *Detroit Free Press* reported, "Hours before the funeral home was opened, lines formed and traffic jammed near the mortuary. Extra help were hired to handle the crowd," which was described as mainly teen-aged girls. Barron's body, dressed in a white western suit with red piping and fringe, was sent to Richton for the funeral and burial next day. The

222 / DETROIT COUNTRY MUSIC

Mississippi service was attended by four thousand people, many traveling from Michigan.[29]

After the burial, Jim Barron returned to South Carolina and found a postcard from his late brother in his mailbox. Written by hand the previous week, Barron's last note read, "I've just been to Nashville, where I signed a recording contract with Columbia Records."[30]

Through the spring, WDOG allowed the Farm Boys (Chuck Thompson, Al Wilson, Terry Bethel, and Rockey VanGieson) to raise funds for Barron's grave marker. As many as fifty letters a day arrived at the station in support of Barron's memory. Paul F. Mabley, Barron's attorney, told the *Detroit Times* that he had been doing great business for someone who had nothing a few years before. Barron was twenty-four years old at the time of his death and worth ten to twelve thousand dollars (close to one hundred thousand in today's economy).

On January 31, after St. Clair County Prosecutor Wilbur V. Hamm prepared a substantial case against him, thirty-six-year-old Fetting admitted to the court he killed Barron. Described in media as an unemployed carpenter, Fetting said he went to have a talk with Barron and to recover love letters his wife had sent the singer. Fetting testified when Barron discovered he had broken into his cottage,

> He came at me with a pitchfork, but I dodged it. Then we sat down to talk. I asked him to tell me all about it. He told me he had four or five letters from [Fetting's wife], but she was the one who was bothering him. Then he went into the bathroom and found some of the letters. He turned around and grinned at me and said my wife didn't love me—that she'd come running to him any time. He said all women are like that—even my sister who is head of one of his fan clubs. When he said he'd had an affair with her, too, I exploded. I shot him once in the head and when he dropped, I shot him again.[31]

During questioning by Fetting's second lawyer, James Hudnut of Roseville, Fetting's wife described an affair she had with Barron to Justice Harry Nelson's courtroom jammed with three hundred fifty observers. A few weeks later, Judge Edward T. Kane charged Fetting with manslaughter, sentencing him to a term of five to fifteen years with psychiatric evaluations in the state penitentiary at Jackson.

Guitarist Chuck Carroll, who had worked with Barron, disagreed with the outcome. "I don't remember how long [Fetting] was in [prison], but he got a good, smart attorney. [The charge] should have been premeditated murder," he said.[32]

EPILOGUE

In the May edition of *Rustic Rhythm* magazine, WFDF Flint disk jockey and bandleader Max Henderson wrote, "I want to say how sorry I felt when I heard of Lonnie Barron's accident. It was a terrible shock to all of us who were his friends. . . . The grapevine had it that he'd just signed up with Columbia records." In the same magazine, Lillian Munz, reporting from Cincinnati, Ohio, also expressed surprise at Barron's death, adding "Please Blue Heart" had just begun to chart.[33]

Writer Ellery Queen prolonged the sensational publicity by writing "Death of a Playboy" in the May edition of *American Weekly* magazine. Part of a series called "Crimes of Passion," the two-page story presented convincing dramatizations of Fetting's jail cell confession to Saunders, as well as his courtroom hearings. Like the Associated Press, Queen depicted Barron as a lusty rock 'n' roller who took advantage of star-struck women.[34]

During the spring of 1957, Barron's friends held concerts at the White Eagle Hall to raise money for the purchase of a granite grave marker. Delano Works in Minnesota designed a five-foot-wide monument, but the price wasn't met through donations. The stone was scaled down to about half the size. Etched below a graphic adaptation of Barron's signature read his favorite motto: "The only way to have friends is to be a friend yourself."

Figure 16. Danny Richards and the Gold Star Cowboys, 1957. From left: Al Allen, Leslie York, Sherman "Wes" Culler (standing), Johnny Osborne (announcer), Richards, and Horace "Horsefly" Wilson. Allen's guitar is at center, with York's to the left and Richards' at right. Used by permission from Keith Cady.

Chapter 16

ONE-WAY TICKET
Danny Richards

> [Jack Luker] was the one that I auditioned for, when I first come up here. . . .
> It was at the Park View [nightclub] on West Vernor. There was a big bunch
> of those out there; Dixie Belle, Park View, Rose [Club], 3-JJJ. Some of 'em
> were pretty nice. And some of 'em, . . . when you walked in, your [health]
> insurance expired! I never had no trouble. . . . I've been lucky. I've met a lot of
> beautiful people and never hurt nobody except myself. And I'm thankful.
>
> —DANNY RICHARDS[1]

Two young men wearing western clothes, Red and Stan, stood talking softly
near a stage door while WLS *National Barn Dance* favorites Lulu Belle and
Scotty sang a duet at the Carmichael Auditorium in downtown Clarksburg,
West Virginia. The men had opened the show with their group, Patsy Jean
and Her Hillbilly Pals. Patsy Jean's husband, Mel Steele, nearly disrupted
the band's performance. If it weren't for the musicians' sober dedication to
their craft and Patsy Jean's stage presence, Steele might have embarrassed
them with his drunkenness.

"Don't know if I can take much more of this," said Red. "It's like living in
a damn prison."

Stan nodded. Red pushed his cowboy hat to the back of his head.

"We play all his jobs and don't get paid," said Red. "He forgets to pay us
and we got nothin' to buy food, let alone rent, and guitar strings. Can't get
away, 'cause we ain't got the price of the fare. And what do you think he's
doin' now? He's out back with the moonshiners—and our pay!"

After a pause, Stan said, "I reckon I'm ready to leave town."

Red shifted his hat down to his forehead. "Buddy, I would welcome the opportunity."

"C'mon. Let's go see if we can talk to him." With a wink, Stan walked out the back of the theater. They spotted Steele laughing with a group of men gathered at the open trunk of a car.

"Hey Mel," Stan got the attention of his boss. "We found good stuff over here that you ought to try. Like a Chesterfield, it satisfies!"

With wide grin and expectant eyes, Steele excused himself and strode with Stan and Red around a corner of the theater, into the shadows.

Seven hours later, carrying a worn leather grip and his guitar case, Red boarded a train to Detroit. He rode all day, watching the landscape grow wintry, until he reached the Michigan Central Station in the middle of the night. Dropping one of his few remaining coins in a public telephone, he dialed a number scribbled on a scrap of paper. Thirty minutes later, two old ladies with scarves tied around their heads picked him up in a pre-war model car. After driving to an east side apartment building, one of the women led him upstairs. Red removed his hat, dropped himself on the couch, fell asleep, and plunged into dreams before his mother found blankets to smother his goosebumps.

Joseph Daniel Richards was born September 11, 1927, in Twinton, Tennessee, northeast of Cookeville. His parents separated when he was nine months old, and Richards' mother raised him in Pennington Gap, Virginia—in Lee County, bordered by Kentucky (Harlan County) to the north, and Tennessee (Hancock County) to the south. Through the 1930s, Richards enjoyed listening to country artists on radio, including the WSM *Grand Ole Opry* in Nashville and the WNOX *Midday Merry-Go-Round* from Knoxville.

He purchased his first guitar at age fifteen and soon found a job playing and singing with Roy Sykes and His Blue Ridge Mountain Boys at WNVA Norton, Virginia. The young men performed music full-time, with daily broadcasts and personal appearances around the region. The group included guitarist Carter Stanley (following his military discharge in 1946), Gaines Blevins (steel guitar), and Darrell "Pee Wee" Lambert (mandolin). They played a mix of traditional mountain ballads and cowboy, religious, and popular tunes. Known as "J.D." in the band, Richards worked with the group for three years, before heading to WWVA Wheeling, West Virginia. In October 1946 Ralph Stanley took Richards' place in the Blue Ridge Mountain Boys. The Stanley Brothers performed together for a few months at WNVA before moving on to greater fame from there.[2]

SUNNY, SHADY SIDES OF THE MOUNTAIN

In 1946 the broadcast schedule at WWVA included country music entertainers during the week and a jamboree variety show on Saturday nights. During fifteen- or thirty-minute programs, musicians sold rose bushes, live baby chicks, and other items listeners purchased through the mail. Artists such as Doc Williams and His Border Riders, Stoney and Wilma Lee Cooper, Lee and Juanita Moore, and a host of others kept audiences tuned in.

Harold "Hawkshaw" Hawkins joined the WWVA roster just before Richards arrived. "I worked with Hawkshaw," said Richards. "And Big Slim, he's the one that wrote all those songs for Hawkshaw ([such as] 'Sunny Side Of The Mountain'), Doc Williams . . . Red Belcher . . . Smokey Pleacher, he was a comedian . . . Budge and Fudge Mayse . . . Honey and Sonny Davis [the Davis Twins]. . . . But Hawkshaw, he was very good to me."[3] Hawkins taught Richards about stage presence and comedy.

> He called me out—"J.D., . . . I bet that I can ask myself a question and answer it, and you can't." I said, "You can ask yourself a question and answer it, and I can't?" He said, "Yeah." I said, "That's impossible! Let's see you do it." He said, "OK. Why is it that a mole leaves no dirt at the top of the hole?" I think about it, and I said, "I don't know. Why?" He said, "He starts from the bottom and digs up." I said, "How in the heck does he get to the bottom?" He said, "That's your question." [*laughs*] People liked that. We'd do that two or three times a week.

In 1947 Hawkins signed a contract with King Records, and he began flying airplanes to bookings in other states. "That's one thing I'm afraid of: heights," said Richards. "I can't fly." He took a job at WSAZ Huntington, West Virginia, with Patsy Jean and Her Hillbilly Pals, an act managed by seasoned bandleader Mel Steele.

Born in 1910 on a farm in Utica, Pennsylvania, Steele played guitar, bass, old-time fiddle, and comedy. He got into radio in 1931. During the late 1930s, Steele led the Oklahoma Ramblers, which included Casey Clark on fiddle. They station-hopped from Bristol, Tennessee, up through Kentucky and the Virginias. The band provided a teen-aged Jimmy Dickens with his first break. After the Ramblers fell apart, Steele and his wife Patsy Jean (married in 1935) worked with John Lair's Renfro Valley tent shows through the end of World War II.[4]

"Patsy Jean played guitar, mandolin, fiddle, banjo, and bass. She was a granddaughter of 'Devil Anse' Hatfield," said Richards. William Anderson "Devil Anse" Hatfield was patriarch of the Hatfield clan during their famous nineteenth-century feud with the McCoy family on the Kentucky and West Virginia border.

In Huntington, Steele booked shows with Cowboy Copas, Grandpa Jones, Bill Monroe, and the York Brothers. In late 1947 the group moved to WPDX Clarksburg, West Virginia, where they performed every day, and Saturday nights at the Carmichael Auditorium with top country artists.[5]

Richards, who was known as "Red" Richards at the time, remembered Steele as "an older guy. . . . He drank too much. Me and another guy in the band began to suspect that he wasn't paying us fair. [He] was taking our money to buy his booze. So one night, after a show with Lulu Belle and Scotty, me and this other guy in the band cornered him, and we persuaded him to give us money that he owed us," he said. Richards left Clarksburg on a train the next morning. He arrived at his mother's apartment in the wee hours of February 20, 1948.

Shortly after the departures of Richards and Stan Carson, a report in the March 13 *Billboard* magazine noted Steele and his wife had left WPDX.[6]

EAST JEFFERSON INTRODUCTIONS

Since 1941 Richards' mother had lived in an east side Detroit neighborhood of white laborers from the South. She worked at the Chrysler facility a few blocks north of her apartment building at East Jefferson and Glover.

Guitarists Chuck Oakes and Emerson Lee "Happy" Moore, recently arrived from Dayton, Ohio, lived nearby. "The next morning, Chuck was gettin' up," said Richards, "and she hollered at him. She said, 'Hey, Chuck! I got someone over here.' He come over and looked at me. She said, 'He's a singer.' Chuck was workin' at a club called Vandewall's. We got introduced, and I went down one Sunday and sat in a set."

When he heard that Jack Luker was looking for a bass player, Richards auditioned for him at the Park View club on West Vernor and Clark Street (near Clark Park). Luker led the Tennessee Valley Boys, one of the hottest bands in town, playing a mix of honky tonk and western swing. Richards failed the audition. "Don't quit singin'," the lanky Luker said to Richards with a smile. "I can't use ya. I like ya, but I need someone to play bass."

Richards found a steady job with rowdy Jack Dowdy at the Bellevue Inn on Bellevue Street and East Lafayette, near the MacArthur Bridge to Belle Isle. Musician Bill Hayes said Dowdy sang rocking country music during the 1940s.[7] "Jack was from Arkansas," said Richards. "I never seen him back down from anyone. He was rough! And that was the roughest bar I ever worked in. There were fights every night. The cops used to send three or four patrol cars for every call they got. After the fight was broken up, the cops would leave and the guys would go over to the Windmill 'slaughterhouse' across the street [at Bellevue and East Jefferson], . . . and start fightin' all over again!"

FIRST RECORDINGS

Richards eventually became a fixture with the Chuck Oakes band at Vandewall's. His technique on bass improved, but it was Richards' vocals and manly good looks (he had a thick mane of wavy red hair) that won over audiences. By age twenty-one, he possessed masterful control of his voice. Guitarist Joyce Songer, who played at Vandewall's, said, "Ooh, I had a crush on him [*laughs*]."[8]

Jack and Dorothy Brown of Fortune Records asked Oakes to record for them, and he cut "Hey! It's Chuck's Boogie," an instrumental. The session was made at United Sound Systems in Detroit. "I was playing rhythm [guitar], . . .

and the man said, 'Dan, you're too loud!' I was just playing like I always did," said Richards. "I backed up about ten feet. He said, 'You're too loud!' I went out in the damn hall, and he said, 'That's just right. Stay out there' [*laughs*]."

The grooves on the A-side of the 78-rpm record held "Waltz Of Virginia," a song by Dorothy Brown. Issued during a vogue for waltzes (e.g., "The Tennessee Waltz"), the record sounded very commercial. Richards' vocal was smooth, light, and warm with longing. A woman simply billed as Sylvia sang harmony, although her part was overdubbed during a follow-up session. Born in Canada, Sylvia Cadeski played piano and performed comedy, pop, jazz, and classical music. She spent 1946 to 1949 hosting *Sylvia Sings* at WLW Cincinnati, Ohio, before moving to Detroit for a few years. After working nightclubs across North America, she settled in Newport, Rhode Island.[9]

The label on "Waltz Of Virginia" credited Danny Richards and Sylvia. "Chuck Oakes started calling me Danny [instead of "J.D." or "Red"] when I came up here," said Richards. Disk jockey Jack Ihrie played both sides of the record on his *Sagebrush Melodies* program at WEXL Royal Oak. Richards said he heard the instrumental side played as theme music during Nelson King's late-night country music show on WCKY Cincinnati, Ohio.

With a record under his belt, Richards started booking gigs for himself. Eddie Jackson played lead guitar for him at the Calumet Bar on Third Street and Calumet. "He was no lead guitarist, but we got by," said Richards. "We fooled 'em [*laughs*]. That was around 1950." Richards also worked with guitarists Tracey White and Bill Merritt.

During his first year in Detroit, Richards met the York Brothers, George and Leslie, when they worked at Ted's 10-Hi on East Jefferson at Fairview. "'Swanee' [Henry Swan] played bass with them," he said. "They asked if I wanted to sit in. I did a song with them. Les said, 'I like what you're doing,' and so on. . . . We'd visit each other and just kept on like that."

ROOSEVELT LOUNGE

On nights he wasn't working, Richards attended country music shows all over Detroit, in hopes of sitting in and attracting attention. This was a common practice among musicians. Richards favored the Roosevelt Lounge (on Mack Avenue near Montclair), the biggest nightclub featuring country music in town. Chief Redbird, Ricky Riddle, and Tommy Cantrell led house bands at the Roosevelt, hosting the likes of Moon Mullican, Ernest Tubb, Merle Travis, Skeets McDonald, Jim Reeves, Goldie Hill, and Lattie Moore. One night in May 1952, Cantrell offered Richards his job.

> Chief Redbird was working the Roosevelt when I [first] went in there. I worked with him quite a bit. Tommy Cantrell came in. . . . He was the one that actually gave me the job. Chief . . . turned it over to Tommy. I went over there, after Tommy had been there six or eight months. He come out one night and said, "Dan, you want a job here?" I said, "Why? What's the matter?" "I'm leaving." He talked to Joe Prinzi [who operated the nightclub with Mike Prinzi]. He said, "I've never heard them, but if you say they're good, bring them on." That was me and Al [Allen] and "Whitey" [Franklin] and "Happy" [Moore].

Al Allen, a guitarist from Bluefield, West Virginia, had been in Detroit for just a couple of years, playing with Tommy Cantrell, Chief Redbird, and others. Steel guitarist Marvin "Whitey" Franklin arrived in Detroit around 1949. Franklin and his brother Jimmy had worked with Chuck Oakes and Happy Moore in Dayton, Ohio, before following them north.

"Cowboy Copas used to [use] the name the Gold Star Rangers [for his band]," said Richards. "He came up here, and I said, 'Copas, I want to use part of your name for my band.' He said, 'Use it all. I don't use it no more.' So I used Gold Star Cowboys." Richards' band backed country stars for a week or two per booking. One of Richards' favorites was Texas piano pounder Moon Mullican.

> He was a sweet man, boy. It hurt me when he passed away 'cause I just heard from him. He lived there in Murfreesboro [Tennessee], and moved again to another town. He begged me to go down there and stay with him. He said, "I'll introduce you to everybody on the *Grand Ole Opry*. I guarantee you will be heard," and all that. I said, "Moon, I don't want that. I appreciate it, but I don't want that life." What little I did in West Virginia with Hawkshaw and them, that done me.[10]

Just a few shakes of a leg up the road, Casey Clark and the Lazy Ranch Boys held weekend jamborees at 12101 Mack Avenue. Clark's daughter Evelyn Harlene said, "I used to love listening to Danny when he came to the barn dance to sing, . . . when he could sneak away from where he was playing. . . . We were always happy to see him. He was such a good singer."[11]

MOTOR CITY JAMBOREE

After a few months at the Roosevelt Lounge, Richards' band was hired for the *Motor City Jamboree* at the Madison Ballroom (on Woodward and Forest, now demolished). The barn dance ran Friday and Saturday nights (with an hour-long radio broadcast Saturday) and Sunday afternoons, featuring a different *Grand Ole Opry* talent every week, local guest artists, and square dances. Having recently left WSM Nashville, Tennessee, for bookings downriver from Detroit, Milton Estes hosted the show. Singer Mary Ann Johnson, from the Detroit suburb of Redford, also joined the cast. Other local acts, such as Montana Frank and California Joe with their trained Hereford bull, filled out the show.

The *Motor City Jamboree*'s first radio broadcast occurred on December 19, 1953, over WXYZ. Around that time, George Morgan headlined, bringing steel player Donald Davis with him. Local singers Flash Griner and Dixie Walker performed songs, and Estes kept the program moving with jokes, introductions, and commercials. Despite its excellent production, *Motor City Jamboree*'s final radio listing in the *Detroit Free Press* appeared February 13, 1954.[12]

At the invitation of Tommy "Butterball" Paige, Richards spent a few weeks in Baltimore. Paige played an engagement in Detroit and left town with Richards in tow.[13]

[Paige] worked with Ernest Tubb. He was one of his first guitar players. . . . Then we came back to the Roosevelt and stayed another year, then went back up to Baltimore again. And that's the last I heard from Butterball. . . . He was a good showman. You wouldn't think he'd be. [You'd] think he just played guitar. But he's a good talker—funny—a joke man.

While in Baltimore the second time, Richards ran into fiddle player Chubby Wise, who worked for Bill Monroe, the York Brothers, Hank Snow, and others. Wise took a liking to Richards' song "Nobody's Crying For Me" and produced a recording session in Washington, D.C. "I had another side. I forget what it was. Anyway, it didn't do nothing," said Richards.[14]

LESLIE YORK IN DETROIT

Things rolled along at the Roosevelt until 1955, when the club owners started booking modern jazz acts. Richards and his band moved around to different venues, including the Dixie Belle on West Vernor and Hatfield's Old Town Tavern at Cadieux and Harper. It was during a booking at Hatfield's when Leslie York joined the group.

"He and his brother George moved to Texas [in 1953], and started a restaurant," said Richards. "They'd come back to Detroit and leave their wives down there to run it." The York Brothers returned during summer 1954 to appear in clubs and work local barn dances. In 1955 Leslie traveled to Detroit without George. Richards said Leslie York wintered in Texas and summered in Detroit for several years.

In 1956 Leslie York took Richards and Whitey Franklin to Cincinnati, Ohio, where King Records had scheduled recording sessions for the York Brothers. York overdubbed his voice in place of his brother's and soloed on a few recordings. "That's me doing a dab on 'Lightning Struck My Heart,' and a couple others," said Richards. Besides "Lightning," cut in January, "Blue River" from October also featured Richards' voice. Franklin played steel guitar at the sessions.

TUNE TRADE-OFF

During 1956 Leslie York ran into Sage and Sand Records producer Pat Nelson one night. Nelson promoted artists in Michigan and Ohio, and distributed records from the trunk of his car. He helped several Detroit artists record for Sage and Sand, including Casey Clark and Lonnie Barron. While

York, Richards, and Nelson conversed, Nelson threw out a line and hooked Richards into lending him money.

Because the grapevine said Nelson did not make good on his debts, Richards ran down Nelson next time he was in Detroit. Instead of paying Richards the money he borrowed, Nelson offered him a Sage and Sand record deal for four sides. In early 1957 the Gold Star Cowboys cut a session where Richards sang two songs and York sang two. Nelson orchestrated a temporary studio in an empty building on Selden, near Woodward. "The engineers set up their equipment," said Richards, "we cut the songs, they dismantled everything, and we left."

Richards and Chuck Oakes wrote "Better To Be Safe," one side of his record. "Les wrote 'The Last Curtain' for me," said Richards. York sang harmony with Richards on the refrain, and Richards harmonized with York on his "I'll Cry Again Tomorrow" (backed with "River Of No Return").

Sage issued both singles in spring 1957. Richards sold his record mainly from nightclub stages in Detroit. A few years later, "Better To Be Safe" and "I'll Cry Again Tomorrow" appeared in a series of country budget albums compiled by Sage (later reissued by the Crown label).[15]

BROADCASTING FROM THE MOUNT

In a 1956 *Country Song Roundup* "Editor's Memo," Norman Silver wrote that WWJ Detroit disk jockey Bob Maxwell, "former manager of Jimmy Dickens," was looking for "Hillbilly bands" to work at WBRB, a new radio station in Mount Clemens scheduled to go on the air June 1. The 500-watt station would serve Detroit and its northeast suburbs.[16]

Danny Richards, Leslie York, and the Gold Star Cowboys opened WBRB radio with a performance at sunrise May 18, 1957. For eighteen months they broadcast daily from the basement of the Colonial Hotel (now demolished), south of downtown Mount Clemens, playing requests, plugging gigs, and selling items such as a plug-in insect killer called the Bug Blaster.

A recording of a WBRB broadcast from the summer of 1957 featured York speaking for the band, with station announcer Johnny Osborne guiding the show through song requests, commercials, and appearances by guests

Curly Hickson and the Rhythm Busters, Hollis Manly, and Bill Hayes. York stated the band performed "anything you want to hear. Just let us know, and we'll play it for you," including country, rock 'n' roll, pop (York performed Pat Boone's hit "Love Letters In The Sand"), and square dances.

Of rock 'n' roll, Richards said, "We had to do a little bit of it—'Johnny B. Goode,' 'Blue Suede Shoes.' . . . I tried to do a country song and make it rock 'n' roll."

In 1959, Maxwell and his partners sold WBRB and live music programs at the station ended. Richards cruised to Los Angeles, California, and worked for bandleader Deke Kirby for a few months. He then traveled to Secaucus, New Jersey, to join Shorty Warren, "King of Eastern Swing," at his Copa Club.

He returned to Michigan around 1960–61. Remarkably, his voice remained free of the rough edges that many singers developed through years of performing. "I've seen so much of it," said Richards. "I was in the clubs all of my life. . . . I never had no dope or nothin'. . . . I had a beer or two when I wanted it, but I never got out of line. And I never was a drunk. I done a lot of things, but I never done nothin' like that."

ONE-WAY TICKET

Around 1963, while Richards played a booking at the O'Mack Bar on St. Jean and Mack Avenue, club owner Arnold Boyd paid for the production of a single pressed by Fortune. With Chuck Carroll on guitar, Whitey Franklin, a drummer, and himself playing upright bass as he sang, Richards recorded "The Love I Used To Know." The flipside, "You Can't Stop Me From Loving You," was a Dorothy Brown composition that Chuck Hatfield and the Treble-Aires cut with a western swing arrangement in 1955 for Fortune. Richards' version emphasized a backbeat that, along with a blues guitar riff by Carroll, gave it a more stripped-down, rock 'n' roll feel. "I didn't care for it," said Richards. "We didn't have the right band for it. . . . It sounded empty." Despite Richards' opinion, "You Can't Stop Me" fared well among music fans, becoming the best-known version of the song.

For his next record, Richards asked Chuck Oakes to play guitar on "One

Way Ticket." "I wrote that song back when the automobile plants were goin' big in Detroit," said Oakes. "A lot of guys were coming up here to work and I said, 'Well, you guys get homesick and then go back home.'" With lyrics about leaving the South for work in the North, Oakes addressed a theme that had been on records since the 1930s. For the flipside, Chuck Carroll replaced Oakes as Richards sang Butterball Paige's "They're Talking About You."

During the 1960s, Richards worked Detroit stages with singer Tommy Kato. Chuck Oakes introduced them at the O'Mack Bar. "You talk about a showman," said Richards. "You'd walk in the club, . . . I don't care what you're doing, nobody [applauds] or nothing. That son-of-a-gun walks in and he'll tear 'em up." Richards sang harmony on Kato's sole Fortune record in 1964. "He moved back to North Carolina in the 1970s," said Richards. "Died of cancer. He was a young man, too."

THREE STRIKES

By the late 1960s, Richards found a day job driving a truck and entertained on weekends. Just a handful of bandleaders from Detroit's postwar country music scene performed regularly in the city, including Eddie Jackson, Casey Clark, and Swanee Caldwell. Southern-born people still made up a substantial part of the local population and audience for live country music.[17]

One day in 1975, investigators for the Internal Revenue Service called on Richards at his home. He was a longtime member of the American Federation of Musicians, which paid the government taxes from his performance earnings. The line of questioning turned to his musician friends. "I said, 'I don't know if they pay taxes or not. I pay mine. What they do is their business,'" said Richards. "Casey Clark said they checked him. I know he was in the union, too. . . . Half the guys wasn't in it. But [the IRS agents] was asking me, 'Do they pay taxes? You've worked with them.' I said, 'I pay mine, buddy. That's all I worry about.'" Apparently, the IRS agents dropped Richards' name when they visited other Detroit C&W musicians. This led a few of Richards' friends to believe he turned the IRS onto them.

A few months later, Richards was unloading a truck when the chain binding a pallet of car parts broke. The pallet crashed down on him, damaging his hip. Following the IRS incident, his accident, and Whitey Franklin's death in 1974, Richards retired from entertaining in nightclubs and settled down in Warren, a northern suburb of Detroit.

Danny Richards' recordings stood among the best country music made in the Motor City. "One Way Ticket," a song about people from the South feeling homesick after moving north, might have been a popular anthem had it been issued on records during the 1950s when Richards started singing the song. Billy Grammer's "I Wanna Go Home" and Bobby Bare's "Detroit City"—essentially two versions of the same hit song—related a similar story in 1963. In 2005 Richards was inducted into the Michigan Country Music Hall of Fame. He died on October 22, 2011.

Figure 17. Performance of the WJR *Big Barn Frolic*, on the stage of the Dairy Workers Hall on Second Avenue in Highland Park, 1953. From left: Chuck Hatfield, "Curly" Ray Cline, May Hawks (obscured), Charlie Cline, Bob Quinn, Ezra Cline, Betty Jack Davis, Paul Williams, Skeeter Davis (obscured), Al Allen, and Betty Lee "Boots" Gilbert. Used by permission from Trevon Hatfield.

Chapter 17

EGG HEAD
Al Allen

> Jack [Scott] was recording a song, and they asked George [Barnes, guitarist] to do his thing on it. Then they asked me to do spur of the moment stuff, to see what I came up with. They chose me to do it.
>
> —AL ALLEN[1]

Guitarist Al Allen had spent ten years working radio shows, theaters, nightclubs, and some television in Detroit, Michigan, when he found himself at a routine recording session in New York City with his friend Jack Scott. Together they had cut several pop hit records, and Allen felt they might do more during the next couple of days. Perched on a stool in a large sound studio, Allen waited for the other musicians.

Suddenly a short, mustached man wearing pants up to his chest bounced in carrying a guitar. A quick look in Allen's direction was the only acknowledgment the man offered as he sat down and proceeded to tune his instrument. Allen wasn't aware of another guitarist playing the session. He watched the man strum open chords and ping-ping notes up and down his strings. "Who is this guy, anyway?" thought Allen, who warmed up playing sophisticated progressions from jazz standards.

"George," barked an engineer from the recording booth. "George Barnes."

At the name, Allen realized he was sitting opposite a guitarist he'd listened to and studied on radio and records for the past twenty years. His eyes popped wide as his body broke into a sweat. Nervous tremors forced him to stand up to keep from blowing his cool. But when the red studio light came on, Allen didn't choke. When he phoned his wife that evening, the first words to leap from his lips were "George Barnes!"

Within sight of the Bluestone River in southern West Virginia, Al Allen, a.k.a. Albert Punturi, was born February 6, 1927, in the small town of Montcalm, near the ridge-lined epicenter of West Virginia coal country and the cosmopolitan city of Bluefield. His Italian immigrant father, sixty-five years old at Allen's birth, worked in the local mines, as did thousands of European immigrants living in the region. The youngest of seven children, Allen was ten when his father suffered a stroke and had to stop working. Papa Punturi survived another ten years, long enough to hear his youngest boy picking and singing from WHIS Bluefield.

WHIS KIDS

Like many musicians of his generation, Allen grew up watching Gene Autry musical cowboy films at a local theater. He began singing and playing mandolin and guitar "as soon as I could understand [how it was done]," he said. "My father bought me a mandolin in 1938." Around 1940, Allen and his brother Sesto Punturi performed at WHIS. Allen played mandolin, his brother a guitar, and together they sang songs of the Blue Sky Boys (the Bolick brothers), among others.

Allen excelled at sports in school. "I had a speech hesitation," he said, "so sports was another way I expressed myself." Drafted into the army in 1945, Allen's knowledge of the Italian language helped place him with a team located in the former estate of Benito Mussolini, the late dictator of Italy. He earned the rank of sergeant, and in 1947 Punturi returned to civilian life in Bluefield. After enrolling in business college, Punturi joined the Lonesome Pine Fiddlers at WHIS, playing electric guitar and mandolin with the group. At the time, the Fiddlers' sound was a mix of country-western and old-time songs.

Ezra Cline first organized the Fiddlers around 1938 in Baisden, West

Virginia, when he and his cousins Ireland "Lazy Ned" Cline and "Curly" Ray Cline got together with singer Gordon Jennings. Jennings departed before the United States entered World War II. Ned Cline died during the Allied invasion of France in 1944. When Curly Ray Cline's multi-instrumentalist brother Charlie joined him and Ezra Cline in 1946, they re-established the group in Bluefield.

Allen sat in with other WHIS entertainers, such as Rex and Eleanor, a husband and wife team, and Ernest Fulcher, whose singing favored Ernest Tubb. Ezra Cline's niece Kathleen sometimes sang with the Lonesome Pine Fiddlers. She wished to be a beauty operator, and after a few dates, Allen offered to pay for her school tuition if she'd pay him back. They married and moved to Detroit in late 1949. "She never did pay me back," chuckled Allen.

TOMMY CANTRELL

With some college courses under his belt, Punturi looked for employment in Detroit, while his wife enrolled in beauty school.

Allen met Tommy Cantrell, a singer who had worked at WCHS Charleston, West Virginia, and WHTN Huntington. In 1949, Cantrell worked with singer Red Sovine (a Charleston native) at WFSA Montgomery, Alabama. Cantrell probably moved from West Virginia to Detroit in summer 1950.[2] Allen's first gig with Cantrell occurred at Don's Bar on Gratiot, between Van Dyke and McClellan. "I was playing lead guitar and he was playing rhythm," said Allen. "It was just a little bitty ol' bar." To avoid confusing bandleaders and promoters with his Italian surname, he started calling himself Al Allen on stage.

CHIEF REDBIRD

In 1950, Joe and Mike Prinzi's Roosevelt Lounge on Mack Avenue opened its doors to country-western entertainers. Chief Redbird and Tommy Cantrell each led bands at the nightclub, where nationally recognized acts mounted its broad stage for extended engagements.

"I met Chief Redbird real fast," said Allen, who probably began with Redbird in 1950. "He really liked my playing. He said, 'I want you to work with me on my jobs. But, I'm gonna take you down to the union [American Federation of Musicians]. You gotta join the union, because I won't hire anybody who don't belong to the union.' So he took me down, . . . and he knew everybody there. I joined the union, and started working with him, doing shows all over town."

The outgoing Redbird kindly encouraged Allen on and off stage. "He worked in a tool and die shop," said Allen. "In fact, he got me a job there. That's probably what I'd have been doing, but the company moved out of state." Allen enrolled in barbering school and continued playing clubs at night.

For several weeks in 1950, guitarist Chuck Carroll worked with fiddler James "Chick" Stripling and Jimmy and Marvin "Whitey" Franklin at the Roosevelt Lounge. Carroll and Allen swapped nights playing with the group. "He's one of the finest guitar players, I think, in Michigan," said Carroll.[3]

THE AL ALLEN SOUND

In 1952 Allen began developing his peculiar style. He studied guitarists such as Tony Mottola, Les Paul, and Chet Atkins, as well as Detroit jazz guitarist Bob Mitchell. "I bought an early (1952) Les Paul 'Goldtop' [Gibson guitar], and that helped me get close to the sound in my head," said Allen.

Detroit instrument technician Jack L. Matthew also contributed. "He was absolutely the best repairman there was (on instruments), in the city of Detroit," said Allen. Matthew's family owned and operated machine shops in town. "He could have been a Leo Fender on guitar stuff. He made some guitars and sold them in Detroit," he said. "He put pedals on Don Tannison's steel [before pedal steel guitars were widely available]."[4]

Matthew and Allen modified a Rickenbacker vibrato arm originally made for a four-string instrument and attached it to Allen's Goldtop.

The only guys I seen back then, in the late 1940s and early 1950s, that had [a vibrato arm on their guitar] was Chet Atkins, and Les Paul. Now, Chet Atkins had one that worked like the one that we made. . . . But what was different about it was, if you pulled the arm up, the strings went up. And you had to push the arm down to make the strings go down. (I'm trying to get this right in my head now.) Well anyway, it was the opposite of how I thought a vibrato should work.

With the new mechanism, Allen produced a shimmering vibrato when he played. At times, his standard six-string guitar sounded like a twelve-string. During the early 1950s, it was an incomparable sound that Allen and Matthew continued to refine. Evidence of their early work was captured by 1953 radio transcriptions of some of Allen's appearances with the Davis Sisters on the WJR *Big Barn Frolic.*[5]

FROLICKING GUITAR

In early 1952, WJR Detroit began broadcasting a segment of the Saturday night *Big Barn Frolic,* a weekly barn dance held at the Dairy Workers Hall in Highland Park. Casey Clark and his band left the show later that year, and vocalist Bob Quinn hired the Lonesome Pine Fiddlers. They moved from West Virginia to Detroit in January 1953, with Charlie Cline leaving a position in Bill Monroe's Bluegrass Boys to join his brother Curly Ray and cousin Ezra, as well as guitarist and singer Paul Williams. The musicians found day jobs in Detroit while performing weekend showcases.

Before the start of 1953, steel guitarist Chuck Hatfield and his wife, bassist and comedian Boots Gilbert, hired into the show. After the Fiddlers arrived, Quinn hired Allen to play guitar.

Chuck Hatfield's Treble-Aires, a quintet that included his wife, her sister Dee, and Dee's husband Vic Cardis, recorded several sessions at Fortune Records. Allen claimed he wasn't an official member of the group, but Hatfield often called him for nightclub gigs and recordings. Before the Davis Sisters signed with RCA-Victor Records and left Detroit in the spring of

244 / DETROIT COUNTRY MUSIC

1953, Allen backed them with the Treble-Aires at the Fortune studio. On "Steel Wool," an instrumental on the B-side of the Davis Sisters Fortune single "Heartbreak Ahead," the steel guitar, fiddle, and electric guitar traded hair-raising solos on a fast-swinging jam.[6] "Heartbreak Ahead" showcased the sensitive side of Allen's technique.

On August 4, 1953, Allen played mandolin for the Lonesome Pine Fiddlers at a session for RCA-Victor in Chicago. Allen took brief solos on two songs, "Honky Tonk Blues" and "I'll Never Change My Mind." Allen's low-key performances at the session revealed a disciplined musician who knew when to play a flourish and when to hold back and support the group. In 2009 the International Bluegrass Music Association Hall of Fame in Nashville, Tennessee, recognized the Lonesome Pine Fiddlers as a pioneer bluegrass act.[7]

Allen played bookings across Southeast Michigan with the cast of the *Big Barn Frolic* through summer 1953, when the show ended. Before winter arrived, Ezra Cline moved his group to WLSI radio Pikeville, Kentucky.

After Danny Richards took over the house band at the Roosevelt Lounge in 1952, Allen maintained a long association with the singer. The band worked several nights a week for a few years. Members included Emerson "Happy" Moore playing rhythm guitar, Whitey Franklin on steel, and Horace "Horsefly" Wilson on bass. "That Al Allen," said Richards. "At the end of the night, he'd grab his guitar and rush out the door with the case half-closed, to get on home [*laughs*]."[8]

"I met a lot of nice people, up on the bandstand," said Allen, who told a story of getting along famously with Jim Reeves during a multi-week booking at the Roosevelt Lounge. Allen received offers from a few guest stars to work the road, but he preferred to remain in Detroit with his family.

In autumn 1953 Richards' band worked the *Motor City Jamboree* at the Madison Ballroom in Detroit. Hosted by emcee Milton Estes, square dances followed stage shows every Friday and Saturday night, and Sunday afternoon, with different guests from Nashville every week. WXYZ radio aired an hour of the Saturday night show from December 1953 through February 1954. Despite its slick presentation, the *Motor City Jamboree* ceased altogether around March 1954.

FREELANCE AT FORTUNE, FOX

Allen's guitar graced several Fortune singles in 1954, when the Treble-Aires backed vocalists May Hawks, Lester Thomas, Forest Rye, Boots Gilbert, and Bobby Sykes. "It may have been sometimes that Dee and Vic weren't available," said Allen, "and they would use Bob Sykes for rhythm. If they'd get stuck and they wanted a lead man, they usually would call me."

In 1954 Allen and his wife purchased a house on Detroit's east side, near Eight Mile Road. He began crafting recordings of himself playing standards such as "Twilight Time" and "Birth Of The Blues," using overdubbing techniques he discovered on Les Paul's groundbreaking records. By trial and error, Allen learned how to make recordings worthy of commercial release with his basement setup.

Allen worked "Saturday nights only" for a while with Lonnie Barron at White Eagle Hall on Gratiot Avenue near Richmond. In late 1954 Allen played lead guitar on Barron's first record "I Better Go" backed with "A Memory Or Two" for the Western Chuck-Wagon label of Flint. Flint radio disk jockey Jimmy Minor split the session with Barron and used the same band for his own single. Casey Clark, leader of the Lazy Ranch Boys in Detroit, played fiddle. "I worked two shows, two nights with Casey Clark, when he had Buddy Emmons [playing steel]," said Allen. "I didn't like his pay, so I didn't go back."

Clark may have offered Allen his standard sideman deal: a weekly salary in exchange for being available whenever Clark might call. A busy man like Allen would have easily turned it down. By then, he and his wife operated their own salon, while he worked at another barbershop. If not cutting hair or playing guitar, "I used to take care of all of the business side and all the handy work. I'd do my accounting and payroll," said Allen. Time spent playing guitar in local recording studios with Bob Quinn, Tommy Whisman, and May Hawks also contributed to Allen's growth. In 1955 Allen purchased a new black Gibson Les Paul custom guitar, commonly referred to as the "fretless wonder." "That really did it, for me," said Allen, indicating he'd come close to perfecting his style.

Allen's 1956–57 gigs with pianist and accordionist Don "Lucky Lee"

Larsh marked his first foray into music with a big beat, when Lee formed a rock 'n' roll group with his younger brother Dave Larsh (guitar), Wilf La-Salle (steel), and William "Rockey" VanGieson (bass). With Joe Coccia on drums and a saxophone player, they sounded like early rock 'n' roll bands of the Northeast United States, especially Bill Haley and His Comets.

Allen played on several singles and demonstration recordings with the group. In 1957, Lucky Lee cut his own singles for the Fox and Chant labels of Detroit real estate broker George Braxton. Lucky Lee's band also backed vocal groups the Romeos, the Four Clippers, and the Larados. Allen did not appear on the Four Clippers sides, and he played on just one of two sessions Lucky Lee made with the Romeos: "Fine, Fine Baby" backed with "Moments To Remember," reissued on Atco. Allen played lead guitar on the Larados' first single, "Bad, Bad Guitar Man" backed with "Now The Parting Begins."

He also worked with Danny Richards and Les York, who shared billing during summers when York visited from his home in Dallas, Texas. Allen played with Richards and York at WBRB radio Mount Clemens, where the band performed a live broadcast every day at noon, 1957–58.

JACK SCOTT

In early 1958, singer Jack Scott invited Allen to join him at his weekend dance in Hazel Park. In 1936 Scott was born Giovanni Scafone Jr. in Windsor, Ontario. Ten years later, his father moved the family to Hazel Park. Fascinated by country music, Scott learned guitar while emulating his idol, Hank Williams, singing and writing songs. Disk jockey Jack Ihrie befriended Scott in 1952, after Ihrie witnessed a performance of him and his sister at Hazel Park High School. Ihrie hosted the popular *Sagebrush Melodies* program weekday afternoons on WEXL Royal Oak, and emceed country music showcases in Detroit. Thanks to Ihrie, sixteen-year-old Scott was soon making appearances with the likes of Marty Robbins, Carl Smith, and Moon Mullican in Detroit theaters.[9]

With a group of schoolmates called the Southern Drifters, Scott performed every weekend at Bill's Barn, a hall on Van Dyke in Utica, in 1955.

By 1956 Scott hosted a weekend dance called "Jack Scott's Dance Ranch" (formerly known as May's Barn) on Rochester Road and Big Beaver in Troy.

In 1957 Scott's band, then known as the Rock-A-Billies,[10] cut four songs at United Sound Systems in Detroit. Scott took acetate disks of them to Carl Thom, owner of the Harmony House record shop in Hazel Park, who gave copies to a local ABC-Paramount records distributor. In May the company purchased Scott's session tapes and issued two singles. Neither disk hit the national charts, but they received promising airplay in Detroit. The records seemed as close to Carl Perkins' Dixie-fried sound as a group north of the Mason-Dixon Line could get. When he called Allen, Scott had shaken up his country band with the addition of a saxophone player and vocal group, the Chantones.

CARLTON CAPERS

"I never thought what we did with Jack was rock 'n' roll," said Allen. "I equate rock 'n' roll with Fats Domino, Carl Perkins, and early Elvis [Presley]. What Jack did was more like pop music." Joe Carlton, a New York City music businessman, purchased Scott's next set of master tapes and started the Carlton record label. Scott's first single for Carlton, "Leroy" backed with "My True Love," climbed to the top of pop music charts in summer 1958. Allen carefully arranged his guitar parts for Scott's songs, as opposed to taking a spontaneous approach like Carl Perkins might have. Allen said the Jack Scott band rehearsed songs prior to recording them.

Their protocol proved successful, as Scott followed "My True Love" with a string of hits including "With Your Love," "Geraldine," "I Never Felt Like This," "The Way I Walk," and "Goodbye Baby."

GIBSON VIBRATO

In late 1958, Allen and Jack Matthew approached the Gibson Guitar Company in Kalamazoo, Michigan, about licensing the guitar vibrato they had just patented. Soon after, Gibson began building the so-called sideways vibrato on their SG (Standard Guitar) model. As partial payment, Allen received a custom ES-355 with the new vibrato attached.[11] Gibson also gave Allen a guitar bridge made of steel, which helped him sustain a tone longer than wood guitar bridges allowed.

Allen's reputation expanded across the Detroit music community. When Jimmy Franklin lined up a session at Fortune Records to record his savage "Hey Mr. Presley," he called Chuck Carroll, who suggested Allen for the job.[12] Without a rehearsal prior to the session, Allen's guitar picking sounded inspired by true rock 'n' roll—improvised and explosive.

As Jack Scott rode the crest of his first nationwide hits, the U.S. Army called him to report for service at the start of 1959. Scott's mid-tempo rocker "Goodbye Baby" played over radios across the nation when he left behind civilian life. While Scott settled into Fort Knox, Kentucky, Carlton released a couple more singles that climbed into the middle of Billboard's top one hundred pop singles chart. Scott returned to Detroit by May, however, after receiving a medical discharge.

AL ALLEN AND THE SOUNDS

During Jack Scott's service, Joe Carlton personally invited Allen to cut a session of instrumentals. Allen wrote four numbers that could have given guitarists Duane Eddy and Link Wray a run for the money. With Dominic Scafone (Jack Scott's cousin) on drums, Allen booked time at Special Recordings downtown. Allen overdubbed several guitar parts, obscuring the musical connection with Jack Scott's records by mixing them into a wall of biting riffs. Around March 1959 Carlton issued "Egg Head" backed with "I'm Beat." Billboard reviewed Allen's record, noting the "interesting guitar sound" and Allen's "unusual guitar sound effect."[13]

Allen organized a band called the Sounds, with Dominic Scafone (drums), Nick Harris (second guitar), Alex Colburn (saxophone), and sometimes a piano man. He appeared in nightclubs, teen-oriented radio programs, and local television. "I had a lady—I think her name was Kay—

that would take me around and they would plan all this for me," said Allen. He met WXYZ disk jockey Mickey Shorr and plugged the record on
Shorr's television dance party. Allen also met top WJBK jockey Tom Clay,
who offered to play the record on his show in exchange for a percentage of
record sales. Allen didn't speak with Clay again.[14]

"I did some interviews for different radio shows," said Allen, "but when
I started to receive phone calls at my home at all hours of the night, I asked
Joe Carlton to release me from my contract." With a business to run and
family to support, Allen didn't consider himself a pop star and wasn't interested in the lifestyle of his friend Jack Scott. Carlton let him go, returning
the master tapes to Allen, who relished the midnight silence that returned
to his household.

TOP-RANKED GUITARISTS

In 1959 Scott's record "The Way I Walk" climbed into pop charts through the
summer, peaking at number thirty-five nationwide. Allen played an unfor-
gettable, mellow solo that fit the cool, strolling groove of the song perfectly.

When Scott's management moved him over to the Top Rank label in
1960, he came up with two more hits: "What In The World's Come Over
You" and "Burning Bridges." "Bridges" was coupled with "Oh Little One,"
featuring Allen's guitar prominently. Allen was unable to attend the session
that produced "Bridges," due to the death of his mother. The producer hired
jazz guitarist Al Caiola in his stead. Allen said he later heard that Caiola was
instructed by Scott and the producer to "play like Al Allen."

Scott retained his band through the transition to Top Rank, at least in
the studio. He wound up traveling without them in a Dick Clark package
tour that year, leaving Allen to gig around Detroit with the Sounds, as well
as with country musicians.

Scott's record labels often brought him and Allen to New York City to
record, and during one episode they met legendary guitarist George Barnes.
Although he played on hundreds of pop, rock, country, and New York City
doo-wop records through the 1950s, Barnes was not the most photographed

musician, and Allen didn't recognize him at first. "I can't remember the song we cut," said Allen, but Scott and the producer chose Allen's performance. "He was on [the final cut], but he was just picking a little rhythm," said Allen.

AL ALLEN PRODUCTIONS

Singer Everett "Swanee" Caldwell, who held a job in a Ford factory by day and led C&W groups in Detroit by night, cut his first records in Allen's basement studio in 1959. Caldwell gave John Henson of the Troy-based Clix label four songs engineered by Allen in stereo, but Henson mastered the records in mono.[15]

In 1961 Top Rank ceased making records, and Jack Scott moved to Capitol Records. In 1962 Scott and Allen performed on the Merv Griffin Show in New York City. "Al Caiola was probably the nicest one of all I met up there [in New York City]. I used his amplifier on Merv Griffin's show," said Allen. "Here they come with a stand, . . . and they put your music on it. I told Al, 'I can't read music that well.' He said, 'Don't worry about it. I'll tell you when to come in.' So I was sittin' there, and the fiddles are playing, and Jack's a-singing, and Al's hunched beside me whispering, 'All right.—Now!' And I started picking [*laughs*]."

SCOTT FREE

When Jack Scott signed a contract with RCA subsidiary label Groove in 1963, he and Allen parted ways but remained friends. After 1963 Scott's music rarely attracted the attention it received in 1958 through 1962. One exception, "You're Only Getting Better," on Dot Records, appeared on *Billboard* country charts in 1973. Allen remained active in local music, gigging with Danny Richards, Swanee Caldwell, and others, besides the occasional house party with Chief Redbird.

Allen and Jack Matthew continued tinkering with their guitar vibrato, too. "After we licensed our vibrato to Gibson, we came up with one even better than that," said Allen. "You could lower or raise a string two tones and it would go back in tune. There was a choice of a bridge. . . . When you worked it, the swinging bridge would always come back to a level, and your strings would always be in tune. Or you could get the other type of bridge, with the rocker on it."[16]

They approached Gibson with the new mechanism in 1963. "They didn't want to change, because they spent a lot of money on building the one they had going," said Allen. Gibson ended production of the 1958 vibrato in 1964. The second-generation Matthew-Allen vibrato kit was never mass-produced.

Allen and his wife retired after forty years in business, though Allen kept up his guitar picking to satisfy his own curiosity about the instrument. Every era in music has its historical markers. Al Allen was the first C&W guitarist to provide a uniquely identifiable style from Detroit. Just as Jack Scott's vocals immediately identified his records to radio listeners, Allen's ethereal, space-age guitar and tastefully spare performances played an essential role in the "Jack Scott sound." In 2003 the Michigan Country Music Hall of Fame added Al Allen to its honor roll. Scott's induction followed in 2004.

Figure 18. Hugh Friar and the Virginia Vagabonds, 1959. From left: Chuck Friar, Jimmy Kirkland, Louis Weddle (seated), Hugh Friar, and Dave Morgan. Used by permission from Hugh Friar.

Chapter 18

ROCKIN' VAGABOND
Hugh Friar

> After country really started dying, . . . I went to work for Artists Corporation
> in Milwaukee. . . . I sent them a tape of the band, and the guy called me and
> said, "Hugh, you got a good band, but we can't book country bands." I had a
> five-piece band. He said, "If you'll drop a couple of those guys, and have lead
> guitar, rhythm guitar and drums, we'll book you."
>
> —HUBERT "HUGH" FRIAR[1]

It wasn't a stretch for Hugh Friar to change his band from country to rock 'n'
roll in 1960. Friar witnessed first-hand the evolution of country music from
folk and cowboy tunes to the widespread use of amplified instruments and
drums. With a group he called the Virginia Vagabonds—a band that lasted
only a couple of years—Friar was best remembered for two records on John
R. Henson's Clix label. Friar's Clix singles represented the sound of modern
country music played in nightclubs across Southeast Michigan at the time.
As the band clowned for photographs with their first Clix record in spring
1959, Friar was only a few years away from leaving the music business.

Born September 16, 1927, and raised on a farm in Claiborne County, near
Tazewell, Tennessee, Friar's first musical experiences included square dances. But he didn't go just to dance. "They used to play music at pie suppers. . . .
Anywhere they was playin' music, if I didn't get with the band, I'd stand in
the background and play, and try to learn what I could," he said.

Around 1944, Friar attended a radio broadcast sponsored by grocer Cas Walker on WROL Knoxville, Tennessee. "I started goin' down there and appearing on his program," he said. Friar hosted his own show at WHLN Harlan, Kentucky, before he moved to Detroit, Michigan, where an uncle lived.

Friar's neighbor in Tennessee, Rufus Shoffner, traveled with him. "We grew up on adjoining farms," said Friar. "We went up there together. Then Rufus, he went back south and I stayed. . . . It was a few years before we played [music] together, again." He worked a variety of jobs, punching time cards at a candy maker's, the Hudson Motor Car Company, Chrysler, and the U.S. Rubber Company.

"The first people that I got acquainted with, was George and Leslie York, the York Brothers. They were playin' at a place called Ted's 10-Hi," said Friar. "Leslie played [lead] guitar, and if George was gonna take a night off or something—gonna be out of town—I would sit in with Leslie. We got to where we could do pretty good duets together. I knew all of their songs and we could do 'em pretty good.

"There was a man there (in Detroit) by the name of Ray Brown. He was a good singer and a good guitar player," said Friar. "I went to a Democratic convention for some local politicians and he was there. I got up and sang a few songs with him. He was playin' at a little place called Allen's Tavern [John R. and Milwaukee]." Former *Grand Ole Opry* star "Fiddlin'" Arthur Smith sometimes worked with Ray Brown and Friar at Allen's Tavern. Smith had moved north because two of his sons lived and worked in Michigan. In 1957 Smith joined Merle Travis in California.

"Chief Louis . . . was a real good fiddle player. He was almost full-blooded Indian," said Friar. "Chief Louis was the uncle to Ray Brown, and to Joe Baumgardner, a mandolin player that worked with me for a long time.

"Then we had [guitarist] Shug Dowdy and [singer] Jack Dowdy, they were brothers from Arkansas," he said. "And [singer] Luke Kelly had bad eyes and had to wear real thick glasses. They got into a fight one time, just a drunken brawl, Jack, Shug, and Luke Kelly. Luke lost his glasses. . . . Luke said, 'Just keep talkin', I'll find ya!' Shug would say something and Luke would swing at him [*laughs*]."

HILLBILLY HICKS

Friar jammed with guitarists Jeff Durham, Glen Ball, and Chuck Oakes, and singers Skeets McDonald, Danny Richards, and Bobby Sykes. In October 1950 *Billboard* magazine noted Hubert Friar and His Hillbilly Hicks signed a contract with Fortune Records of Detroit.[2] "Jack Brown [Fortune owner] came in where I was playing one night," said Friar. "He was gonna make a star out of me. I learned later that all he wanted was the price of making the record, 'cause he didn't have no distribution, no means of pushing the records. . . . But I sold quite a few of the records where I was playing."

The Hillbilly Hicks included Joe Baumgardner (mandolin) and Henry "Swanee" Swan (bass). Swan had played with the York Brothers since 1946. The band cut Friar's song "Heartaches And Teardrops," released late 1950. The flipside, "Joe's Mandolin Boogie," was made up on the spot, with lyrical references to country bars on Mack Avenue and the York Brothers' "Highland Park Girl."

> We were out there getting set up for the recording session and we were just warming up. [Baumgardner] started playing that [boogie], and Jack [Brown] really liked it. He said, "I'd like to have that on a record. . . . What's the words to it?" Joe told him, "That's an instrumental. There's no words to it." So Jack said to me, "Hugh, why don't you write some words to that, and let's record it?" So that's what we done.

Buster Turner, a native of New Tazewell, Tennessee, then living in Monroe, Michigan, ran into Friar at the Fortune studio as Friar worked on a follow-up session. "I remember we went up there one time, and we got in there and [Jack Brown] had the engineer there and was recording Hugh," said Turner. "Hubert was trying to sing like Ernest Tubb, and finally [Jack] come in there and said, . . . 'Hey buddy, we've got an Ernest Tubb. We don't need another one.'"[3] Brown's and his wife Dorothy's attempts to influence Friar's ambitions rubbed him the wrong way. "She knew all the legal aspects and everything," said Friar. "She tried to tell me that I had to do this and I had to do that. I told her, 'I don't have to do anything.' So I picked up my guitar and left."

During the early 1950s, Friar performed with West Virginia guitarist George Upton at the J-B bar on Mack Avenue, near the Chrysler facility where Upton worked during the day. Other musicians who played with Friar included bass player Horace "Horsefly" Wilson and guitarist Tracey White. Jimmy Work, who lived in the neighborhood, sometimes sat in with the band, as did Bill Callihan, the disabled steel guitarist who lived in a basement apartment in Detroit. "He had a little recording studio. Just recorded for the local people," said Friar. "He played steel guitar, and whatever Jerry Byrd played, however Jerry Byrd played it, he copied it."

VIRGINIA VAGABONDS

Guitarist Jim Kirkland recalled meeting Friar and his wife at a jamboree around 1958. Kirkland had just given up a bid for stardom with his rockabilly "I Wonder If You Wonder" on the local Fox label. Guitarist Dave Morgan, steel guitarist Louis Weddle, and bassist Charles Friar (Hugh's brother) rounded out Friar's new group, called the Virginia Vagabonds. Kirkland and Morgan traded leads on most songs, with Kirkland's finger-picking complementing Morgan's flat pick technique.

Friar booked a long-term contract at the Tradewinds club in Lansing, and in early 1959, John Henson and his wife spent an evening digging the band. Henson invited Friar to record for his Clix label.

On March 21, 1959, Friar and band, plus pianist Freddie Bach, gathered at Henson's home in Troy. "He had a couple of rooms built onto his house that he used. . . . It was set up good. It was soundproofed and everything.

Had good acoustics," said Friar. The band cut four Friar originals that Henson issued on two 45-rpm singles. The mid-tempo bopper "I Can't Stay Mad At You" included a rocking guitar solo by Kirkland. The flipside, "Crazy Dreams," featured a slow, romantic beat.

Friar wrote "I Can't Stay Mad At You" with the Davis Sisters (Betty Jack and Skeeter) in mind. He got acquainted with them when they lived in Detroit in 1952 and 1953. "[After] they left Detroit, I lost contact with Skeeter for several years," said Friar. "When I played that for John Henson, he said, 'Man, we need to record that!' And I said that's for a woman. 'Aw,' he said, 'Nobody will ever [notice] the difference. That's got a good beat.'"

Friar's second Clix single, issued the same year, included another dance number, "Empty Arms," backed with the heart song, "You Didn't Forget," with Weddle singing tenor harmony.

Kirkland used a tape echo effect with his guitar, assembled from a Voice of Music tape recorder that musician and sound engineer Stan Getz modified for him. "You had to combine the fast and slow speeds," said Kirkland. "I could just stand there and chord the guitar, and I could make it do whatever I thought it should have done."[4] Like his picking on his Fox record, Kirkland's notes sounded sharp and punchy, almost "scratchy," with the echo effect. Its edge contrasted well with Hugh Friar's smooth vocals.

Although Henson made use of formal contracts for the recordings and copyrights, Clix had no widespread distribution established for product. As with his Fortune record, Friar sold most copies at personal appearances. "[Henson] asked me if I had some more songs that I wanted to record," said Friar. "But he wasn't a-doin' anything with what I already recorded, so I didn't figure it was worthwhile getting into it."

ROCKIN' THREE

Friar sent a tape of the band to Artists Corporation in Milwaukee, Wisconsin, and a representative offered to book Friar but wanted a three-piece act that played rock 'n' roll. "I finished out my contract at the Tradewinds," he said. "Jimmy Kirkland, he had a good job there in a factory. He couldn't go on the road, so I hired Jimmy Kelly, Luke Kelly's son. . . . He had a friend [who] was a real good drummer. . . . Gary Diamond was the boy's name. We went on the road as the Rockin' Three.

"I lived in Dearborn at that time and they'd just call you and tell you where you was booked and you went there. They wouldn't book you over two weeks at one place. They wanted you to be hot. Usually, you played Tuesday through Saturday. They'd call you Friday or Saturday or something, and tell you where you were goin' from one place to the other. Sometimes we'd go home, sometimes we'd go directly to the other spot," he said.

After a few months, Friar disbanded. "I quit that and come back to Toledo, Ohio, and managed a club for Rufus Shoffner. He had a place in Toledo called the Cadillac Club," he said. "My wife and I managed that and [I] also played music. We was there probably eighteen months, then I bought a nightclub in Toledo called the Flamingo Club."

While Friar and his wife ran the Flamingo, he played in the house band and booked acts such as George Jones, Jimmy Newman, and Jimmie Skinner. An old contract revealed Jones performed one night for two hundred dollars. "Nowadays, the stars won't even talk to you for that much [laughs]," said Friar.

"We were working day and night, my wife and I, and just barely paying the bills," he said. "We had two small boys. And when I paid the band, a lot of the time I didn't get anything.

"The place was out in the country," said Friar. "Had a big dance floor, and with a band you'd have a good crowd. A lot of the customers came from Bowling Green, Ohio, from the college over there. . . . They'd come and sit, . . . and dance all night, but they didn't spend a lot of money.

"Then I found out that it might be ten years before [we could acquire] a liquor license, 'cause what you had to do in Ohio, . . . they went according to the population. I found out I wouldn't get no liquor license until the population out in Wood County . . . built up enough to permit it. . . . With just beer and wine, there's not that much profit. And then you had the entertainment tax, . . . We was working for nothing. So we got out of it, and I didn't play any music for thirty years. Just sat around the house and played," he said.

Friar sold the nightclub in 1962 and hired into a railroad company. He retired and moved to northern Georgia, where a local church became Friar's main venue for his singing, which he continued into his eighth decade.

Figure 19. Ford Nix, ca. 1966. Used by permission from Cranford Nix.

Chapter 19

AIN'T NO SIGN I WOULDN'T IF I COULD
Ford Nix

> I had my job back at Chrysler, . . . and I never really intended on going into music full time. I wished I had. You know how you do, you keep puttin' things off and first thing you know, it's over with.
>
> —CRANFORD "FORD" NIX[1]

A young man in dust-covered leather shoes slowly walked an empty highway shoulder headed north. The orange sun blazing over the western horizon shot shadows across the surrounding grassy hills as he carried a small grip of essentials and a battered banjo case. As a car approached from behind, he turned and signaled the driver with his thumb that he needed a ride. It rolled by him without slowing. A little further up the road, another car pulled over for the hitchhiker. He thanked the old man behind the wheel as he settled onto the seat of a late-model Studebaker.

"Where are we?" asked the hitchhiker, as the car pulled onto the road.

"About two miles south of the Ohio line," said the old man. "In Kentucky, of course. You been walking for very long?"

"All day—without a ride, until you come along."

"Well, I wouldn't blame the folks around here."

"Huh?"

"Everyone here figures you're as well off where you are, as where you're a-goin."

"There's truth in that," chuckled the musician. "That's a good 'un. I'm gonna remember it."

Blairsville, Georgia, is a village of nineteenth-century buildings situated smack dab in the middle of the Chattahoochee National Forest. Once known as Cherokee territory, Blairsville serves as the county seat in Union County, where American settlers first discovered gold in the nearby Blue Ridge Mountains more than two hundred years ago. Off Highway 180, Brasstown Bald, the state's tallest mountain at 4,784 feet above sea level, also has a Blairsville address. In November 1932, when Ford Nix was born, his hometown was somewhat isolated from the rest of the world, although the Carolinas and Tennessee were a hop, skip, and jump away, and the Alabama state line was just a few hours' drive.

Nix grew up among nine siblings—five boys and four girls. A few of his uncles played music. But it was Earl Scruggs picking banjo on stage with guitarist Lester Flatt at a show in West Virginia that inspired a teen-aged Nix. "I thought, 'I ain't never heard no music like that!' Even though they was on the *Grand Ole Opry*, we didn't even have a radio a lot of times, when I was a kid. But I got interested in it at that point and never did quit," he said. "Any kind of bluegrass music I could hear, it suited me just fine. But it was hard to hear on the radio at that time. There wasn't that many bands going. The Stanley Brothers was a good 'un but they was so far away. They were up in Bristol [Tennessee] and you couldn't hear 'em where I lived. Then Charlie Monroe, he was on WNOX [Knoxville, Tennessee]. He influenced me a lot."

Just a couple years later, Nix won a banjo contest in Birmingham, Alabama. Medicine show troubadour "Ramblin'" Tommy Scott offered Nix his first paying gig. "He was a guy that would sell herb medicine.... He made pretty good money at that because people thought they were going to be helped by taking it," said Nix. Scott's musicians would perform free shows to gather a crowd, then sell snake oil remedies.[2]

Nix and some friends formed a band called the Georgia Mountain Boys, but at age seventeen he followed the hillbilly highway to Detroit, where he found a job at Chrysler. "I came up here because all my buddies was leavin' down there to come up here for a job," he said.

BARN DANCE BANJO

In early 1952 the WJR *Big Barn Frolic* Saturday night barn dance premiered at the Dairy Workers Hall in Highland Park, Michigan. Casey Clark and His Lazy Ranch Boys served as the main music makers, until they left the show to start their own barn dance in December.

"I met Casey Clark, . . . and he gave me a job," said Nix. At first, Nix's style of music was unheard of in Detroit radio. Casey Clark, a Kentuckian from the eastern region of the commonwealth, recognized and appreciated the sound Nix brought to the show. Telling jokes also helped Nix step into the spotlight and become known as a solo act. A story about hitchhiking through Kentucky on his way to Detroit proved an evergreen crowd pleaser.

"Casey was a good man. I admired him a lot," said Nix. "He had a couple of people there known as the Davis Sisters, and I started playing around with them a little bit in their band. . . . I'd just go over to their house and help 'em pick. . . . And I used to know Roy Hall. He had a jamboree a-goin' up here at that same time." After Clark left the *Frolic*, Roy Hall and His Cohutta Mountain Boys played for several weeks. Nix found opportunities to appear at both barn dances.[3]

SOUNDS OF THE USAF

With the Korean War weighing on his mind, and the draft removing friends from circulation every day, Nix enlisted in the U.S. Air Force, reporting for duty January 1953. While stationed in Japan he operated radios, transmitting and receiving coded messages. Nix also joined a musical group. One of the members was an Arkansas man named Harold Jenkins, who later changed his name to Conway Twitty.

"We played service clubs, airmen's clubs," said Nix. "At that time, me and another boy from Virginia, we got together, and he knew Conway, so we went down and got him and we called ourselves the Pike County Boys. You know, just a bluegrass band. Conway played the guitar. He sang stuff like Johnnie and Jack, Louvin Brothers songs."

When his service ended, Nix landed in Southern California. He visited all the country music shows he could find. "Mac Wiseman was out there on the 'Town Hall Party,' and I met Mac. He told me to come back to Richmond, Virginia, and he'd give me a job," said Nix.

He returned to Michigan, checked in at Chrysler, and hopped a bus to Richmond, where Nix discovered "Mac had gotten a promotion from Dot Records and he . . . disbanded. But his band, we all got together and we played it on out for three or four months. We played the [WRVA] *Old Dominion Barn Dance*. I'd ride the bus down there on the weekends and play the show, then come back and work all week," he said.

After eleven years, the *Old Dominion Barn Dance* closed in 1957 and Nix turned his attention to Nashville. Through the next ten years, he appeared occasionally on the *Flatt and Scruggs TV Show*, and on the WSM *Ernest Tubb Midnight Jamboree*.[4]

DETROIT, PART TWO

Back in Detroit, Nix visited the city's nightclubs and jamborees regularly. "I'd go around and sit in with all of 'em. . . . [The musicians] really enjoyed me coming in, you know. It gave them a break," he said. In 1957 Nix met Ray Taylor, a singer and musician who worked at his aunt Lou's nightclub, Taylor's Bar, at Milwaukee Street and John R. "[Ray] had a boy named Eddie [Fraley]. . . . I played the banjo and we had a bass fiddle player named Hollis Hamm. . . . [I'd] pretty much get there on Friday night and play 'til Monday morning."

Taylor was born in Smithville, Tennessee, and grew up in Athens, Alabama, from the age of five. He learned to play guitar and fiddle, and performed on WJMW Athens at age sixteen. In 1956 he moved to Detroit, playing music in country bars. Eventually he operated his own nightclub in the city.[5]

NIX CLICKS

Nix tracked down John Henson, who ran Clix Records from his home in Troy, Michigan. "I met John 'cause my buddy I was playing with from Mac Wiseman's band, he knew John, and he told me about him hunting for talent," said Nix.[6] Henson purchased country and rock 'n' roll recordings made at local studios, but he also recorded bands in a large room at his house.

Nix brought Ray Taylor to Henson's attention, and Taylor and his band, the Alabama Pals, made three singles for the label. Taylor's first, with Nix on banjo, included "Kentucky Girl" and "Clocking My Card," which described the industrial lifestyle of many Detroiters.[7]

After Taylor's record had run its course (reportedly selling five thousand copies), Nix wrote "Ain't No Sign I Wouldn't If I Could," and "Nine Times Out Of Ten." "Those were the first two songs I had written," he said. "Only thing was, I don't think I was all that talented, like Conway Twitty." At the time, Twitty's rock 'n' roll wasn't much more sophisticated than Nix's down-home humor: *I ain't been runnin' around with the prettiest girl in town / But it ain't no sign I wouldn't if I could.*[8]

Local bluegrass singer and guitarist "Curly" Dan Holcomb and an unknown bass player participated in the session. "[The] guy playing the bass I had never seen. . . . He really played the bass like a hot band would," said Nix.

Nix borrowed Eddie Fraley's electric guitar and played it as he would pick a banjo, finger style. Curly Dan's percussive rhythm and the bass added a fitting bounce to Nix's humorous lyrics and the drone of the electric guitar. The resulting sound was remarkably full, with Henson achieving a slight echo from the room on Nix's vocals. "John had a nice house. . . . He had a big fireplace and cut them records there in the living room. . . . You could hear that fire in the record. I don't know if John ever noticed it or not," said Nix. "I bought five hundred records and I guess I sold about twenty-five [*laughs*]."

Henson issued the record in 1959. It represented the sound of electrified bluegrass, a peculiar genre that cropped up in Clix and Fortune records during the late 1950s. The hybridized sound helped bluegrass music gain a foothold in Detroit, with practitioners such as Nix, Curly Dan, Buster Turner, Rufus Shoffner, Ray Taylor, and Wendy Smith performing in Detroit nightclubs such as the All States, B-21, Yale, the Pullman, and Taylor's. Nix's record demonstrated how in Detroit bluegrass was open to interpretation before a nationwide folk music trend coincided with (or led to) a purification of bluegrass by defining it as a strictly acoustic genre. "See, what made me do it like that was, I had it set up to cut, but some of the boys didn't show up," said Nix. "I just played my own guitar. Everybody didn't know me then, so they weren't expecting a banjo to be on the record."

LEWIS LEADS

Around that time, Nix signed a contract with promoter Victor Lewis. Born in 1922 in Johnson City, Tennessee, Lewis left home at age twelve and settled in Detroit. By the mid-1950s Lewis promoted country music shows, bringing *Grand Ole Opry* talent to Ford Auditorium in Detroit and the Hazel Park Raceway. In 1958 Lewis sent Hank Williams' ex-wife Audrey and her Hank Williams Memorial Show on a nationwide tour. The next year he produced a multi-talent showcase called Country Music Hit Parade Jamboree in Michigan, where amateur singers competed for prizes.[9]

"He booked me out in Kansas and everywhere, on the weekends," said Nix. "I was lucky, because the people I worked for at Chrysler would give me a day off, where I didn't have to get right back the next day."

Among many artists Nix encouraged, singer Patti Lynn gained her first nightclub experience with him at Taylor's and the Pullman, located on Manchester Street, across from a Ford Motor Company facility in Highland Park. In 1960 Lynn and Nix joined Billy Martin's Rhythm Wranglers and spent six months performing on the *Michigan Jamboree* at WILX-TV Channel Ten Jackson, Michigan.

When Stonewall Jackson toured the Midwest in 1962, Nix worked in his band through Michigan, Indiana, and Ohio. Michigan bluegrass promoter

Fay McGinnis said, "Ford played every show with Stonewall. Stonewall said, 'Boy, that banjo fits so well in "Waterloo."'" [Nix] traveled some with Minnie Pearl. She wanted Ford to go to Nashville. . . . And Little Jimmy Dickens he traveled with, and George Morgan. . . . When they needed anybody, they'd call up here and Ford would take off from Chrysler, . . . and go with 'em."[10]

Nix met Wandell "Wendy" Smith, singing and playing mandolin at the All States bar, and they organized a quartet called the Windy Mountain Boys. "We stayed together about four or five years," said Nix. The band recorded a single for Fortune Records around 1963. "High, Wide And Handsome" backed with "John Henry" became one of the finest examples of Motor City bluegrass—driving, steady, and tight.

MOTOWN BLUEGRASS

During 1963 Nix entered the Motown Records studio on Grand Boulevard to pick his banjo for the Supremes. "(The Man With The) Rock And Roll Banjo Band" appeared as the B-side to the 1963 hit "A Breath Taking Guy." After leaving the air force, Nix enrolled at the RETS Electronics School in Detroit. "I had that GI Bill and I was taking up electronics. I thought I could do something with it, but it was too hard for me," he said. Motown founder Berry Gordy Jr. took some of the same courses, and he remembered Nix when the Supremes' producers were looking for someone to play banjo.

"I just done it to help 'em out," said Nix. "They had an old house, and they took out the kitchen floor, and they had a big, high ceiling; and they recorded it back in the basement, but they had all that room (above). They got some good sound, Motown did. I met Berry Gordy, and I got signed up on a contract with Motown Records. They never did do anything with me. At that time, they had a tough time selling hillbilly music."

After the Motown session, Nix formed a group called the Motown Mountain Boys and returned to Hitsville, U.S.A. (Motown Records headquarters) with Billy Gill and Carl Vanover.

"It was just a try-out session," said Gill.[11] "It was fun to do because, you know, they had a great sound there at Motown. 'Course, Ford didn't have anything worked up, really. Just went in there and played several instrumentals. . . . We knew the chorus to a song, so Carl and I just sang the chorus on it as a duet or a trio with Ford singing baritone. . . . You'd think because all [the producer] did was rock 'n' roll, he wouldn't know much about bluegrass, but he knew harmony, I'll tell you. . . . We had a black jazz bass player, and drummer. Them guys, even though they never played bluegrass, . . . they had their part, I'm telling you. We didn't have to show them nothin'.

"It was Ford's project," said Gill. "He made a deal with 'em, . . . about putting out a bluegrass album. . . . It wouldn't have been enough to make an album, . . . five songs or so. . . . You don't think about jazz people playing bluegrass, but I guess good jazz musicians can play anything."

"They paid me for the one [session] I cut," Nix said. "We done four or five songs. . . . They still could release it some day." The recordings remain in the vault of Motown Records.

ROVING PICKER

Nix worked *Grand Ole Opry* shows at Cobo Arena, besides regional tours with Patsy Cline, Ferlin Husky, and Billy Grammer. He joined Frankie Meadows at WKBD-TV Channel Fifty on a country variety show during the mid-1960s. While working with Meadows, Nix cut a single for the Glenn label based in Hammond, Indiana.

Nix's Glenn record included the traditional "Roving Gambler" retitled "Gambling Man" backed with "Five String Boogie," an instrumental. "Now, that 'Five String Boogie,' I wrote that song," said Nix. "I got the boogie woogie from everybody else, though.

"Billy [Gill] helped cut that, 'Five String Boogie.' He played the guitar and he's singing tenor on 'Gamblin' Man.' We cut that out at Sound Inc. [in New Haven]," he said. "They used to play that on WEXL [radio Royal Oak]." Like the Clix single, the Glenn record barely made it out of the Midwest. Unfortunately, the artist's name was misprinted "Ford Nick" on the labels.

In 1967, Nix won third place in a talent contest at Paul Wade's first annual Michigan Country Music Convention, held in Michigan's Irish Hills. The following year, Nix teamed with guitar and mandolin picker and singer Frank Buchanan to cut "Ford Nix and Frank Buchannan [*sic*] Sing And Play Folk Songs And Bluegrass." Released by Fortune, Roy McGinnis (husband of Fay) and his band the Sunnysiders helped Nix and Buchanan cut the album in two days. The driving performances made up the first long-playing album of bluegrass made in Detroit.[12]

Nix worked by day and picked by night through the next decade. He booked country shows with WEXL radio's Joe Patrick and Bobbie Williams in 1973, when the pioneering radio station celebrated fifty years.[13] During the 1970s and 1980s Nix appeared regularly with disk jockey Deano Day on his programs at Detroit's top country radio stations.

Nix retired from Chrysler in 1981. Detroit's *Country in the City News* reported, "Ford Nix is a well known name in the bluegrass field in not only Michigan, but also Nashville and around the country. He says he plans now to devote full time to the music business and try to become a regular on the *Grand Ole Opry*. Ford also owns a chicken farm down south that has been very prosperous for him over the years."[14]

In retirement, Nix continued performing at a wide variety of venues, from small jam sessions to country music jamborees, and bluegrass festivals, always finding acceptance for his down-home jokes and expert banjo picking. Ford Nix passed away October 14, 2012.

CURLY DAN & WILMA ANN
and the
DANVILLE Mt. BOYS Radio & Recording artist
BMI WRITERS

Figure 20. Curly Dan and Wilma Ann, 1965. Top row, from left: Wandell "Wendy" Smith, Sonny Nelson, and Charles Palmer. Used by permission from Ricky Dan Holcomb.

Chapter 20

YOU CAN HEAR THE OLD FOLKS SING
Curly Dan and Wilma Ann

> I'm from a family of twelve kids. We didn't even have a radio in the house
> when we were growing up. You talk about poor folks, we was that! . . . I al-
> ways said, if I ever get married, I'm gonna marry a man that played the guitar.
> And I did.
>
> —WILMA ANN HOLCOMB[1]

A Southeast Michigan legend tells that folks back home in Kentucky once
taught their kids a variation of the three R's: Readin', Ritin', and Route 23.
With a steady stream of workers headed north, U.S. Route 23 brought tra-
ditions and values of Southern people to Michigan's industrial cities during
the twentieth century. Curly Dan and Wilma Ann drove Route 23 north
from West Virginia to Hazel Park, Michigan, in 1952. From the late 1950s
through 1984, the duo remained a fixture of area bluegrass events.

Fame took the Holcombs by surprise in 1963, after the Happy Hearts
label issued their song "South On 23." Its success in the Midwest and parts
of the South turned heads in Nashville, Tennessee, where Curly Dan and
Wilma Ann recorded a second version for Starday Records subsidiary label Nashville. They also made a guest appearance on the WSM *Grand Ole
Opry*.

Curly Dan and Wilma Ann cut more than a dozen singles for Detroit labels such as Fortune, Clix, Happy Hearts, and Dearborn. During the 1960s
and 1970s, they cut three albums for Old Homestead Records.

SOUTH ON 23

Densile Holcomb, a.k.a. Curly Dan, was born in 1923, in Clay, West Virginia. Wilma Ann Lowers was born in Charleston, West Virginia, the following year. In 1936 at age thirteen, Curly played mandolin for country gospel trio Cap, Andy, and Flip at WCHS Charleston, West Virginia.[2]

The couple met in Maryland, where both had moved seeking work in 1941. They wed Christmas Eve 1942 and returned to West Virginia, where Curly worked in a coal mine for ten years. In 1952 they moved to Michigan. Curly took a job in a Chrysler factory, but after a couple of years he was laid off. "He knew he'd be off for a long time," said Wilma Ann, "and we had to bring our daughter up to Henry Ford Hospital. She had a serious illness. So he went to the school board." Curly accepted a job as a stationary engineer at Royal Oak public schools, which he kept through retirement.

They invited local musicians to their house for picking sessions, often meeting new talent such as mandolinist Bill Napier. When they found long-time collaborator Jim Maynard, "he was sitting in his backyard playing a banjo," said Wilma Ann, "and we stopped and met him."

Within a few years after moving to Michigan, Curly assembled the Danville Mountain Trio. "He never cared that much for a fiddle," said Wilma Ann. "We used a fiddle a lot at the festivals, just pickup guys, you know, that wanted to play. We had two fiddle players, good ones, in our time, and that was it." During the 1950s, the Danville Mountain Trio (Curly Dan, Napier, and Maynard) played mainly at the All States bar, at Michigan and Cass in Detroit. They also appeared as occasional guests at Casey Clark's barn dances.

In 1956 Curly Dan's first record, "Sleep, Darling" backed with "My Little Rose" (including Napier and Maynard), on Detroit's Fortune label, reintroduced American music uncompromising in its acoustic folk influences to Detroit's music scene.[3]

As Curly made the rounds of Detroit nightclubs, he sometimes jammed with local mandolin players such as Wandell "Wendy" Smith and Frank Wakefield, who lived in town for a couple of years.[4] "Curly played in the bars with Frank Wakefield," said Wilma Ann. "But I didn't play any with him.

[Wakefield] was always gonna come to our house and eat [*laughs*]. He never did come. Curly said that every time he'd go on stage he'd say, 'I'm gonna go home with Curly and eat!'"

Working all day and playing music at night started getting old for Curly, who missed spending time with his wife and family. Eventually he convinced his wife to pick up an instrument and join him on stage.

> I didn't want to leave the kids and get a babysitter just to go every time he wanted to go. He said, "If you don't start playing something, well, I'm gonna quit." . . . So I told him, "Well, if I play anything, I want to play a bass fiddle." I didn't think I'd ever get one. That was the reason I said it. And I came home from work and there she lay on the floor. I asked him, "Why'd you get an old cheap thing like this one for?" He said, "What do you mean cheap?" I said, "Look at them ole big strings on there!" I had never seen one, only a picture. And then I thought, "I'll do what I can with it."
>
> He said if I would get real serious, he said, "You'd be a real good bass player." He always said I didn't have a serious bone in my body. And I said, "If you have to be serious and not be able to have a good time, I don't want to play. I'm gonna play the best I can and have my fun." And I did.

In 1959 Curly Dan and the Danville Mountain Boys recorded for John Henson's Clix label in Troy. A line in Jimmy Martin's 1954 RCA-Victor record "I Pulled A Boo Boo" inspired Curly's "I Flubbed My Dub."

It was around that time when Wilma Ann began performing in public. She felt ready to join them at the Clix session, but her husband and Jim Maynard thought otherwise. "I told 'em I was gonna go," said Wilma Ann. "They said, 'Well, when you go, they're gonna put you over in a cardboard box.' And I said, 'I can stay at home and get in a cardboard box [*laughs*].'"

After Wilma Ann joined the act full-time, they gradually moved out of nightclubs, performing at jamborees and festivals. Local bluegrass booster (and Stanley Brothers fan club president) Fay McGinnis, whose husband Roy led the Sunnysiders, booked the act.

In 1963 LaVerne Wright, Happy Hearts Records owner, recorded Curly Dan and Wilma Ann at his house in Wayne, Michigan. He issued two singles. The first, "South On 23" (backed with "Original Ballad Of Jesse James"), grew so popular Wright sold out of it quickly and had to press more. They followed "South On 23" with "I Guess I'm Going Insane," a blues about a heartsick lover (backed with "Poor Little Farmer Boy"). Banjo player Ronnie Ewert joined them for the recordings, along with Billy Gill (guitar) and Charlie Tuttle (mandolin).[5]

Support from local radio stations such as WEXL Royal Oak and WYSI Ypsilanti helped establish "South On 23" as an evergreen in Michigan bluegrass circles. In the last verse of the song, Curly compared the road to heaven like a gold-paved Route 23. With lyrics about a nostalgic trip to visit family in West Virginia, "South On 23" caught the attention of a wider country music audience.

Their version for the Nashville label featured a dobro solo played by Wayne Honeycutt. Starday Records probably helped bring the act to the *Grand Ole Opry*, where they performed "South On 23" and the flipside of their Nashville single, "A Visit Back Home." "I was so nervous, there was no use to ask me nothing," said Wilma Ann.

They recorded "South On 23" four different times for as many labels.[6] The last version was cut as the title track of an album for Old Homestead Records in 1972.

NORTH ON 23

In 1965, the couple wrote "North On 23," a sequel to their bestseller, pressed by Fortune Records. They performed with *Opry* stars on shows in Detroit and the Midwest, as well as bluegrass festivals and programs booked by the United Service Organizations (USO). Around this time, Carmen Flatt, a second cousin of Lester, joined the group on banjo, and Wendy Smith played mandolin.

In 1967 Curly launched his own Danville label with a single by the Hall Brothers. The brothers, Buddy (five-string banjo, age twelve) and Jimmy (guitar, age eleven), cut Jimmy Dickens' "I'm Little But I'm Loud" and the Holcomb's "Poor Little Farmer Boy" with fiddle player Bobby Adkins.

Curly cut the Danville records in his garage, turning out professional-sounding recordings. He pressed a series of six singles, ten sides of which featured Curly Dan and Wilma Ann. Their Danville performances sounded unhurried and fresh, amounting to some of the finest of their career.

In 1968 Curly Dan and Wilma Ann crafted another jewel of a record with the traditional "Pretty Polly" backed with "Another Lonely Heart" for the Dearborn label. While the band played loud and soft for dramatic effect, Curly's straight vocal delivery contrasted well. The session included WYSI disk jockey Big Bill Evans on harmonica. For several months, Curly Dan and Wilma Ann performed with Evans at the radio station.[7]

The act played a series of shows produced by musician and comedian Ford Nix around 1970. Guitarist Kiester Duty worked with the band during the 1970s and 1980s. "He said he carried my bass for ten years in order to get in the band," said Wilma Ann, "and finally worked his way in. But he just went with us—I mean he wasn't classed as one of the band."

In 1976, Curly suffered a heart attack. "For a while there, he didn't play—not a long while. I think two months after he got out of the hospital, he was down there playing at the Lincoln High School," said Wilma Ann. Around 1984 the couple decided to retire.

> I had an aneurysm in the brain, and I was having a hard time. He had had that heart attack, and he wasn't the healthiest in the world. . . . He was put in the Bluegrass Hall Of Fame in Salt River.[8] . . . Then we quit and I'd say, "Well, why don't we go to the festivals?" And he'd say, "No, it's just like an alcoholic trying to quit drinking. If you go, they'll be hollering, 'Just go up and do one!'" He said, "I'm not gonna do it. I'm gonna stay away from it."

A disabling stroke afflicted Curly in 1992, and he died in 1999. "He sat for seven years and never drank a drop of nothing," said Wilma Ann. "He even wrote songs while he was sitting there. He put them all on a tape for his daughter. He couldn't hardly sing, you know, but she wouldn't take the world for it." After Curly's death, Wilma Ann's bass stood in a corner of her home untouched, until she passed away in 2008.

APPENDIX A

Related Music in Print

Some music described in this project may be found online at video sharing sites and posted as sound clips on independent music blogs. The following list of titles represents music recently available on compact disc.

Otto Gray and His Oklahoma Cowboys. *Early Cowboy Band*. British Archive of Country Music, 2005.
This disc features Chief Redbird's first recordings, when he performed as Chief Sanders.

York Brothers. *Long Time Gone*. Ace Records, 2006.
From sessions for King Records made in 1947 through 1950, this disc presents original releases mixed with previously unissued outtakes.

Skeets McDonald. *Don't Let The Stars Get In Your Eyes*. Bear Family Records, 1998.
Five disc box set includes McDonald's earliest recordings for the Fortune and Citation labels in Detroit.

Arizona Weston. *Early Country In Detroit*. Old Homestead Records, 2006.
Collection of Weston's commercial singles plus studio outtakes and demonstration recordings.

Eldon Baker and His Brown County Revelers. *When The Roses Bloom In Dixieland*. British Archive of Country Music, 2006.
This set of 1930s–1940s Midwest swing includes Bronson "Barefoot Brownie" Reynold's first recordings of "Lost John" and "Chokin The Reeds."

Gene Starr. *The Boy With The Golden Voice*. Old Homestead Records, 2006.
Starr's voice on WKNX Saginaw in 1947–48 is digitally restored from radio transcription disks, which also feature Casey Clark's Lazy Ranch Boys.

Various artists. *That'll Flat Git It, Vol. 27 (Sage & Sand)*. Bear Family Records, 2011.
This retrospective of rock 'n' roll on Sage and Sand Records includes the Lazy Ranch Boys, Evelyn Harlene, Joannie King, and Lonnie Barron.

Roy Hall. *Roy Rocks*. Bear Family Records, 2005.
A collection of Roy Hall's rock 'n' roll recordings, including sides made for Fortune
    Records.

Lonnie Barron / May Hawks. *A Memory Or Two*. Old Homestead Records, 2003.
Disc includes all eight of Barron's commercial recordings, plus commercial and previ-
    ously unissued demonstration records by May Hawks, many featuring the Treble-
    Aires.

Davis Sisters. *Memories*. Bear Family Records, 1993.
This double compact disc set includes radio transcriptions of Betty Jack and Skeeter
    Davis singing on the WJR *Big Barn Frolic* with Roy Hall, and the Treble-Aires.
    Also includes recordings made in Detroit studios, including Fortune Records.

Earl and Joyce Songer. *Earl & Joyce Songer*. Old Homestead Records, 2000.
Disc includes the Songers' commercial output, with recordings for Fortune, Coral, and
    Imperial labels.

Jimmy Work. *Making Believe*. Bear Family Records, 1993.
Besides compiling Work's major label recordings, this double compact disc set features
    Work's earliest cuts issued by the Trophy and Alben labels in Detroit.

Jack Scott. *The Way I Walk*. Bear Family Records, 1992.
Five compact disc box set compiles Scott's recordings from 1957 to 1977. A good por-
    tion feature Al Allen on guitar.

Jimmy Kirkland. *Cool Daddy*. Rollercoaster Records, 2007.
Disc compiles Kirkland's 1958 rock 'n' roll recordings, along with two tracks from Hugh
    Friar's Clix session, plus hillbilly swing by Kirkland's wife, Cecelia Boron, and
    Harry Perry's band.

APPENDIX B
Bibliography and List of Interviews

Bibliography

Books

Bjorn, Lars, and Jim Gallert. *Before Motown: A History of Jazz in Detroit, 1920–60.* Ann Arbor: University of Michigan, 2001.

Bogdanov, Vladimir, Chris Woodstra, and Stephen Thomas Erlewine. *All Music Guide to Country: The Definitive Guide to Country Music.* San Francisco: Backbeat, 2003.

Bond, Marilyn, and S. R. Boland. *The Birth of the Detroit Sound: 1940–1964.* Charleston, S. C.: Arcadia, 2002.

Carson, David. *Rockin' Down the Dial: The Detroit Sound of Radio (From Jack the Bellboy to the Big 8).* New York: Momentum Books LLC, 1999.

Chlouber, Carla. *The Oklahoma Cowboy Band.* Charleston, S.C.: Arcadia, 2008.

Davis, Skeeter. *Bus Fare to Kentucky, the Autobiography of Skeeter Davis.* Secaucus, N.J.: Carol Pub. Group, 1993.

Escott, Colin. *Roadkill on the Three-Chord Highway: Art and Trash in American Popular Music.* New York: Routledge, 2002.

Green, Douglas B. *Singing in the Saddle: The History of the Singing Cowboy.* Nashville: Country Music Foundation, 2002.

Gregory, James N. *The Southern Diaspora: How the Great Migrations of Black and White Southerners Transformed America.* New York: University of North Carolina, 2005.

Hawkins, Martin. *A Shot in the Dark: Making Records in Nashville, 1945–1955.* Nashville: Vanderbilt University Press and Country Music Foundation, 2006.

Kienzle, Rich. *Southwest Shuffle.* New York: Routledge, 2003.

Malone, Bill C. *Singing Cowboys and Musical Mountaineers: Southern Culture and the Roots of Country Music.* Athens: University of Georgia, 2003.

Russell, Tony. *Country Music Records: A Discography, 1921–1942.* New York: Oxford University Press and Country Music Foundation Inc., 2004.

Sparks, Jacob B. *Jacob's Well of Life: The Autobiography of Jacob B. Sparks.* Detroit: Self-published, 1948.

Tosches, Nick. *Unsung Heroes of Rock 'n' Roll.* New York: Harmony Books, 1991, revised edition.

Tribe, Ivan M. *Mountaineer Jamboree: Country Music in West Virginia.* New York: University Press of Kentucky, 1996.

Turner, Buster, and Stewart Collingswood. *Music in My Soul.* Jacksboro, Tenn.: Self-published, 1995.

Wolfe, Charles K. *Kentucky Country: Folk and Country Music of Kentucky.* New York: University Press of Kentucky, 1996.

Wolfe, Charles K., and James Edward Akenson. *Country Music Goes to War.* New York: University Press of Kentucky, 2005.

Vintage Periodicals

The Billboard. The Billboard Publishing Co. New York.

The Cash Box. Cash Box Magazine, Inc. New York.

Country and Western Jamboree. Maher Publications, Inc. Chicago.

Country & Western Jamboree. Country & Western Jamboree, Inc. Chicago.

Country Gentlemen. Maclean-Hunter Pub. Co. Ltd. Toronto.

Country in the City News. Country in the City Inc. Wayne, Mich.

Country Song Roundup. American Folk Publications, Inc. Derby, Conn.

Cowboy Songs. American Folk Publications, Inc. Derby, Conn.

The Detroit Free Press. Detroit.

The Detroit News. Detroit.

The Detroit Times. Detroit.

Folk and Country Songs. American Folk Publications, Inc. Derby, Conn.

Hoedown. Artist Publications, Inc. Cincinnati.

The Mountain Broadcast and Prairie Recorder. Rialto Music Publishing Corp. New York.

The Mountain Broadcast and Prairie Recorder (New Series). Mountain Broadcast Pub. Co., Inc. New York.

Music City News—Michigan Supplement. Music City News. Wayne, Mich.

The National Hillbilly News. Orville and Jenny Via. Huntington, W.Va.

Record Roundup. King Record Dist. Co. Cincinnati.

The Richmond Review. Richmond, Mich.

Rustic Rhythm. Rustic Rhythm, Inc. New York.

Song and Picture Barn Dance Magazine. Chicago.

Interviews

Keith Cady

Al Allen (Albert Punturi). Personal interview. 2003.

Al Allen. Personal interview. 2004.

Jim Baker. Telephone interview. April 22, 2003.

Don Beeler. Personal interview. August 2001.

Terry Bethel. Telephone interview. April 29, 2003.

Al Burnette. Telephone interview. June 22, 2000.

Sudie Mae Callaway. Telephone interview. August 2002.

Chuck Carroll. Telephone interview. April 24, 2000.

Marvin Cobb. Telephone interview. July 11, 2002.

Ralph Davis. Telephone interview. Aug. 12, 2003.

Jimmy Dickens. Personal interview. June 29, 2002.

Jimmy Dickens. Telephone interview. July 16, 2002.

Gene Edwards. Telephone interview. May 17, 2000.

Red Ellis. Telephone interview. April 1, 2002.

Buddy Emmons. Telephone interview. Jan. 26, 2007.

Lee Nolan Faulkner. Telephone interview. May 2, 2001.

Hubert Friar. Telephone interview. Jan. 24, 2001.

Billy Gill. Telephone interview. March 29, 2001.

Forrest Green. Telephone interview. Nov. 24, 2000.

Grace Hall. Telephone interview. Aug. 2, 2001.

May Hawks. Personal interview. June 29, 2001.

May Hawks. Telephone interview. July 6, 2006.

William Hayes. Telephone interview. July 15, 2001.

Donnell Hemminger. E-mail message. 1998.

Wilma Ann Holcomb. Telephone interview. June 28, 2001.

Eddie Jackson. Telephone interview. December 1999.

Okie Jones. Telephone interview. Nov. 8, 2000.

Jimmy Kirkland. Personal interview. Nov. 10, 2001.

Dave Larsh. Personal interview. 2002.

Roy Maxedon. Telephone interview. 2001.

Dick McCobb. Telephone interview. Feb. 1, 2007.

Gene McDowell. Telephone interview. April 12, 2000.

Fay McGinnis. Telephone interview. April 12, 2000.

Frances Mitchell. Telephone interview. May 28, 2003.

Ford Nix. Telephone interview. Jan. 23, 2002.

Chuck Oakes. Telephone interview. May 12, 2000.

Jimmy Odell. Telephone interview. 2000.

Bobby Osborne. Telephone interview. July 11, 2001.

Dusty Owens. Telephone interview. March 27, 2002.

Faye Griner Phillips. Telephone interview. July 2001.

Ray Price. Telephone interview. Oct. 8, 2002.

Buddy Ratcliff. Telephone interview. Nov. 7, 2003.

Chuck Rich. Telephone interview. Aug. 1, 2002.

Danny Richards. Telephone interview. April 11, 2000.
Danny Richards. Telephone interview. April 13, 2000.
Skeet Ring. Telephone interview. April 16, 2004.
Sandy Salyers. Telephone interview. May 16, 2000.
Jim Sauber. Personal interview. Aug. 22, 2003.
Leon Seiter. Telephone interview. March 12, 2005.
John Sykes. Personal interview. 2002.
Hank Thompson. Telephone interview. March 12, 2003.
Buster Turner. Telephone interview. May 21, 2001.
Tommy Venable. Telephone interview. June 1, 2001.
Frank Wakefield. Telephone interview. June 4, 2001.
Arizona Weston. Telephone interview. Nov. 19, 2003.
Bud White. Telephone interview. July 26, 2001.
Jimmy Lee Williams. Telephone interview. May 12, 2003.
Lawton Williams. Telephone interview. March 14, 2000.
Paul Williams. Telephone interview. May 2, 2001.
Paul Williams. Telephone interview. May 17, 2001.
Al Wilson. Telephone interview. March 29, 2002.
Jimmy Work. Telephone interview. Feb. 24, 2000.

Craig Maki

Al Allen (Albert Punturi). Telephone interview. Oct. 18, 2009.
Al Allen. Telephone interview. Oct. 27, 2009.
Linda Austin. E-mail interview. June 20, 2012.
James Barron. Telephone interview. July 11, 1995.
Jim Benson Jr. E-mail interview. Sept. 16, 2011.
Dorothy Cardis. Telephone interview. Aug. 31, 2006.
Casey Clark. Telephone interview. March 20, 1994.
Casey Clark. Personal interview. 1995.
Casey Clark. Radio broadcast interview with Dan Moran. April 22, 1995.
Casey Clark. Personal interview. 1997.
Trampas Ferguson. E-mail interview. March 6, 2007.
Hubert Friar. Telephone interview. Sept. 17, 2009.
Ernie Harwell. Personal interview. Nov. 10, 2008.
Trevon Hatfield. Telephone interview. June 1, 2006.
Robert James Hogg. Personal interview. June 2, 2005.
Robert James Hogg. Personal interview. August 26, 2012.
Virginia Hollar. Telephone interview. June 13, 2005.
Jeff Howell. Telephone interview. 2009.

Eddie Jackson. Telephone interview. May 30, 1995.
Eddie Jackson. Radio broadcast interview. July 19, 1998.
Eddie Jackson. Personal interviews, 1995–2001.
Joan King. E-mail interview. June 22, 2006.
Carolyn Linnington. Telephone interview. 2009.
Patti Lynn. Personal interview. Nov. 12, 1995.
Don Rader. Personal interview. 1994.
Don Rader. Personal interview. 1995.
Della Redbird. E-mail interviews. 2010–11.
Danny Richards. Personal interview. Jan. 29, 2006.
Danny Richards. Telephone interview. Dec. 8, 2006.
Danny Richards. Telephone interview. June 15, 2007.
Danny Richards. Telephone interview. Aug. 14, 2007.
Danny Richards. Telephone interview. Feb. 22, 2008.
Danny Riddle. E-mail interview. Sept. 11, 2007.
Laura Riddle. Telephone interview. 2009.
Speedy Rogers. Telephone interview. Nov. 7, 2005.
Mimia F. Singo, a.k.a. Joyce Songer. Telephone interview. Feb. 24, 2008.
Mimia F. Singo, a.k.a. Joyce Songer. E-mail interview. March 11, 2008.
Bill Sterling. E-mail interview. Sept. 21–22, 2005.
Arizona Weston and Margueritte Breeding (spouse). Personal interview. June 4, 2006.
Jimmy Work. Telephone interview. Oct. 13, 2011.
Jimmy Work. Telephone interview. July 25, 2012.

Craig Maki and Keith Cady

Al Allen (Albert Punturi). Personal interview. June 26, 2005.
Evelyn Atkins. Personal interview. Aug. 4, 2011.
Mary Clark. Personal interview. Sept. 17, 2000.
Jimmy Kirkland. Personal interview. March 31, 2001.
Tommy Odom. Personal interview. July 2, 2001.
Johnny Powers. Personal interview. February 2001.
Don Rader. Personal interview. Dec. 2, 2000.
Della Redbird. Personal interview. Nov. 4, 2009.
Danny Richards. Personal interview. June 26, 2005.
Hank Thompson. Personal interview. Nov. 2, 2002.
Arizona Weston. Personal interview. March 12, 2006.
Jimmy Williams. Personal interview. April 2003.

NOTES

Chapter 1

1. "Risque Records/30 Years of Double-Entendre Debate," *Billboard* (April 1, 1967. Vol. 79, No. 13), 69.

2. "Hamtramck Mama" was also issued with labels of black ink on red paper, which included the address of Universal Recording Studios.

3. "Turning Back the Clock—Ten Years Ago This Week (Chicago. May 25, 1940)," *Billboard* (June 3, 1950. Vol. 62, No. 22), 113. Harry Graham, head of Marquette Music in 1940, stated one of his firm's custom records caused a 15 percent improvement in gross sales. Judging by sales numbers of "Hamtramck Mama" reported in later years (300,000 in Detroit), we might conclude that was the record in question. No other record produced by Marquette Music is so easily identified. *Billboard* did not review records with double entendre or risqué lyrics, which probably accounts for the reporter not naming the record in his article.

4. Another address in the same vicinity, 519 Lenox Street, south of East Jefferson at Essex Avenue, was printed on labels for Universal 114, a jazz record featuring "She Won't Turn Over For Me" by Chick Fowler.

5. "Martin-McCoy Migrants Boom Hillbilly Talent in Detroit," *Billboard* (Dec. 4, 1943. Vol. 55, No. 49), 20.

6. James N. Gregory, *The Southern Diaspora: How the Great Migrations of Black and White Southerners Transformed America* (New York: University of North Carolina, 2005).

7. "American Folk Tunes," *Billboard* (Sept. 2, 1944. Vol. 56, No. 36), 62. "American Folk Tunes," *Billboard* (Sept. 20, 1947. Vol. 59, No. 37), 121.

8. Charles K. Wolfe, *Kentucky Country: Folk and Country Music of Kentucky* (New York: University Press of Kentucky, 1996).

9. Dennis Flannigan, "Texas Jim Lewis, The Man With The Hootnanny," http://www .seattlewesternswingmusicsociety.com/jimlewis.html (Accessed 2005). Texas Jim Lewis' parents and siblings moved from Florida to Detroit in 1931. Jim and his half-brother Jack entertained in blind pigs run by the Purple Gang in Detroit until 1932, when Jim moved to Texas. He returned in 1934.

10. "Coinmen Retailing Platters," *Billboard* (Jan. 19, 1946. Vol. 58, No. 3), 81. "Coinmen You Know," *Billboard* (Aug. 31, 1946. Vol. 58, No. 35), 120.

11. "Coinmen You Know," *Billboard* (March 22, 1947. Vol. 59, No. 12), 111.

12. "Coinmen You Know," *Billboard* (June 24, 1950. Vol. 62, No. 25), 171.

13. Joe Martin, "Dealer Doings," *Billboard* (May 22, 1954. Vol. 66, No. 21), 61. Detroit record collector Cappy Wortman visited the Mellow Music Shop around 1960. He confirmed the Mellow Records scene of the 1940s was long gone.

14. Jimmy Work interviewed by Craig Maki in 2012.

15. Bill Graham, "Notes from Nashville," *Record Roundup* (March 1948. Vol. 2, No. 2), 5.

16. Jacob B. Sparks, *Jacob's Well of Life: The Autobiography of Jacob B. Sparks* (Detroit: Self-published, 1948).

17. http://issuu.com/boxoffice/docs/boxoffice_122251/111 (Accessed 2009). The Hollywood Theater was a venerable vaudeville house. Earl and Joyce Songer and Slim Hagerman worked the weekend jamborees in 1951–52.

18. Justice "Cowboy" Colt was son of Brace Beemer, the voice of WXYZ radio's original Lone Ranger serials. For more information, see http://www.detroitkidshow.com/Justice_Colt.htm (Accessed 2011).

19. Jimmy Williams interviewed by Craig Maki and Keith Cady in 2003.

20. "Station Sets Golden Anniv. With Fair," *Billboard* (May 26, 1973. Vol. 85, No. 21), 46.

Chapter 2

1. Chief William A. Redbird quoted from a 1966 home tape recording.

2. Carla Chlouber, *The Oklahoma Cowboy Band* (Charleston, SC: Arcadia Pub., 2008), 42.

3. T. B. Neddles, Department of the Interior, *Commission to the Five Civilized Tribes* (Pryor Creek, Indian Territory, Sept. 11, 1900), File: Cher 2485. Interview with William D. Sanders. The commission denied Sanders' claim for citizenship in the Cherokee nation.

4. Della Redbird interviewed by Craig Maki and Keith Cady in 2009 and 2010. Modern science finds measuring blood degrees an antiquated method of determining a person's race.

5. Redbird 1966 home tape recording.

6. Chief Redbird went by the name Chief Sanders publicly when performing with the Oklahoma Cowboys.

7. Glenn Shirley, "Daddy of the Cowboy Bands," *Oklahoma Today* (Fall 1959. Vol. 9, No. 4), 6–7, 29.

8. Newspaper Enterprise Association Service, "Oklahoma Singing Cowboys Make Hit Over WGY." Clipping from unknown newspaper. Unknown date. Source: Redbird scrapbook.

9. Unattributed newspaper clipping from Redbird scrapbook. The scrapbook included an entry form to the 1931 Madison Square Garden rodeo. Chlouber's book features a photograph of the Oklahoma Cowboys made in 1933 in Michigan. These clues, along with the

reporter's reference to Redbird as Chief Sanders, may point to the WJBK job as something he and his friends took when the Oklahoma Cowboys were on hiatus.

10. When Redbird went solo, he wore a traditional Sioux headdress in his promotional photos.

11. Danny Richards interviewed by Keith Cady in 2000, and by Craig Maki in 2005.

12. "Guinan Maps New Label in Detroit," *Billboard* (Jan. 1, 1949. Vol. 61, No. 1), 39.

13. The first Shelby single included "When We Say Goodby In Algiers" (vocal trio led by Redbird) backed with "I Don't Mind" (vocal by Blackie Blackburn). The second included "Every Afternoon At Four" (vocal by Maria Cummings) backed with "They're Gonna Hang Old Pappy Tomorrow" (vocal by Chief Redbird). During World War II, Blackburn led a band called the Roving Cowboys on WCAR Pontiac.

14. Arizona Weston interviewed by Craig Maki in 2006.

15. BR5-49's arrangement of "Cherokee Boogie" followed closely that of Johnny Horton's 1959 recording for Columbia Records.

16. Gene Roe, "Sincerely, Couzin Gene," *National Hillbilly News* (November–December 1949. Vol. 5, No. 2), 16. Roe contributed news from Detroit to *Country Song Roundup* magazine during the early 1950s.

17. From March through December 1954, Girard and Dannon also performed on the WWJ-TV *Michigan Barn Dance* country music show.

18. Helen Fogel, "Old Cherokee Trouper Gets Whoops from Kids," *Detroit Free Press* (Dec. 1, 1975). Scrapbook clipping.

19. Jim Crutchfield, "Proud Indian Wants To See Chief Carter," *Detroit Free Press* (1978). Scrapbook clipping.

Chapter 3

1. Paul Wade, "What Ever Happened to Mountain Red?" *Music City News—Michigan Supplement* (October 1966. Vol. 1, No. 1), 1. Wade promoted country music in Michigan and operated a talent agency from the 1960s until his death in 1988.

2. Robert James Hogg interviewed by Craig Maki in June 2005.

3. Genealogy information obtained from Virginia Hollar, and from 1968 notes by Carl Breeding, posted by Glenn Hogg online at http://worldconnect.rootsweb.com/cgi-bin/igm.cgi?op=GET&db=gwh&id=I0862 (Accessed 2007).

4. Wade, op. cit., 1.

5. *Mountain Broadcast and Prairie Recorder* (November 1939. Vol. 1, No. 3), 2, 10.

6. Virginia Hollar (born Ferree) interviewed by Craig Maki in June 2005. Red and Skeets McDonald had each been married before. Red spent a few years in Detroit married to Juanita Howard. McDonald and Opal Clark of Pontiac had a son before they divorced.

7. *Music City News—Michigan Supplement* (January 1967. Vol. 2, No. 1), 5.

8. Jerry Yates, "Mt. Red Receives Award," *Music City News—Michigan Supplement* (October 1967. Vol. 1, No. 10), 1.

Chapter 4

1. Tommy Venable interviewed by Keith Cady in 2001.

2. *Hillbilly Stars Scrapbook of 1952* (Thurston Moore Enterprises, 1952). "Their mother and father were great musicians, and helped them along in their chosen careers."

3. Ivan M. Tribe, http://www.countryworks.com/artist_full.asp?KEY=YORK (Accessed 2009). Dorse R. Perry, "The York Bros," liner notes to York Brothers, *Early Favorites Vol. 1*, Old Homestead OHCS 324, 1987, phonograph album. Courtesy John Morris.

4. History of Hamtramck. http://www.hamtramck.us/History.htm (Accessed 2005). Paul R. Kavieff, "The crosstown mob wars of 1930–31," http://info.detnews.com/history/story/index.cfm?id=157&category=life (Accessed 2005).

5. "Risque Records / 30 Years of Double-Entendre Debate," *Billboard* (April 1, 1967. Vol. 79, No. 13), 69.

6. "Marquette Into New Showrooms For Open House," *Billboard* (March 16, 1946. Vol. 58, No. 11), 106.

7. "Hamtramck Mama" (Leslie York–George York), Trianon Publications (Fortune 120, 1949).

8. Les York's "Hamtramck Mama" riff is also prominent in "Gamblers Blues" and "Going To The Shindig."

9. Besides gigging with the York Brothers, Art Brooke played steel guitar with Chief Redbird's Western Aces during the 1940s. Taft "Rosebud" Blevins played fiddle and steel, and sang on stages with various hillbilly acts around Detroit.

10. "Market Reports—August Biz Good," *Billboard* (Sept. 12, 1942. Vol. 54, No. 36), 75.

11. "American Folk Records," *Billboard* (Dec. 26, 1942. Vol. 54, No. 52), 64.

12. "American Folk Tunes," *Billboard* (April 1, 1944. Vol. 56, No. 14), 72.

13. "The York Bros," *National Hillbilly News* (January 1947. Vol. 2, No. 6), 2, 3.

14. Hugh Friar interviewed by Keith Cady in 2001. Robert Russell "Chubby" Wise worked with Bill Monroe's Bluegrass Boys from 1942 to 1948, playing fiddle on Monroe's Columbia records. The York Brothers probably got to know Wise while working with Monroe during 1947.

15. Eddie Jackson interviewed by Craig Maki in 1995 and 2000.

16. "Folk Talent and Tunes," *Billboard* (Sept. 18, 1948. Vol. 60, No. 38), 34.

17. Bill Graham, "Notes from Nashville," *Record Roundup* (March 1948. Vol. 2, No. 2), 5.

18. Johnny Sippel, "Folk Talent and Tunes," *Billboard* (July 23, 1949. Vol. 61, No. 30), 31.

19. Fortune issued "Detroit Hula Girl" backed with "Going Home" at the same time as records by May Hawks and Boots Gilbert. All three acts performed on the WJR *Big Barn Frolic*. Danny Richards recalled the location of the York Brothers' apartments during a 2007 interview.

20. Chuck Oakes interviewed by Keith Cady in 2000.

21. George's wife, Valencia Dawson, wrote "River Of Tears." Leslie's wife, Roberta Yates, was often credited on York Brothers King releases, as was the team of "Dawson-Yates."

22. WJR radio transcription disc (June 24, 1953). On the night of June 8, a tornado tore

through the Beecher community near Flint, killing dozens of people and causing tremendous damage to properties. WJR raised money for the Red Feather Disaster Fund with an on-air campaign.

23. Mary Clark interviewed by Craig Maki and Keith Cady in 2000.

24. Danny Richards interviewed by Keith Cady in 2000. Richards stated Al Allen played electric guitar at the King sessions he attended, but Allen was sure he didn't go. Allen's trademark tremolo sound is absent from those recordings, so Richards may have been mistaken.

25. David Carson, *Rockin' Down the Dial: The Detroit Sound of Radio (From Jack the Bellboy to the Big 8)* (New York: Momentum Books LLC, 1999).

26. Various artists, *Straight Outta Boone County*, Bloodshot BS 019, 1997, compact disc. Detroit's Volebeats remade "Hamtramck Mama."

27. Paul Williams interviewed by Keith Cady in 2001.

Chapter 5

1. Arizona Weston, a.k.a. William Harvey Breeding, interviewed by Keith Cady in 2003, and with Craig Maki in 2006.

2. This was a year before Cowboy Copas moved to WNOX Knoxville and fronted the Gold Star Rangers. In 1943 he began singing at the WSM *Grand Ole Opry* with Pee Wee King's band. Copas' first hit record, "Filipino Baby," appeared on King Records in 1946.

3. For more about Skeets McDonald, see Charles K. Wolfe's profile in *Classic Country: Legends of Country Music* (New York: Routledge, 2000). Colin Escott included a feature on McDonald in his book *Roadkill on the Three-Chord Highway: Art and Trash in American Popular Music* (New York: Routledge, 2002). Also see Nick Tosches' story "Whom In The End The Tattooed Lady Slew" in his book *Unsung Heroes of Rock 'n' Roll* (Harmony Books, revised edition, 1991).

4. Harry Mack, Ford Motor Company executive and associate of the notorious Harry Bennett, headed the Dearborn sales branch before Henry Ford II forced him out of the company in 1945.

5. Oklahoma sang "Bessie Cut Your Toenails (You're Ripping My Bed Sheets)," which included farm animal calls by Tony Gray for comedic effect, backed with "Rosebud's Boogie," a guitar boogie where Rosebud Gailey demonstrated one of the slickest techniques ever heard.

6. *Mountain Broadcast and Prairie Recorder* (March 1945. New Series, No. 3), 30, 33.

7. *Country Music Review* (January 1964. Vol. 1, No. 5), 27. Arizona Weston appeared (unidentified) in a snapshot with Skeets McDonald and Bobby Sykes backstage at the *Grand Ole Opry*. The magazine ranked McDonald's "Call Me Mr. Brown" number four in its top fifty records of the month.

8. Conversation with Karen Cusumano and Craig Maki in 2007.

9. Singer Dottie Moore, born in Arkansas, lived in Flint. Her records attracted a significant following in the Midwest. Starday released a single and she appeared on Ralph

Emory's radio program at WSM Nashville. Plagued by diabetes, Moore grew blind at age thirty-four and died three years later.

10. Charlotte Harden, born in Arkansas, finished her schooling in Flint. She made records for a variety of labels during the late 1950s and 1960s.

11. Archie Grammer's Emcee record included Bobby Brandon's "The Beginning Of The End" backed with Billy Martin's "I Couldn't Believe."

12. Other local entertainers who recorded for Glenn included Frankie Meadows, Patti Lynn, Ford Nix, Jim Mitchell, and Earl Roach (from Windsor, Ontario).

13. Carter Stanley took ill in October and passed away in Bristol, Tennessee, December 1, 1966.

14. An avid baseball fan, Weston probably named his shop after Lakeland, Florida, the winter home of the Detroit Tigers.

15. In Nashville Weston also cut "Don't Walk Away" and "Your Birthday Waltz."

Chapter 6

1. Chuck Oakes interviewed by Keith Cady in 2000. Lou's Loan Office was a pawnshop located on East Jefferson Avenue.

2. William Hayes interviewed by Keith Cady in 2001.

3. Smilin' Ernie (Studly) and his wife, Shy Ann (a.k.a. Mary Studly) were featured in the pages of *National Hillbilly News* (September 1945. Vol. 1, No. 4), 7; (June 1946. Vol. 2, No. 6), 12. They called their act the Radio Rodeo Variety Show and performed at WDRO Augusta, Maine.

4. Johnny Sippel, "Folk Talent And Tunes," *Billboard* (June 9, 1951. Vol. 63, No. 23), 30. Jimmy Franklin's wife was Dimples Darlene. Chuck Hatfield, who played steel guitar, and Boots Gilbert, Hatfield's wife who played bass and performed comedy, worked together in Detroit from 1952 through 1958.

Chapter 7

1. Casey Clark interviewed by Dan Moran in 1995, WCBN *Down Home Show* in Ann Arbor, Michigan.

2. Cranford "Ford" Nix interviewed by Keith Cady in 2002.

3. Conversation between Casey Clark and Craig Maki in 1994.

4. Moran.

5. Jimmy Dickens interviewed by Keith Cady in 2002.

6. Mary Clark interviewed by Keith Cady and Craig Maki in 2000.

7. www.hillbilly-music.com/artists/story/index.php?id=14664 (Accessed 2009). After the Oklahoma Ramblers broke up, Steele and his wife worked John Lair's Renfro Valley tent shows and radio stations in West Virginia through the early 1950s.

8. *Mountain Broadcast and Prairie Recorder* (September 1940. Vol. 2, No. 1), 10–11. Bert Layne and Riley Puckett played for Gid Tanner's Skillet Lickers during the early 1930s.

9. Eddie Stubbs, "'Little' Jimmy Dickens," liner notes to "Little" Jimmy Dickens, *Country Boy*, Bear Family Records BCD 15848, 1998, compact disc.

10. Hugh Cross recorded with guitarist Riley Puckett and fiddler Clayton McMichen in 1927. During a session for Columbia Records, they made the first commercial recording of "Red River Valley."

11. Nat Green, "American Folk Tunes," *Billboard* (Oct. 21, 1944. Vol. 56, No. 43), 65.

12. Casey Clark said Smiley Burnette dedicated the song "It's My Lazy Day" to him. A song about taking a day off from any sort of exertion, Clark proudly sang it at personal appearances.

13. Tim Doolittle, who had performed on WJR since the 1920s, entertained with members of the Goodwill-Billies (such as Clark) Saturday mornings.

14. http://archive.lib.msu.edu/MMM/JT/04/b/JT04b010.pdf (Accessed 2009). "Goodwill Billies [*sic*] Will Be Attraction At Sheep Show," *The Manchester Enterprise* (Manchester, Mich. March 7, 1946. Vol. 79, No. 24), 1.

15. Arizona Weston interviewed by Craig Maki and Keith Cady in 2006.

16. Mary Jean Shurtz, "I've Been Listenin'," *Mountain Broadcast and Prairie Recorder* (October 1946. New Series, No. 10), 21.

17. "American Folk Tunes," *Billboard* (Oct. 12, 1946. Vol. 58, No. 41), 106.

18. Stubbs, op. cit., 8.

19. Richard H. Keeler, "News From Old New England," *Mountain Broadcast and Prairie Recorder* (June 1946. New Series, No. 8), 26.

20. Luke Byron "Buddy" Ratcliff interviewed by Keith Cady in 2003.

21. Evelyn Harlene (Clark) Atkins interviewed by Craig Maki and Keith Cady in 2011.

22. Trampas Ferguson, e-mail message to Craig Maki, March 6, 2007. Buddy Starcher, "Here and There," *Mountain Broadcast and Prairie Recorder* (December 1944. New Series, No. 2), 20.

23. May Hawks interviewed by Keith Cady in 2001 and 2006.

24. Jim Sauber interviewed by Keith Cady in 2003. "Jackson prison" refers to the State Prison of Southern Michigan, located near Jackson. The name Jimmie Dawn appeared next to Casey Clark's and Coy Crank's on the record label.

25. "Uncle Don" Andrews (Andrew D. Lynar, 1924–2001) left WKNX in May 1950 for WSGW. He worked in Saginaw radio until retiring to Florida in 1982. Bob Shaffer was featured in "Your Good Neighbor—Bob Shaffer." *Country Song Roundup* (June 1950. Vol. 1, No. 6.), 23. In 1949 Bob Maxwell left WKNX for WWJ radio Detroit.

26. The Centralia radio station was probably WCNT, which opened in 1946. Clark and his family lived there from February to March 1949.

27. http://www.ihesm.com/Loudermilk1.html (Accessed 2010). A photograph on this website shows Joe Tanner wearing the same cowboy shirt he wore in the band photo for Clark's book of sacred songs.

28. "Folk Talent and Tunes," *Billboard* (Sept. 22, 1951. Vol. 63, No. 38), 36. "Red Kirk, who was at WSM Nashville, returned to WIMA Lima, O., where he is working with Barefoot Brownie Reynolds, Casey Clark and Bob Pauly. Kirk is also working a d.j. show there."

29. Chuck Carroll interviewed by Keith Cady in 2000.

30. Chuck Oakes interviewed by Keith Cady in 2000.

31. In 1948, Rusty McDonald toured with Tex Ritter in a band that included Spud Goodale, Boots Gilbert, and Tommy Durden.

32. http://www.hillbilly-music.com/artists/story/index.php?id=12568 (Accessed 2010).

33. Skeeter Davis, *Bus Fare to Kentucky: The Autobiography of Skeeter Davis* (Secaucus, N.J.: Carol Pub. Group, 1993).

34. "Radio-TV Show Charts / Top 5 Radio Shows Each Day of the Week in Detroit," *Billboard* (August 16, 1952. Vol. 64, No. 33), 10.

35. Don Rader interviewed by Craig Maki and Keith Cady in 2000.

36. Betty Glynn, "The Oahu Publishing Co.—Harry Stanley," *Aloha International Steel Guitar Club Newsletter* (April/May/June 1989), 11. Oahu Publishing operated in Cleveland until 1968, when Harry Stanley moved to Sun City, Arizona. After Stanley's death in 1970, Oahu Publishing stayed in business until 1985.

37. Russ Waters played steel on several recordings by Max Henderson and his band (which included Charlie Flannery on fiddle) for the Serenade label around 1952. Waters purchased the Flint Honolulu Conservatory in 1956. When he died in 1962, he had taught music for twenty-seven years.

38. Jim Baker interviewed by Keith Cady in 2003.

39. "Charlie and Honey featured at WCHS," *National Hillbilly News* (April 1946. Vol. 2, No. 4), 24.

40. "Radio-TV Show Charts / Top 5 Radio Shows Each Day of the Week in Detroit," *Billboard* (June 20, 1953. Vol. 65, No. 25), 8.

41. Sudie Mae (Callaway) Baker interviewed by Keith Cady in 2002.

42. Buddy Emmons interviewed by Keith Cady in 2007.

43. Bobby Osborne interviewed by Keith Cady in 2001.

44. Jimmy Work interviewed by Keith Cady in 2000.

45. "Butcher Paper List," http://www.standelamps.com/about_us/story/story_p06 .html (Accessed 2011).

46. Dick McCobb interviewed by Keith Cady in 2007.

47. E-mail written by Hemminger in 1998, forwarded to Keith Cady by Harold Skidmore of Lindsey, Ohio, in 2001.

48. "On The Trail," *Country & Western Jamboree* (July 1955), 35.

49. Terry Bethel interviewed by Keith Cady in 2003.

50. "Five Favorites," *Cowboy Songs* (December 1956. No. 49), 20.

51. Okie (a.k.a. Oakie) Jones interviewed by Keith Cady in 2000.

52. Jimmy Murrah worked in Detroit with Eddie Jackson's band for a few years. Murrah moved to Lansing during the 1960s and eventually retired to Florida.

53. Bill Sachs, "Folk Talent and Tunes," *Billboard* (March 3, 1956. Vol. 68, No. 9), 72.

54. Bill Sachs, "Folk Talent and Tunes," *Billboard* (March 10, 1956. Vol. 68, No. 10), 60.

55. Lonnie Barron, "Lonnie's Country Corner," *Richmond Review* (April 5, 1956), 2.

56. Lonnie Barron, "Lonnie's Country Corner," *Richmond Review* (May 3, 1956), 2. Bar-

ron wrote, "I told you we'd cut a new record to be released about May 1. Well, we had to recut it. We worked on it Sunday and Monday. Now it will probably be another two or three weeks before it's released."

57. Kay Starr had a pop hit with Pee Wee King's "Bonaparte's Retreat" in 1950. Her 1950 duet with Capitol Records label-mate "Tennessee" Ernie Ford, "I'll Never Be Free," also reached the top of pop and country charts.

58. *Country and Western Jamboree* (March 1956). Released in early 1958, Roy Moss' Fascination record included "Yes, Juanita's Mine" backed with "Wiggle Walkin' Baby."

59. Effie Burrus, "Personable Joannie King Visits Teen Life Editor," *Teen Life* (Jan. 6, 1958. Vol. 3, No. 1), 5. Joannie King's Sage single included "History" backed with "OK Doll."

60. Paul Williams interviewed by Keith Cady in 2001. The nightclub in Pontiac was probably Spattafiore's.

61. "WNAX Missouri Valley Barn Dance," http://www.hillbilly-music.com/programs/story/index.php?prog=540 (Accessed 2011).

62. "Country Round Up," *Cash Box* (Oct. 4, 1958), 51. *Broadcasting* (Oct. 27, 1958. No. 53), 2. WNAX radio full-page advertisement.

63. "Country Round Up," *Cash Box* (Aug. 23, 1958), 49.

64. Evelyn Harlene didn't work in nightclubs until after the family moved to Ohio.

65. Willie G. Moseley, "Jody Payne—'Family' member for a quarter-century," *Vintage Guitar* (February 2000). Casey Clark introduced Willie Nelson to Jody Payne around 1963, when Nelson played bass for Ray Price at a show arranged by Clark in Detroit.

66. Johnny Paycheck recorded Bill Merritt's "It Won't Be Long (And I'll Be Hating You)" in 1968.

67. Gary McMullen interviewed by Craig Maki in 2011. Fred Flowerday, Sr. worked as sound effects engineer at WXYZ radio on 1930s and 1940s productions of the *Lone Ranger*, *Green Hornet*, and *Sergeant Preston of the Yukon*. Flowerday first launched Special Recordings downtown.

68. *Country in the City News* east side reporter Tom Tesnow started the monthly *Magazine of Country Music* after Atkins ceased publishing CCN.

Chapter 8

1. Bud White interviewed by Keith Cady in 2001.

2. Martin Hawkins, liner notes to Roy Hall, *Roy Rocks*, Bear Family BCD16747AR, 2005, compact disc.

3. Grace Hall interviewed by Keith Cady in 2001. "He could hear something on the radio for the first time and play it," she said.

4. Nick Tosches, "See, We Was All Drunk," *Unsung Heroes of Rock 'n' Roll* (New York: Harmony Books, 1991, revised edition), 109–13. Greg Paulus, *Rock-A-Billy, Or Else!* liner notes to Barrelhouse BH-016, 1981, phonograph album. In Hawkins' notes to BCD16747AR, the only black musician Hall mentioned to him was Piano Red, but only as an artist whose records he admired.

5. In his notes to BCD16747AR, Hawkins quoted Hall from 1974 and 1975 interviews in which Hall stated he played piano for Uncle Dave Macon when he was eleven years old. Macon (1870–1952) was a banjo picker and entertainer from middle Tennessee who had been with the WSM *Grand Ole Opry* since the 1920s.

6. *Mountain Broadcast and Prairie Recorder* (December 1941. Vol. 2, No. 7), 2. A letter to the magazine from Don Parsons described himself as a guitarist and emcee of the group. He also listed the band's personnel: Duke Caldwell (vocalist, guitar, bass), Bud (published as "Budd") White (fiddle), Geeter Coker (mandolin), Billie Ross (steel guitar), and Howard Ross (comedian).

7. Certainly there was live country-western music in Detroit before World War II, though not as widespread as it grew after war's end.

8. *Country Song Roundup* (March/April 1954. No. 30), 26.

9. While working at the Park View Inn (on West Vernor, near Clark Park), Arlee Barber (singer, rhythm guitar), Tommy Odom, and Frankie Brumbalough earned a mention by Gene Roe in his column for the *National Hillbilly News* (July–August 1949. Vol. 4, No. 6), 20.

10. Bud White said Brumbalough and Odom initially worked with the Roy Hall band for "about two or three weeks." Labels on their Fortune 78-rpm records listed musicians on recordings. Bandleader Jack Luker played rhythm guitar on some sides, while Arlee Barber and Bud White played rhythm guitar on others.

11. Frankie Brumbalough sang lead on most Cohutta Mountain Boys records. Bud White wrote and sang "We Never Get Too Old To Cry" and "My Freckle Face Gal."

12. "Dirty Boogie" (Roy Hall), Trianon Publications (Fortune 126, 1949).

13. William Hayes interviewed by Keith Cady in 2001.

14. Hawkins. Bullet was an independent label opened in Nashville in 1945.

15. The discography in BCD16747AR lists Tommy Odom as guitarist at the Bullet session, but the guitar solos sound like Hal Clark, who played a less sophisticated style than Odom. White said Odom was drunk during most of their trip to Nashville, which may explain his absence from most of the session.

16. Johnny Sippel, "Folk Talent & Tunes," *Billboard* (May 27, 1950. Vol. 62, No. 21), 33.

17. "Our Album of Country Song Folk," *Country Song Roundup* (February 1951. No. 10), 11.

18. Johnnie White, Benny Walker, and Skeets McDonald also recorded the tune for Citation.

19. Vic Cardis and the Westernaires (the Gilbert sisters, Boots and Dee) played at Caravan Gardens in winter 1949–50.

20. Other country artists who recorded for Citation included Bob Quinn and Jack Luker (Luker's sides featured Roy Hall on piano). Bud White said Lou Parker died during the mid-1950s.

21. Conversation with Al Allen and his wife Kathleen, a niece of Ezra Cline of the Lonesome Pine Fiddlers, and Craig Maki, November 6, 2011.

22. Davis Sisters, *Memories*, Bear Family BCD15722BH, 1993, compact disc. On the

double compact disc set, four tracks featured the Davis Sisters with Roy Hall's band, from live performances at the WJR *Big Barn Frolic*. Discography compilers made some educated guesses at the personnel by including members of the Lonesome Pine Fiddlers. Bud White said he played on the show. Before the fiddle solo during the Davis Sisters' performance of "Jambalaya," Hall exclaimed, "That's Rusty boy!" referring to Myrl "Rusty" McDonald.

23. Jim Benson Jr., e-mail to Craig Maki, September 16, 2011. Jim Benson and the Rhythm Ramblers (his brother Leon, guitar; Johnny Burnell, fiddle; and Cliff Southers, steel) drove to Detroit to cut their record at Fortune. Jack and Dorothy Brown had invited Hall to record with the Davis Sisters that day, and, at the Browns' suggestion, Hall performed with the Rhythm Ramblers. Jim Benson, Cliff Southers, and Hall backed the Davis Sisters on "Jealous Love."

24. *Country Song Roundup* (March–April 1954. No. 30), 26. http://www.hillbilly-music.com/artists/story/index.php?id=12568 (Accessed 2010). Detroit C&W vocalist Mary Ann Johnson was a member of the tour. Montana Frank was a sharpshooter, and skilled with a whip. California Joe led Pinto and El Toro through tricks on stage.

25. Interviews with Don Rader by Craig Maki in 1995, and with Keith Cady and Craig Maki in 2000. Christine's last name is unknown, as are her whereabouts.

26. Hank Crawford later directed Ray Charles' band.

27. Tosches.

28. Interview with Billy Gill by Keith Cady in 2001.

29. Jack Brown published song credits to Chuck Berry's "Little Queenie" to Dorothy Brown and Andre Williams. Williams made rhythm and blues records on Fortune during the 1950s, and the vocal sounded a little like him, but probably wasn't. If guitarist Armand Hernandez worked with Hall in Detroit, then the recording probably featured him playing lead guitar and singing the song.

30. "Rockabilly Tunesmith Roy Hall, 61, Buried," *The Tennessean* (March 6, 1984), 5-D. Source: Grace Hall scrapbook.

Chapter 9

1. May Hawks interviewed by Keith Cady in 2001 and 2006.

2. "Uncle Don" Andrews worked as a country disk jockey spinning records in the Saginaw Valley at WKNX and WSGW radio stations.

3. "The History of Martha White," http://www.marthawhite.com/heritage/mwhistory.asp (Accessed 2006).

4. Jimmy Dickens interviewed by Keith Cady in 2002.

5. Milton Estes arrived at WSM and the *Grand Ole Opry* as a member of Pee Wee King's Golden West Cowboys in 1937. He worked the *Opry* with his band after the war, until 1953 when Estes entertained in Detroit nightclubs and as emcee of the *Motor City Jamboree*, a barn dance broadcast Saturday nights on WXYZ radio from the Madison Ballroom.

6. Skeeter Davis, *Bus Fare to Kentucky: The Autobiography of Skeeter Davis* (Secaucus,

N.J.: Carol Pub. Group, 1993), 130. "High harmony" was Skeeter Davis' term for her style of singing.

7. Gene Roe, "News From the Four Corners," *Country Song Roundup* (January 1954. No. 28), 24. Roe noted Hawks' recording of "Jealous Love" and referred to her as "the former Miss Martha White." Roe covered the Great Lakes region in CSR 1953–54. Originally from McVeigh, Kentucky, he lived in Melvindale, a suburb of Detroit.

8. Gene Roe, "News From the Four Corners," *Country Song Roundup* (June 1954. No. 32), 26. "May Hawks and Casey Clark are gaining recognition as record spinners on Detroit's WJR."

9. "Women In the News," *Cowboy Songs* (September–October 1954. No. 37), 18.

10. Bill Sachs, "American Folk Tunes," *Billboard* (January 29, 1955. Vol. 67, No. 5), 50. Al Allen said he played lead guitar; Don Tanisson, steel guitar; Boots Gilbert, bass; and Bob Sykes rhythm guitar at Hawks' Label "X" session. Gilbert and Sykes sang the background vocals on the flipside, "Pastime Girl."

11. In 1951–52, the Spellbinders hosted a show on WJR. In 1954 the group signed with the William Morris talent agency. They sang on Patti Page's television show as the "Page Five" in 1955.

Chapter 10

1. William Hayes interviewed by Keith Cady in 2001.

2. Al Allen interviewed by Keith Cady and Craig Maki in 2005.

3. Danny Richards interviewed by Keith Cady in 2000.

4. "From Music to Marines / Beat of Drum Replaces Rhythm of Guitar," *The Flint Journal* (1952). Clipping source: Hatfield family scrapbook.

5. On February 8, 1938, Chuck Hatfield received a certificate from the Flint Honolulu Conservatory of Music, marking completion of studies on the "Hawaiian guitar." Source: Hatfield family scrapbook.

6. Robert James "Dusty Owens" Kucharski interviewed by Keith Cady in 2002. Dusty Owens, "It's Me Again—An Autobiography," http://www.hillbilly-music.com/artists/ story/ index.php?id=11598 (Accessed 2009).

7. In 2008 steel guitarist Bob Anderson, who was stationed at Ford Madison in 1949 with the U.S. Army, said Manning joined his group on stage and sang "I'm A Fool To Care." *Song and Picture Barn Dance Magazine* (No. 5, 1948). "On The Cover / Bob Manning / America's Smilin' Cowboy," *National Hillbilly News* (September–October 1947. Vol. 3, No. 1), 2. "Bob Manning," *National Hillbilly News* (November–December 1948. Vol. 4, No. 2), 31. Hank Ray Harwood, "Lloyd Reading—'Bakersfield sound originator,'" http://www .bakotopia.com/home/ ViewPost/67295 (Accessed 2008). Manning was on the radio in Bakersfield during the mid-1950s at KPMC.

8. Jim Beck produced recordings with a studio he built himself.

9. During the 1940s steel guitarist Jerry Byrd worked at John Lair's Renfro Valley, with the Goodwill-Billies on WJR Detroit, with Red Foley on the WSM *Grand Ole Opry*, and

the WLW *Midwestern Hayride* in Cincinnati, Ohio. While in Cincinnati, Byrd recorded with stars such as Cowboy Copas, Hawkshaw Hawkins, Hank Williams, the York Brothers, and Grandpa Jones.

10. Hank Thompson interviewed by Keith Cady in 2003.

11. "Bob Manning," *National Hillbilly News* (November–December 1949. Vol. 5, No. 2), 8, 10. Manning died in 1993 in California.

12. Sons of Texas flier. Source: Hatfield family scrapbook.

13. Hank Thompson and Tennessee Ernie Ford both recorded for Capitol Records.

14. Johnny Sippel, "Folk Talent and Tunes," *Billboard* (June 3, 1950. Vol. 62, No. 22), 33.

15. Eddie Jackson interviewed by Craig Maki in 1997. Hank Thompson interviewed by Keith Cady and Craig Maki in 2002.

16. Johnny Sippel, "Folk Talent and Tunes," *Billboard* (November 18, 1950. Vol. 62, No. 46), 29.

17. Trevon Hatfield interviewed by Craig Maki in 2006.

18. Dorothy Cardis interviewed by Craig Maki in 2006.

19. Charles K. Wolfe and James Edward Akenson, *Country Music Goes To War* (New York: University Press of Kentucky, 2005), 68.

20. Bill and Kathy Jameson, "Tommy Durden / Legend Within a Legend," *Goldmine* (March 1, 1985. Vol. II, Issue 5, No. 120), 26.

21. "American Folk Tunes," *Billboard* (May 1, 1948. Vol. 60, No. 18), 119.

22. Jameson.

23. Richard L. Cole, "Humor Earthy, Or Humor Mild," *The Washington Post* (July 23, 1948), 22.

24. Various artists, *Guys of the Big 'D' Jamboree*, Dragon Street Records DCD 70102, 2002, compact disc. Vic Cardis appeared in a photograph with Lefty Frizzell, taken in 1950 at the Jim Beck Studio in Dallas. Frizzell cut "Always In Love" and "Steppin' Out" with the musicians in the photo.

25. Kevin Coffey, "Biography of Skeeter Elkin," http://www.texasplayboys.net/Biographies/skeeter.htm (Accessed 2009). Elkin "spent some time playing in drummer Hal Black's jazz band at the Top of the Hill Club at Grantham Lake at Shreveport, a group that featured jazz saxophone veteran Pud Brown and Black's vocalist wife Penny, who with Black and her sisters (who were then married to steel guitarist Tommy Durden and fiddler Vic Cardis, respectively) had earlier toured with Tex Ritter (Black would also later work as drummer with Houston Western Swing bandleader Benny Leaders)."

26. Bud White interviewed by Keith Cady in 2001.

27. The Four Star record included "That's Where You Dropped Your Candy" (vocal duet with Boots Gilbert and Tommy Durden) backed with "There's A Lock Upon Your Heart." The Freedom record featured "Hula Boogie" (on which Boots Gilbert played mandolin) backed with "Crossroads."

28. These Westernaires were not associated with Don "Sonny Boy" Sexton's Musical Westernaires of Flint, who were active from the 1940s through the 1970s.

29. Unattributed clipping from unknown (Minnesota) newspaper. Unknown date, al-

though a description of the Westernaires playing "How High The Moon," a 1951 hit by Les Paul and Mary Ford, may provide a clue to the year. Source: Hatfield family scrapbook.

30. Arizona Weston interviewed by Keith Cady and Craig Maki in 2006.

31. Margueritte Breeding interviewed by Craig Maki in 2007.

32. Roy Hall backed the Davis Sisters on their first record for Fortune, "Jealous Love," around December 1952. Contrary to copy printed on the labels of "Sorrow And Pain" and "Kaw-Liga," which stated Roy Hall provided the music, the Treble-Aires played on both numbers. Songwriter Dorothy Brown owned Fortune Records with her husband Jack.

33. "Radio-TV Show Charts / Top 5 Radio Shows Each Day of the Week in Detroit," *Billboard* (June 20, 1953. Vol. 65, No. 25), 10.

34. Al Allen interviewed by Keith Cady and Craig Maki, November 6, 2011.

35. Joel Friedman, "Folk Talent and Tunes," *Billboard* (February 13, 1954. Vol. 66, No. 7), 57. "Johnny Maddox currently appearing at the Roosevelt Lounge, Detroit."

36. Bill Sachs, "Folk Talent and Tunes," *Billboard* (September 25, 1954. Vol. 66, No. 39), 57.

37. Wink Gilbert and Hal Black started careers in television production during the 1950s, from which they retired decades later.

Chapter 11

1. James Edward "Eddie" Jackson interviewed by Craig Maki in 1995 and 1996.

2. During the 1940s and 1950s, Bill Callihan played Hawaiian steel guitar and made recordings at his home in Detroit. During the 1950s he lived in a basement apartment at 700 Delaware, north of Grand Boulevard.

3. In 1942 Eveline Haire and Her Swingtime Cowgirls cut four sides for the Mellow and Hot Wax labels of Detroit. Jackson did not participate in the recordings.

4. The *Mount Clemens Daily Monitor-Leader* newspaper owned and operated radio station WMLN. It broadcast at 106.3 FM from May 1, 1947, through early 1954.

5. Clogging, a dance associated with bluegrass and mountain music, was also common at country music bars in Detroit.

6. Red Foley cut "Chattanoogie Shoe Shine Boy" on November 8, 1949, at Castle Studio in the Hotel Tulane. Doyle "Ricky" Riddle (1920–88) recorded for the Tennessee label, Coral, M-G-M, Decca, Rio Grande, and Dixie. After living in Michigan, Tennessee, and Arizona, Riddle settled in Detroit during the 1970s. Around 1980 a thief hit him in the head outside a Detroit bar, and Riddle spent the rest of his life in a nursing home.

7. Following his return from the navy, Jackson courted a nurse and married her. They had two children before divorcing.

8. A tape of vintage recordings that steel guitarist Dwight Harris assembled for Jackson included several 1951 performances of Harris, Jackson, and Bob Norton together at

the Roxy bar. Norton took masterful bass solos, joked, and sang with Eddie. The trio performed western songs, a polka, and instrumentals.

9. Three Brass Rail restaurants operated in Detroit; the downtown location featured burlesque shows. Bass player Jimmy Franklin sang his "You Are The One" on the flipside of "Rock And Roll Baby."

10. Prior to working with Eddie Jackson, Herb Ivey fronted his own group in Detroit. Jackson discovered Jimmy Knuckles playing piano in a dive on Third Street. "He was from Kentucky and always drinking. I had to drive him everywhere," said Jackson. "We put him to good use in the band, though, and Jim worked with me for nineteen years. . . . When we recorded for Shelby, they had sheet music for us. Jim was the only guy in the band who could read music, so he wrote lead sheets for the rest of us with the names of chords marked on the beat."

11. Bobby Sykes and Jackson grew up together in the same Detroit neighborhood (near New Center). "Bobby and [guitarist] Jeff Durham used to work shows on the same circuit as I did during the forties. Bobby's favorite singer was Red Foley, and you can tell by listening to his records," said Jackson.

12. Danny Richards interviewed by Keith Cady in 2000.

13. Jackson wrote "Blues I Can't Hide" for Patti Lynn, but he cut it first. In 1964 his band helped Lynn cut her version. Lynn's single, retitled "Same Old Blues," was issued on Fortune subsidiary label Hi-Q. Interesting to note: Detroit rhythm and blues singer Hank Ballard cut "I'm Learning" for King Records in January 1962.

14. The original Harmony House record shop located on John R. at I-75 in Hazel Park closed in 2003.

15. Jackson said Special Recordings was on Duffield, near Woodward, downtown (138 Duffield).

16. Norm Childs, "Jean Shepard brightens 'Blue Monday,'" *Music City News—Michigan Supplement* (Nov. 1966. Vol. 1, No. 2), 4.

17. Everett "Swanee" Caldwell performed country music in the Detroit area for fifty years. To escape working in coal mines, he left his hometown of Logan, West Virginia, and moved to Detroit around 1950. A singer and bass player, Caldwell worked as a line foreman in a Ford factory by day. He cut singles for local labels such as Clix and Happy Hearts (1959–61) before signing with King Records of Cincinnati, Ohio, where he scored a small hit in 1963 with "Tear Stained Guitar." He later recorded for Boone, Evers, Rich, and other labels. Caldwell led bands several nights a week until a year before his death in 2000.

18. Caldwell's Caravan single included "An Old Pair Of Shoes" backed with "A Good Woman Has Gone Again."

19. Sound Inc. was owned and operated by William Howard Walker, Larry Lick, and Stan Getz (not the famous jazz artist).

20. Originally from Pontiac, Michigan, guitarist Marvin Weyer played lead guitar for rock 'n' roll group Nick and the Jaguars. They had records on Jack Brown's Hi-Q and Berry Gordy's Tamla labels in Detroit around 1959. Weyer served in Vietnam with the U.S.

Marine Corps. He moved to Nashville and worked with Barbara Mandrell, among others, for several years before returning to Michigan during the 1970s.

21. The latest versions of the Swingsters included Marvin Weyer (guitar), Nick Harris (bass), Joe Coccia (drums), Joe Pistorio (drums), and Eddie's son William (bass). Harris and Coccia first played with Jackson during the 1960s. Coccia also played with Detroit acts such as the Lucky Lee Trio and Walkin' Tony Lee.

Chapter 12

1. Frances Mitchell interviewed by Keith Cady in 2003.

2. Eveline Haire cut recordings for Mellow Records in 1942: "Prairie Sweetheart" backed with "I Have Done You Wrong," and "My Pal, My Pinto And I" backed with "Triflin' Woman." Mitchell didn't perform on the records.

3. Sam and Kirk McGee were born and raised on a farm in Franklin, Tennessee, at the dawn of the twentieth century. Inspired by their musician father, the McGee brothers worked on the WSM *Grand Ole Opry* from its early days through the 1970s. They played with Uncle Dave Macon and His Fruit Jar Drinkers, Fiddlin' Arthur Smith (as the Dixieliners), and Bill Monroe.

4. Mitchell worked the day shift at the Golden Greek Lounge on Eight Mile Road (west of Dequindre) in Detroit for many years.

5. Bobby Stevenson and Bob Mitchell may have played in the orchestra for Chick Fowler's "She Won't Turn Over For Me" (Universal, 1941).

6. Bill Randle, liner notes to Bobby Stevenson Trio, *Patterns in Purple*, Label "X" LXA-1024, 1955, phonograph album.

7. Al Allen interviewed by Craig Maki in 2005.

8. Bill Monroe made his first appearance in Detroit at the Masonic Temple in June 1947. James "Chick" Stripling played bass for Monroe for just a few months. He also worked with the Stanley Brothers. Stripling played fiddle in Detroit nightclubs from the 1950s before moving to Virginia during the 1960s. He died in 1970.

9. Besides harmonica, Jimmy Riddle (1918–82) played accordion and grew famous during the 1960s and 1970s for the folk phenomenon called "eephing."

Chapter 13

1. Mimia F. Singo (known as Joyce Songer from 1949 to 1964) interviewed by Craig Maki in 2008.

2. Ivan M. Tribe, *Mountaineer Jamboree: Country Music in West Virginia* (New York: University Press of Kentucky, 1996), 35–37. Bill Cox lived from 1897 to 1968.

3. J.C. "Dude" Towler, "Biography on Earl Songer," *The All Star Revue* (January 1953). Published by Dude Towler, president, Earl Songer Fan Club, Ypsilanti, Mich. By the time Songer arrived in Detroit, solo mountaineer and cowboy acts such as Mountain Red and Gernert Case were well established on radio.

4. The Henley Street Bridge in Knoxville spans the Tennessee River. The bridge opened January 1932. Chet Atkins moved from Tennessee to Georgia in 1936, so Singo probably met Atkins at some point during 1932 to 1936. "Spanish Fire Bells" was the name of an instrumental that Singo recorded in 1950 for Fortune Records. If Atkins made a recording of it, he used another title.

5. In 1948 Vargo issued an instrumental record by Elton Adams and the Blue Ridge Mountaineers ("Philipino Waltz" backed with "Silver Bells") that was also pressed by the Rondo label of Chicago, Illinois. Adams' act also recorded "E. Blues" backed with "Good Old Mountain Dew" for Arcadia, featuring vocals by Red Nix. Singo thought Adams died around 1953.

6. Buddy Starcher recorded "The Fire In My Heart" for Four Star in 1946.

7. Johnny Sippel, "Folk Talent and Tunes," *Billboard* (October 28, 1950. Vol. 62, No. 43), 36.

8. Towler.

9. "Advance Folk (Country & Western) Record Releases," *Billboard* (December 2, 1950. Vol. 62, No. 48), 23.

10. "Det. H'wood Tries Vaude," *Billboard* (December 22, 1951. Vol. 63, No. 51), 14.

11. In 1948, Vargo issued singles by Charlie Jones and the Kentucky Corn Crackers, including "Sweet Georgia Brown" (instrumental) backed with "Cool Water" (Geo. Sikes Trio) and "Darktown Strutters Ball" (unknown vocalist) backed with "I Want A Girl" (Geo. Sikes Trio)—the second was also issued on Rondo.

12. Johnny Sippel, "Folk Talent and Tunes," *Billboard* (October 25, 1952. Vol. 64, No. 43), 67.

13. "Harvester Show Plays To 20,000," *Billboard* (February 21, 1953. Vol. 65, No. 8), 28.

14. "Record Reviews," *Billboard* (April 18, 1953. Vol. 65, No. 16), 45, "Sansoo." "Record Reviews," *Billboard* (October 3, 1953. Vol. 65, No. 40), 46, "Unwelcome Bride."

15. *Country Song Roundup* (May 1954. Vol. 1, No. 31), 4. The feature referred to Singo as Joyce Songer. Also appearing on the page: Betty Amos, Goldie Hill, and "Little Patsy" Elshire.

16. "New Country Label Bows," *Billboard* (January 11, 1964. Vol. 76, No. 2), 28.

17. Speedy Rogers, a.k.a. Forrest Combs, interviewed by Craig Maki in 2005.

18. Bobby Osborne interviewed by Keith Cady in 2001.

Chapter 14

1. Jimmy Work interviewed by Keith Cady in 2000.

2. "Coinmen You Know," *Billboard* (September 4, 1948. Vol. 60, No. 36), 109. Johnny Sippel, "Folk Talent and Tunes," *Billboard* (January 29, 1949. Vol. 61, No. 5), 30. Work's Alben record was his only release on the label. Another Alben record, "Stampede With Van" by Andy Johnson and His Peppermint Sticks, was dedicated to one of Detroit's first black radio hosts, Van Douglas at WJBK.

3. "Alben Albums Repped," *Billboard* (March 19, 1949. Vol. 61, No. 12), 47. Okum resigned his position with the association in March 1949.

4. "Coinmen You Know," *Billboard* (October 16, 1948. Vol. 60, No. 42), 107. "Ben Okum has returned from a business trip to St. Louis in connection with the distribution of the Alben record line . . ." "Music—As Written," *Billboard* (October 30, 1948. Vol. 60, No. 44), 37.". . . Apollo Distributing in New York has taken over distribution for Alben, a Detroit label."

5. "Music," *Cash Box* (unknown edition, 1948). Clipping source: Jimmy Work scrapbook.

6. Vladimir Bogdanov, Chris Woodstra, and Stephen Thomas Erlewine, *All Music Guide to Country: The Definitive Guide to Country Music* (San Francisco, CA: Backbeat, 2003), 845. A version of "Tennessee Border" by Hank Williams first appeared in 1960 on "The Lonesome Sound of Hank Williams," an M-G-M compilation of 1949 radio show transcriptions enhanced by overdubs of new performances by studio musicians.

7. "Record Reviews," *Billboard* (June 25, 1949. Vol. 61, No. 26), 117.

8. Johnny Sippell, "American Folk Tunes," *Billboard* (April 1, 1950. Vol. 62, No. 13), 124.

9. Work's Bullet cut of "Tennessee Border" is lost. Work couldn't remember the title of the other unissued song, also lost. Bullet Recording and Transcription Company went out of business in 1952 but was revived for several years as a custom diskery during the 1960s.

10. Skeets McDonald cut a session for London in Chicago with the same studio band that played with Work in 1950. Although McDonald was a friend of his, Work was unaware of McDonald's recordings for London, probably made before Work's. "So I Cried Myself To Sleep" (London), issued under the name "Skeets" Donald, appeared ten catalog numbers before Work's first London record. When asked if there was a London Records representative in Detroit to recruit artists for the label, Work said there was no such connection. It seems Work and McDonald interacted with London Records independently.

11. Work's other Capitol records included "Crazy Moon" backed with "Out Of My Mind," and "I'm Lonesome For Someone" backed with "How Can I Love You (When You're Not Around)."

12. Ray McKinley, "Biographies of Dot Artists," *Billboard* (October 9, 1954. Vol. 66, No. 41), 48.

13. Al Allen played guitar with country and rock 'n' roll acts in Detroit from 1949 to the mid-1960s.

14. Vladimir Bogdanov, Chris Woodstra, and Stephen Thomas Erlewine.

15. Bill Sachs, "Folk Talent and Tunes," *Billboard* (April 2, 1955. Vol. 67, No. 46), 16. Work and the troupe traveled through Missouri, Arkansas, Tennessee, Mississippi, and Louisiana.

16. Bill Sachs, "Folk Talent and Tunes," *Billboard* (September 29, 1956. Vol. 68, No. 39), 69.

17. Bill Sachs, "Folk Talent and Tunes," *Billboard* (May 13, 1957. Vol. 69, No. 20), 74.

18. Bill Sachs, "Folk Talent and Tunes," *Billboard* (December 1, 1958. Vol. 70, No. 48), 6. All 501 was reviewed in the December 15, 1958, edition of *Billboard*.

19. In 1986 Bear Family Records compiled "Making Believe," an album of Work's Dot recordings. In 1988 the company issued "Crazy Moon," which contained his Decca and Capitol recordings. Bear Family assembled *Making Believe,* a compact disc set of all of Work's commercial output, in 1993.

Chapter 15

1. Lonnie Barron, "Lonnie's Country Corner," *Richmond Review* (January 19, 1956).

2. James Barron interviewed by Craig Maki in 1995.

3. Lonnie Barron, "Lonnie's Country Corner," *Richmond Review* (March 1, 1956).

4. Barron's radio show came on at a quarter past twelve o'clock Monday through Saturday, and a quarter to five on Sunday. In April 1956, the Sunday program moved to a quarter past twelve o'clock. Concerning WDOG, Jimmy Williams said, "First it was WSDC when it went on the air in [December] 1951. Some people in Detroit owned WSDC.... Sawyer, Dreysdale and Coughlin. Jerry Coughlin was one of the owners. The Dreysdale people had Dreysdale Buick in Detroit. Sawyer was a brother-in-law of Coughlin." In 1954 Coughlin changed the station's call letters to WDOG. Jimmy Williams interviewed by Keith Cady and Craig Maki in 2003.

5. Cranford "Ford" Nix interviewed by Donald McCatty in 2004 (unpublished).

6. Terry Bethel interviewed by Keith Cady in 2003.

7. Joannie King sang at Barron's Saturday night dances. E-mail message by King, forwarded to Craig Maki by Gladys Drummond June 23, 2006.

8. Bill Sachs, "Folk Talent & Tunes," *Billboard* (November 13, 1954. Vol. 66, No. 46), 95.

9. Al Allen interviewed by Keith Cady in 2003. Allen identified himself as the guitarist for the recording session. The rest of the band is unknown, except for Casey Clark on fiddle. Les Emery also issued a single by Jimmy Minor from the session.

10. "Local Boy Goes to Hollywood," *New Haven Herald* (January 20, 1955), 1. The article described Pat Nelson as "part owner of the recording company."

11. Pee Wee King's show broadcast Saturday nights on WBBM-TV from the Garrick Theater in Chicago, Illinois. During the summer of 1955, WXYZ-TV Channel Seven Detroit aired King's program. Barron published his impressions of appearing as a guest on the show in his February 9, 1956, newspaper column.

12. Lonnie Barron's photo appeared in *Country Song Roundup* No. 33 (July–August 1954) with a short autobiography, and in No. 39 (July 1955) as part of a salute to RCA Records. His lyrics to "Go On, It's Okay" were reproduced in No. 46 (October 1956).

13. Johnny Powers, a.k.a. John Pavlik, interviewed by Keith Cady and Craig Maki in 2001.

14. Okie Jones was a featured singer in Casey Clark's Lazy Ranch Boys.

15. Sally Massey, "Folk News & Country Views," *Folk and Country Songs* (January 1957.

Vol. II, No. 1), 26. After performing his WDOG radio show, Barron drove to WABJ Adrian to broadcast another show.

16. Lonnie Barron, "Lonnie's Country Corner," *Richmond Review* (May 17, 1956), 2.

17. Lonnie Barron, "Lonnie's Country Corner," *Richmond Review* (May 10, 1956), 2.

18. Advertisement, *Billboard* (July 7, 1956. Vol. 68, No. 27), 47.

19. Bill Sachs, "Folk Talent & Tunes," *Billboard* (September 29, 1956. Vol. 68, No. 39), 69.

20. Bill Sachs, "Folk Talent & Tunes" *Billboard* (October 20, 1956. Vol. 68, No. 42), 87.

21. Don Rader interviewed by Craig Maki in 1995.

22. Tex Clarke, "Letter to the Home Folks," *Cowboy Songs* (April 1957. Vol. 3, No. 51), 28.

23. "Disk Jockey Found Slain," *Detroit Times* (January 10, 1957), 1.

24. Chuck Rich interviewed by Keith Cady in 2002.

25. "Fan Club Dies With Lonnie," *Detroit Free Press* (January 11, 1957. Vol. 126, No. 254), 3.

26. William Sudomier, "Says He Killed Singer For Dating His Wife," *Detroit Free Press* (January 10, 1957. Vol. 126, No. 253), 1.

27. Warren H. Stromberg, "Says He Killed Lonnie After Taunt," *Detroit Free Press* (February 8, 1957), 1.

28. "Radio Singer Killed; Jealous Husband Held," *Marine City News* (January 17, 1957).

29. "3,500 Bid Lonnie Farewell," *Detroit Times* (January 12, 1957). "'He Can't Be Dead,' Girl Sobs," *Detroit Free Press* (January 11, 1957. Vol. 126, No. 254), 3.

30. Terry Bethel knew in autumn 1956 that Barron was negotiating a contract with Columbia Records. He remembered Barron took more than one trip to Nashville to meet with label representatives. Casey Clark witnessed the deal.

31. Stromberg.

32. Chuck Carroll interviewed by Keith Cady in 2000.

33. Max Henderson, *Rustic Rhythm* (May 1957. Vol. 1, No. 2), 29; and Lillian Munz, 31.

34. Ellery Queen, "Death of a Playboy," *American Weekly* (May 26, 1957), 22–23.

Chapter 16

1. Danny Richards interviewed by Keith Cady, April 2000. Richards also interviewed by Keith Cady and Craig Maki in 2005, 2006, and 2007.

2. Darrell "Pee Wee" Lambert played mandolin and sang harmony on Stanley Brothers' recordings for the Rich-R-Tone label in 1947. Lambert later formed the Pine Ridge Boys, a bluegrass combo. Gaines Blevins moved to Georgia to work with "Doc" Ramblin' Tommy Scott in 1950. Blevins played fiddle, bass, and guitar with Scott until his death in 1996. Stanley Brothers biography by Stephen Thomas Erlewine and David Vinopal for All Music Guide, http://www.answers.com/topic/the-stanley-brothers?cat=entertainment (Accessed 2009). Pee Wee Lambert biography by Eugene Chadbourne for All Music Guide,

http://www.answers.com/topic/pee-wee-lambert?cat=entertainment (Accessed 2009). Gaines Blevins information from Tommy Scott biography at http://www.carolinacotton. org (Accessed 2009).

3. Hawkshaw Hawkins sang "Big Slim" Aliff's "Sunny Side Of The Mountain" as his theme song during the earliest days of his career.

4. *Life History of Patsy Jean and Mel* (ca. 1950), self-published souvenir book.

5. *Mountain Broadcast and Prairie Recorder* (June 1946. New Series, No. 8), 23. Steele wrote he had been in the music business for fifteen years. At WDBJ Roanoke, Virginia, Patsy Jean and Mel performed every morning at five minutes past six o'clock.

6. "American Folk Tunes," *Billboard* (March 13, 1948. Vol. 60, No. 12), 105.

7. William Hayes interviewed by Keith Cady in 2001.

8. Mimia F. Singo, a.k.a. Joyce Songer, interviewed by Craig Maki in 2008.

9. http://www.saucysylvia.com (Accessed 2011).

10. Moon Mullican died of a heart attack in Beaumont, Texas, January 1, 1967.

11. Evelyn Harlene (Clark) Atkins interviewed by Craig Maki and Keith Cady in 2011.

12. Gene Roe, "News From the Four Corners," *Country Song Roundup* (May 1954. Vol. 1, No. 31), 26. Mary Ann Johnson went on a tour with Montana Frank and California Joe through July, and recorded for M-G-M records that year.

13. Chuck Oakes interviewed by Keith Cady in 2000.

14. If it was released, the record produced by Chubby Wise has yet to be identified.

15. The Sage/Crown compilations, "Oldies and Goodies (Country and Western)," included several Detroit-based talents who recorded for Sage and Sand.

16. *Country Song Roundup* (June 1956. Vol. 1, No. 44), 3. David Carson, *Rockin' Down the Dial: The Detroit Sound of Radio (From Jack the Bellboy to the Big 8)* (New York: Momentum Books LLC, 1999), 29–31. "Maxwell's Radio Career Reads Like Map of World," *Teen Life* (November 9, 1956. Vol. 1, No. 18), 7. Bob Maxwell first worked with Jimmy Dickens at WKNX Saginaw, Michigan, in 1947. He began his career in 1941 as an overnight broadcaster at WEXL Royal Oak. In 1949 he moved from WKNX to WWJ Detroit. Maxwell also worked at WXYZ and WJLB. After selling WBRB in 1959, Maxwell programmed for WCBS and WABC New York. In 1981 he moved to Los Angeles, landing small roles in movies and making television and radio commercials. Maxwell died in Palm Springs, California, in December 2002.

17. James N. Gregory, *The Southern Diaspora: How the Great Migrations of Black and White Southerners Transformed America* (New York: University of North Carolina Press, 2005), Appendix A.3. P. 332. According to the 1970 population census, more than 455,000 white Southern-born people lived in Michigan.

Chapter 17

1. Al Allen, a.k.a. Albert Punturi, and Kathleen Punturi interviewed by Craig Maki and Keith Cady in 2005, and by Craig Maki in 2009.

2. "Tommy Cantrell," *National Hillbilly News* (March–April 1950. Vol.5, No.4), 43. "Tommy is from Charleston, W.Va., and is now heard daily at 12:05 over WHTN in Huntington, W.Va. With him is Charley Miller, whose hot piano background sparks the half hour show." Ivan M. Tribe, *Mountaineer Jamboree* (Lexington, Ky.: University of Kentucky Press, 1984), 170, 171.

3. Chuck Carroll interviewed by Keith Cady in 2000. Carroll worked with Casey Clark and His Lazy Ranch Boys from 1952 to 1955.

4. Don Tannison was a steel guitarist from Windsor, Ontario.

5. Davis Sisters, *Memories*, Bear Family BCD15722BH, 1993, compact disc.

6. Allen said "Steel Wool" was a warm-up exercise and the band didn't know Jack Brown, owner of Fortune Records, was recording them.

7. Bill Archer, "Goins, Lonesome Pine Fiddlers, going into Bluegrass Hall of Fame," *Bluefield Daily Telegraph* (August 16, 2009), http://www.bdtonline.com/local/local_story_228211834.html (Accessed 2009).

8. Danny Richards interviewed by Keith Cady in 2000, and by Keith Cady and Craig Maki in 2005.

9. An extant ticket stub, good for one day October 23 to 25, 1953, revealed bandleader Herb Ivey and His Carolina Boys hosted Moon Mullican at the Madison Ballroom, along with Bob Quinn, Jack Scott, and Roy Hall and His Cohutta Mountain Boys.

10. "UMO Sponsors Yule Program For a Prison," *Billboard* (January 15, 1957. Vol. 69, No. 1), 64. The Detroit House of Correction hosted a holiday show for prisoners featuring Jack Scott and His Rock-A-Billies and eight other acts.

11. The Gibson ES-355 guitar is still in production.

12. Chuck Oakes interviewed by Keith Cady in 2000.

13. "Reviews of New Pop Records," *Billboard* (April 27, 1959. Vol. 71, No. 17), 41.

14. The payola scandal in Detroit later that year ended high-flying careers of several disk jockeys, including Tom Clay and Mickey Shorr. Shorr maintained he never took payola. He left Detroit but came back to run WABX-FM during the late 1960s. Clay also spent several years "in the wilderness" before returning to radio and voice-over work in California.

15. Swanee Caldwell's Clix singles included "Thrill Happy" backed with "Mixed Up Heart," and "I'm Lonesome Tonight" backed with "Don't Say You're Sorry."

16. Rather than a convex curve like typical guitar bridges, Allen and Matthew's swinging bridge was shaped with a concave curve.

Chapter 18

1. Hubert Friar interviewed by Keith Cady in 2001.

2. Johnny Sippel, "Folk Talent and Tunes," *Billboard* (Oct. 21, 1950. Vol. 62, No. 42), 35.

3. Buster Turner interviewed by Keith Cady in 2001.

4. Jimmy Kirkland interviewed by Craig Maki and Keith Cady in 2001.

Chapter 19

1. Cranford "Ford" Nix interviewed by Keith Cady in 2002.

2. Ford Nix interviewed by Donald McCatty in 2004 (unpublished).

3. McCatty. Nix was familiar with the hall at 12101 Mack Avenue and helped Clark secure it for his barn dances. The U.A.W. Local to which Nix belonged used it as its headquarters.

4. Billy Jo Kennedy, "Ford Nix," *Music City News—Michigan Supplement* (May 1968, Vol. 2, No. 5), 10.

5. Gary Thompson, *Olympic Rock*, liner notes to Dial 004, 1977, phonograph album.

6. Before moving to Detroit in 1955 and recording for Clix Records, Nix's friend Jimmy Lee Williams played mandolin in Mac Wiseman's band.

7. In 1960 Ray Taylor, his seventeen-year-old son Dolphus (drums), and Chuck Reeves (guitar) cut a double-sided rockabilly platter for Clix: "Connie Lou" backed with "My Hamtramck Baby." A year later he made his third Clix record: "I'll Never Let You Worry My Mind Anymore" backed with "That Same Old Fool Again."

8. "Ain't No Sign I Wouldn't If I Could" (Cranford Nix), True Tone Publishing (Clix 813, 1959).

9. Crile Bevington Jr., "'Power of Positive Thinking' Is True Belief Of Nashville Producer," *The Times—Tri-Cities Daily* (Florence, Sheffield, Tuscumbia, Muscle Shoals, Alabama. September 24, 1967. Vol. 108, No. 177), 17. http://news.google.com/newspapers?nid=1842&dat=19670924&id=4CgsAAAAIBAJ&sjid=_scEAAAAIBAJ&pg=769,3470115 (Accessed 2010). "Victor Lewis, 86, died Nov. 13." http://www.musicrow.com/2009/01/nashville-related-music-obituaries-2008/ (Accessed 2010). *Country Music Hit Parade Jamboree Official Program* (1959). Victor Lewis produced a talent show at the Hazel Park Raceway one afternoon, and the winner received a prize during a concert that evening at Ford Auditorium. Lewis moved to Nashville around 1960 and produced country music concerts, including the National Country Music Cavalcade of Stars in May 1964 at Madison Square Garden in New York City. That same year, Lewis launched Marathon Pictures, the first feature film company based in Nashville, with "Country Music On Broadway," starring Ferlin Husky. He died in 2008.

10. Fay McGinnis interviewed by Keith Cady in 2000.

11. Billy Gill interviewed by Keith Cady in 2001.

12. Nix met Frank Buchanan at the WRVA *Old Dominion Barn Dance*. Buchanan worked with Bill Monroe in 1960 to 1962. He also played with Roy Acuff, Ernest Tubb, Jimmy Dickens, Raymond Fairchild, and others. He died in July 2012.

13. "Station Sets Golden Anniv. With Fair," *Billboard* (May 26, 1973. Vol. 85, No. 21), 46.

14. "Ford Retires," *Country In The City News* (February 1981. Vol. 4, No. 3), 34.

Chapter 20

1. Wilma Ann Holcomb interviewed by Keith Cady in 2001.

2. Cap, Andy, and Flip pioneered live music broadcasts on West Virginia radio. Popular during the 1930s and 1940s, the trio appeared on the WWVA *World's Original Jamboree* in Wheeling, as well as WCHS Charleston.

3. On "Sleep, Darling" Curly Dan had the privilege of being the first to record with acclaimed mandolin player Bill Napier.

4. Frank Wakefield, one of the most celebrated mandolin pickers for his skill and unique style, played music in Detroit and Monroe, Michigan, ca. 1955 to 1958.

5. Billy Gill played guitar, sang, and wrote songs in Jimmy Martin's group after the Osborne Brothers left Detroit. After traveling with Martin to Shreveport, Louisiana, Gill returned to Detroit in 1958. He and Pete Gobel teamed up on Happy Hearts records, besides cutting his own songs for various labels. Gill died in 2006.

6. Curly Dan and Wilma Ann recorded "South On 23" for Happy Hearts (single), Nashville (single), Danville (single), and Old Homestead (album).

7. http://faac.us/adf/messages/16041/99471.html?1148223317 (Accessed 2009). See April 2004 forum post by Ron Murphy. Martin & Snyder Distributing, a coin machine vendor based in Cleveland with a branch office in Dearborn, Michigan, operated the Dearborn label. With producer Ed Kaplan (M-S-K Productions), Martin & Snyder recorded many kinds of music to fill the jukeboxes they serviced with their own catalog.

8. Salt River Acres, Inc., of Midland, Michigan, produces bluegrass festivals every summer.

INDEX

Sholes, Steve, 93
Shook, Jack, 192
Shook, Jody, 156
Shorr, Mickey, 249
Short, Jimmie and Leon, 156, 199
"Shotgun Wedding," 194
Sikes, Lucky, 95
Sikes Trio. *See* George Sikes Trio
Silver Sage Buckaroos, 40, 172
Singing Kid (radio artist), 56
Singo, Joyce (Songer), 186–95, 229; Country
    Three, 195; Hi-Jumpers, 193
Siracuse, Jimmy, 73
"Sixty Minute Man," 45
Skinner, Jimmie, 114, 200, 258
"Skinny Minnie From Texas City," 132
"Sleep, Darling," 272
"Sleepwalk," 177
Sliver's Oregon Buckaroos, 32, 56
Sloan, George, 59, 60
"Slowly," 101, 103
Smilin' Ernie's Radio Jamboree, 70
"Smiling Through The Years," 191
Smith, Al, 200
Smith, Carl, 98, 99, 203, 246
Smith, Dewey "Smitty," 76, 103, 168, 173
Smith, "Fiddlin'" Arthur, 254
Smith, Harry (Shorty), 8
Smith, Wandell "Wendy," 266, 270, 272, 274;
    Windy Mountain Boys, 267
Smithers, Carroll, 110, 122
Smithers, Hershel "Cowboy," 88, 110
"Smoke! Smoke! Smoke! (That Cigarette),"
    72
"Smokey Mountain Moon," 202
Smoky and His Guitar (WIBM), 84
Snow, Hank, 43, 201, 233
"So Long, Lone Ranger," 61
"Soft Lips And Poison Kisses," 150
"Someone To Call My Own," 191
Songer, Earl, 187–94
Songer, Joyce. *See* Singo, Joyce
Sons of Texas, 155, 156
Sons of the Pioneers, 59, 66, 72, 86
"Sophroni," 119
"Sorrow And Pain," 92, 164
Sosby, Eddie, and His Radio Rangers, 83, 172
Sound Incorporated, 64, 179, 268
"South On 23," 271, 272, 274
"Southern Fried Chicken," 203
Southern, Hal. *See* Clark, Hal
Sova, Bill, 74, 132, 133, 165
Sovine, Red, 65, 241
"Spanish Fire Bells," 188, 191

"Sparkling Brown Eyes," 188
Sparks, Jacob B., 7
Sparton Records, 215
Spattafiore's, 61, 193
"Speak To Me Little Darling," 40
Spears, Billie Jo, 122
Special Recordings, 124, 178, 248
"Speed Limit," 89
Spellbinders, 150
St. Charles Theater, 160
St. Jean Bar, 58
"St. Joe Boogie," 135
Stairway To The Stars, 212
Stallard, "Indian" Bill, 78, 80
Standel Company, 102, 109, 111
Stanley Brothers, 65, 227, 262
Stanley, Carter, 226
Stanley, Harold G., 94
Stanley, Ralph, 227
Starcher, Buddy, 189, 190
Starday Records, 150, 271, 274
Starnes, Doyle, 180
Starr, Floyd, 90
Starr, Gene, 84, 86, 87, 123
Starr, Kay, 114
Stars of Tomorrow (WTAC), 108
Steed, Hy, 29
"Steel Guitar Rag," 105, 109, 183, 187
"Steel Wool," 153, 164, 244
Steele, Bob, 160
Steele, Mel, 79, 80, 225–28; Oklahoma Ram-
    blers, 79, 228
Steele, Patsy Jean, 79, 225, 227, 228; Hillbilly
    Pals, 225, 227
Steen, Joe, 5, 6
Stevenson, Bobby, 23, 183. *See also* Bobby
    Stevenson Trio
Stewart, Billy, 157
Stewart, Redd, 45
Stockwell, Jack, 59
Storer, Lester. *See* Natchee the Indian
"Stormy Weather," 162
Stover, Jeff, 53, 54
Stover, Smokey, 168
"Straighten Up And Fly Right," 148, 150
Strate-8 Records, 139
String Dusters (band), 201
Stringdusters (band), 158
Stripling, Chick, 184, 242
Studly, Ernie, 71
"Suckin' Cider," 20
"Sugaree," 123
Sullivan, Shorty, 202
Sultan Recording Company, 7